PROUD

PROUD

MY FIGHT
FOR AN
UNLIKELY
AMERICAN DREAM

IBTIHAJ MUHAMMAD

WITH LORI L. THARPS

hachette
BOOKS

NEW YORK   BOSTON

Hachette Books
Hachette Book Group
1290 Avenue of the Americas, New York, NY 10104
hachettebooks.com
twitter.com/hachettebooks

First edition: July 2018

Hachette Books is a division of Hachette Book Group, Inc. The Hachette
Books name and logo are trademarks of Hachette Book Group, Inc.

The publisher is not responsible for websites (or their content) that are not
owned by the publisher.

The Hachette Speakers Bureau provides a wide range of authors for speaking
events. To find out more, go to www.hachettespeakersbureau.com or call
(866) 376-6591.

LCCN: 2018938062
ISBNs: 978-0-316-51896-3 (hardcover); 978-0-316-48723-8 (signed edition);
978-0-316-52549-7 (B&N signed edition); 978-0-316-51895-6 (ebook)

Printed in the United States of America

LSC-C

10 9 8 7 6 5 4 3 2 1

To anyone who has ever been told they don't belong. When you let your light shine, it illuminates everyone around you.

Sometimes, I feel discriminated against, but it does not make me angry. It merely astonishes me. How can anyone deny themselves the pleasure of my company? It's beyond me.

—ZORA NEALE HURSTON

AUTHOR'S NOTE

This book is a memoir, not an autobiography. The stories and opinions recollected in these pages are based upon my memories and are true as I remember them. In some cases, names and identifying details have been changed, and some characters are composites of people who have passed through my life. In order to keep the story moving forward, I have also compressed time in some instances. If I had to describe exactly what this book is, I'd say it is the true story of my life.

PROLOGUE

"Muhammad...?" her voice trailed off. The substitute teacher, Ms. Winter, squinted and brought the list of names on the attendance sheet closer to her face. She was stuck, and I could guess why. She was looking at the seven letters in my first name and wondering how to pronounce it.

"Is your last name Muhammad?" she asked, her eyes fixed on me, the only fourth grader in the classroom wearing a hijab, who happened to be sitting in the front row.

"Yes." I nodded. My eyes stayed glued in front of me.

"And how do you pronounce your first name, young lady?" she asked.

"It's Ib-ti-haj," I said, pronouncing each syllable as slowly as possible. "It's pronounced just like it's written," I added. That usually helped people understand how to say my name, but it didn't help Ms. Winter. She made another face, the kind of face you make when your mouth lands on something bitter.

"Oh, that's too hard," she said, shaking her head no and scribbling something down on the attendance sheet. "We're going to call you Ibti."

"Okay," I said aloud, but the way she said "Ibti" made my cheeks burn. I refused to turn my head to see if my classmates were laughing at me or, worse, pitying me for having a name that was too hard to pronounce.

During recess, I did some quick calculating in my head to

be sure, but I was right. My friend Jennifer had eight letters in her name, and Elizabeth Brewster had nine in hers, and yet their names weren't "too hard." Their names didn't require shortening. Why did mine? Ibtihaj was the easiest name in the world to pronounce. All my friends could say it, and they were all only nine years old like me. Ms. Winter didn't even try to say my name.

———————

The truth is, for as far back as I can remember, this sort of confusion has existed about who I am, and it always starts with my name. Ibtihaj. "How do you say it?" "What does it mean?" And then the way I identify myself leaves some people perplexed: Black but Muslim. Muslim but American. Hijabi but an athlete. I've walked into many rooms and stood on stages where it was clear people didn't know what to make of me. When no one knows where you fit into the social order of color and creed, confusion ensues until order is restored. Until people understand who you really are; that is when they stop and listen.

And that's why I wrote *Proud*. I want people to understand who *I* really am and maybe other Americans like me who feel the same, to get to know the journey behind the headlines of the "first US athlete to compete in the Olympic Games wearing hijab." I wrote this book because I wanted to chronicle my quest to challenge society's limited perceptions of what a Muslim woman, a Black woman, or an athlete can be.

I want people to know that much of my strength as an athlete comes from how high I had to climb to release myself from society's boxes and show up to the party even when an invitation was never extended to me. Along the way, I had to learn how to be tough and tenacious or risk losing the fight before it even started. I had to maximize my expectations for myself because no one else would, and I had to have the guts to pursue what I wanted even though it meant charting my own path. I didn't have any role models to look up to who looked like me in fencing, and there weren't any other Muslim women wearing hijab at the elite levels of sport to inspire my quest. I had myself, my family, and my faith, and that was enough for me to persist.

Proud may seem like a familiar story, as this path I'm on was forged by the men and women who came before me—Muhammad Ali, Jackie Robinson, John Carlos, Althea Gibson, Serena and Venus Williams, Mahmoud Abdul-Rauf—athletes who defied the naysayers and triumphed over mountains of adversity. They had barriers thrust in front of them and doors slammed in their faces, yet they still triumphed both on and off the court. I hope that, when reading Proud, anyone who has had an opportunity taken from them because of their race, religion, or gender can find solace in these pages. I hope people feel empowered by my fight and know that they have every right to demand a place at the table of whatever life is offering.

If someone had told me that my life would unfold the way it has—full of untold blessings and endless opportunities—because I picked up a sword in high school at thirteen years old, I would have called him or her a liar. But I did pick up that sword, and despite the uphill battle, it has been a rewarding journey. It is my hope that everyone finds their own sword to wield in a way that brings them happiness and success, and that the word "no" becomes their motivation to press forward. *Inshallah*, so may it be.

PROUD

CHAPTER 1

In search of my mother's garden, I found my own.

—ALICE WALKER

Come on, Ibtihaj," my best friend, Amy, pleaded. She wanted me to come to her sleepover birthday party, but I knew the chances I would be able to go were slim to none. There was just no way it was going to happen. The rules were pretty clear in our house. No sleepovers. My father had already ruled them out before I even knew what sleepovers were. But I really wanted to go to Amy's party. She was my best friend. Plus, all the girls at school were having slumber parties now, and I was convinced I was the only third grader at Seth Boyden Elementary School who wasn't allowed to sleep over at someone else's house. Usually, on Monday mornings when all the girls were talking about how much fun they'd had together at a party over the weekend, I'd be stuck standing on the sidelines with nothing to add to the conversation.

"Can't you ask your dad? Maybe he'll say yes this time," Amy prodded as we sat on the picnic table bench in her backyard, resting after playing jump rope and riding bikes. Amy always had the best ideas and was so clever.

"You know my dad," I said, sighing. "But I'll ask him anyway."

"Just try to butter him up," Amy suggested. "Give him a hug."

1

I knew I would find my dad in his room getting ready to go to his evening shift at the precinct. He had gotten promoted to detective at work, so he didn't have to wear his regular police uniform like he used to. But he was still a cop through and through, and the strict expectations he had at work for his officers were the same ones he had for his children at home. He ran our household with military precision. We knew not to question his authority or bend the rules. But I still held out hope that I'd change Abu's mind, because I really wanted to go to Amy's birthday party. I knocked on the door. "Abu," I called out quietly. "Can I come in?"

I opened the door to my parents' room and found Abu sitting on the bed pulling on his socks. I put a big smile on my face to get him in the right mood. Remembering Amy's advice, I walked right over and gave him a big hug, wrapping my skinny arms around his compact frame and taking care to avoid the prickly whiskers in his thick beard.

"Abu," I said, pulling away to look into his eyes. "My best friend, Amy, across the street is having a sleepover party for her birthday and wants to know if I can go. Can I?" I rushed out the words like I'd been holding my breath.

Abu didn't even pause before answering. "Ibtihaj, you know the rules. No sleepovers. You won't be sleeping at anyone's house except this one. It's not safe."

"But you let me sleep at Auntie and Uncle Bernard's house," I reasoned.

"That's different. They're family," he insisted, walking past me to head out the bedroom door.

I followed him down the carpeted steps to the living room. My mom was there putting my little sister, Faizah, to sleep on her lap. She still had on her hijab and her work clothes, dark, long, loose pants and a brown cotton tunic top. As a special-education teacher, Mom often found herself having to get on the floor with her students for certain activities.

"What's going on?" Mom asked, noting the frustrated look on my face. She saw that I was fast on Abu's trail, my face a mask of determination.

"Amy wants me to sleep over at her house for her birthday, but Abu said no," I whined, willing my mother to make my father change his mind.

She glanced up at my father and took in what was going on between us. The stoic look on Abu's face made it clear he wasn't going to change his mind. Even I could tell that.

"You know the rules, Ibtihaj," my mother said, echoing my father's words from just a moment earlier. My feelings of hope deflated. Sometimes she could help make Abu see things differently, like the time she convinced him to let us keep a stray cat that we had found in the garage, even though Abu claimed he didn't like pets. The cat ran away after only a few days, but after Abu saw how well we took care of it, he surprised us and brought home a beautiful umbrella cockatoo named Koocah that he rescued while on duty from a group of kids who were abusing her. And even though he still pretended to hate Koocah, she was now a real member of our family. So I knew there was room for my dad to change his mind, and I had inherited his stubbornness.

"Abu, the kids who are coming to the party are just the girls from my class," I said. "There won't be any boys there."

My father was shuffling around the carpeted living room in his socks, collecting his keys, his wallet, and his glasses like he did every time he left the house. He stopped moving and turned to face me. "Ibtihaj, no sleepovers means no sleepovers," he said with firmness in his voice to signal to me that the discussion was over.

The tears started to form in my eyes, and my dad walked over to me. "Ibtihaj, you don't need to cry about this," Abu said, smoothing down the stray hairs that had escaped from my braids.

I was frustrated. We had a lot of rules in our house. There were things we couldn't do, like watch television during the week or listen to music on the radio; things we had to do, like wear our hijabs to school twice a week and pray five times a day; and things we were supposed to do, like get good grades and respect our parents. Some of the rules, I knew, came from the Quran, but some, like the sleepover rule, were simply because Abu was a protective father. He was a cop, and he saw bad things happen to good people every day. And some of the rules we followed in our house were because of where Abu and Mommy came from, which was where they didn't want any of their kids to end up.

My parents were both born and raised in Newark, New Jersey. In 1967, when my parents were teens, the Newark riots broke out, and the city burned with rage. Newark's Black residents were protesting the racism and relentless police brutality endemic to the city. The riots ran unabated for four days straight, and when it was all over, twenty-six people were dead, more than seven hundred injured, and more than a thousand people had been arrested. Most of the victims caught in the crossfire were Black. In the aftermath of the riots, most business owners on Springfield Avenue, the key commercial thoroughfare, didn't bother to rebuild and left their stores abandoned and boarded up. Most of the white people who had the means to do so fled the city, fearing more riots. A lot of people gave up on Newark, and the city became synonymous with urban decay, unemployment, and poverty. Drug abuse and crime were pervasive. When federal dollars poured into Newark to rebuild it in the 1970s, most of that financial capital went to the downtown business districts and did nothing to help the Black residents who still lived in Newark's residential areas. In other words, even after the riots, Newark remained burdened by the dark shadow of its past.

My mother, Denise, watched Newark burn, and it only strengthened her resolve to break free. The violence she witnessed frightened her, but it wasn't wholly unexpected. Violence was something my mother acknowledged as part of the landscape of her neighborhood. But she had a plan. Like her sister, Diana, who was eleven years older and had a good job and lived in New York City, my mom knew she had to do well in school and get out of Newark. She planned to follow in her sister's footsteps.

Mom said her friends and family always called her a prude because she refused party with them. They said she was too serious. But my mother wasn't a prude; she was just afraid of what would happen if she let herself run loose, even for a day. She watched her own mother try to fight her demons with alcohol and lose the battle every time. She didn't want that life. She was determined to do things differently. She didn't want to get stuck like so many of the women she saw on porch steps and street corners looking like they'd been through a war of their own making. Rather than find out what temptation tasted like, my mother sought stability. When she felt the need to hang out, she'd walk just a few blocks to visit her cousin, Sharon.

Sharon was a cousin from her mother's side of the family. She was only a few years older than my mom, but she was living a life my mother admired. Sharon lived with her husband, Karim, and they had a marriage that wasn't punctuated by violent fights and lonely tears like the relationships she witnessed growing up. Inside their small apartment, it felt like an oasis from the chaos in the streets, and it was one of the only places my mother felt really safe. For one thing, Karim was always home by six p.m. Sharon never paced the living room wondering where he was, whom he was with, or when he'd be home. Karim had a good job as a mechanic, and Sharon said he didn't drink or smoke or hang in the streets.

Sharon felt like a big sister to my mom. They'd just watch TV and talk. One night, while hanging out in the kitchen, she asked Sharon how she found a guy like Karim who was not caught up in the streets.

"Girl, Karim is a Muslim," Sharon said. "You have to find yourself a Muslim man to marry. They will always do right by you."

"Karim's a Muslim?" Mom asked. "Like he's part of the Nation of Islam?"

"No, he's Muslim. Karim says those Nation brothas are trippin'. He says they're more interested in starting a revolution than getting right with God."

"Are you going to become a Muslim?" Mom asked.

Sharon shrugged. "I'm thinking about it. Karim wants me to, especially before we have children."

Mom considered the way Karim treated Sharon, with such obvious respect and care, so unlike the way her own father treated her mother, and told her cousin, "Girl, you should think about it, considering what a good man Karim is. That has to mean something."

And it was at that moment that the seed of Islam was planted in my mother's brain. Was converting to another religion a possibility for her, too? She began to study the men and women around the neighborhood whom she knew were Muslim. The men who belonged to the Nation were easy to recognize, standing in front of their storefront mosques with their bow ties and bean pies. The women, too, wearing long dresses and head coverings. They all seemed so sure of themselves, so proud. The Nation of Islam is a religious organization based on Muslim principles, but it is also deeply rooted in Black nationalism. My mom wasn't looking to be political; she was searching for religion.

She started to visit Sharon and Karim more often to talk about Islam. They kept a Quran on their coffee table, and every time she visited, Mom liked to flip through the pages, searching for a message. At the time, she didn't understand much of the Quran's writings; the poetic language went over her head, but still there were enough verses that jumped off the page and spoke to her:

"Islam is the religion of mercy."
"And whoever holds firmly to Allah has [indeed] been guided a straight path."
"Allah does not burden a soul beyond that it can bear."

These simple lines filled my mother's spirit. She fell in love with Islam and the peaceful guidance that it offered. She started thinking about God as Allah. She put her short skirts away and started rethinking what she wore. By wearing long pants and long skirts she was in control of how her body would be perceived. By the time my mom started college at Rutgers University, she knew enough about the religion to know she had found her salvation. She was reinventing her life, rewriting her story. She knew that she wanted Islam in her future and all the honor and beauty it brought. It lifted her soul and gave her more to believe in than what was in front of her. She liked the idea that there was more in the world than the eye could see, that Allah had put us here with purpose, and she was devoted to honoring her newfound relationship with Him. Her soul, her heart, her life was now Muslim.

Unlike my mother, my father, Eugene, discovered Islam from his family members. He didn't have to seek out a new religion on his own; he simply had to follow in his brothers' footsteps. One of twelve children raised by a single mother, my father was the third eldest of the eight boys. All of his older brothers had joined the Nation of Islam before my father hit his teen years. The Nation of

Islam appealed to many Black men in Newark because it offered spiritual guidance in the midst of all the city's recklessness, and it came gift-wrapped in a Black nationalist agenda that uplifted Black men in a world determined to break their spirits. But as Abu matured, he found himself attracted not to the nationalist rhetoric used by certain factions of the Nation of Islam, but by the spiritual guidance and the irrefutable guidelines on how to live a God-conscious life.

Because Abu's parents separated when he was five, my father was attracted to Islam's emphasis on the family and the important role of the father in the family hierarchy. So, along with a group of other friends, Abu founded a new mosque in East Orange, New Jersey, where traditional Islamic precepts would be observed. It was there that he first saw my mother, who coincidentally had come to my father's mosque to officially take her *shahaadah*, or declaration of faith. She seemed so earnest in her love of the religion and so dedicated to learning everything she could in the class for new converts, my father was immediately attracted to her. Sometimes he would peek into the classroom where she was studying and he would just watch her studying as she pored over the verses from the Quran, her glasses sliding down her nose.

My father acted quickly, as he knew a woman as beautiful as my mom with such a naked love of the faith wouldn't be on the market for long. He asked some of his friends to find out all they could about this new convert, and he soon found out her name was Denise, but she had chosen the name Inayah when she converted. Following Muslim tradition, members of the mosque formally introduced my parents, and they went on only a handful of dates to see if they made a good match. They did, on both sides. My mother liked my father's quiet sense of humor and that he had an entrepreneurial spirit. In addition to running the mosque, he also owned two small restaurants in Newark. Complementary to her understated beauty, my father fell in love with my mother's enthusiasm for life and her love of children. She was an obvious nurturer and immediately made my father feel comfortable in his own skin. My father didn't hesitate to make his intentions known, first to my mother's parents and then to her. They were married a short time later, first signing their Islamic marriage contract in a traditional nikah ceremony, and then later they celebrated with a more formal occasion.

As part of their new life, my parents now went by their chosen names Inayah and Shamsiddin. Their new names symbolized their dedication to Allah, and that dedication extended to all aspects of their lives. They were not going to be Muslims in name only. In contrast to the way they were raised, my parents mutually agreed to raise their children following Muslim traditions. It was their gift to us. All meals would be halal, prayer would be observed five times a day, and hijab would be observed for the girls when they came of age. No matter what, family and faith would always come first. My mother vowed her children would never end up victims of the streets. My father vowed his children would always have a father in their lives. And so they found a spacious second-floor apartment in a quiet residential section of Newark and a private Islamic academy for the children to attend. Even though it was a struggle to send three children to a private school, my parents were both willing to sacrifice for their children's spiritual education. Both of my parents wanted more for their children than what Newark—a city still licking the wounds from its past—would be able to provide, more than what Newark had given to them. So they started saving their money, and in just a few years they had saved enough to buy a cozy four-bedroom home in Maplewood, New Jersey.

The picturesque suburban township of Maplewood felt about as far away from urban decay as one can imagine. I was five years old when we drove into town, passing block after block of colonial-style brick homes with tidy lawns and manicured gardens. When Abu stopped in front of our new house, the first thing I noticed was the forest-green front door. The compact three-story home was painted a stark white with frosty mint–colored shutters draping the second-story windows. I wondered if there was a yard in back, because the small, square front yard didn't look big enough for a good game of tag. Abu told us kids—my older sister, Brandilyn; my brother, Qareeb; me; and my little sister, Asiya—to get out of the car so he could show us something special. The four of us scrambled out of the back seat and followed my dad down the long driveway to the back of the house. There in front of us was a huge in-ground swimming pool. The pool took up a large portion of the backyard space, but I wasn't going to complain. I wanted to jump in the water right then and there.

"Can we go swimming, Abu?" I begged.

"Ibtihaj, you don't know how to swim," my father said and laughed.

"I know, but I can do a cannonball, can't I, Qareeb?" I said, trying to get my older brother to vouch for me.

"I don't want any one of you kids even near this pool without me or your mother next to you," my father said. "But I'm going to teach you all how to swim. That's one of the reasons why we bought this house. My children aren't going to be statistics, another Black kid drowning because no one ever taught them how to swim, no way." And that was Abu—strong, focused, determined in his moves.

I didn't know anyone who had a swimming pool in their backyard. In fact, most of my friends lived in apartments like we did, so no one even had a backyard. If we wanted to play outside, our moms usually took us to the park, but even then, they were always worried, telling us to keep our eyes open and pay attention to our surroundings. But everything about Maplewood seemed different than Newark. Newark was gritty, with a lot of pavement and dilapidated buildings. Maplewood was pure, full of trees and parks. Parts of Maplewood literally looked like a stand-in for a 1950s movie set, particularly the downtown area with its restaurants, cafés, bakeries, and bookstores. It looked like a storybook town to my parents. The park in the center of town was designed by John Olmsted and Frederick Olmsted, Jr., sons of the famous landscape architect Frederick Law Olmsted, and had a duck pond and white wooden gazebos dotting the area. My parents knew they made the right decision to raise their family in Maplewood. In addition to all of the family-friendly amenities, including good public schools, libraries, and a community center, Maplewood was also an anomaly because of its racial and economic diversity.

In the early nineties when my family and I arrived in Maplewood, the city was approximately 59 percent white and 33 percent Black. There was only one other Muslim family in town, but the women in that family didn't wear hijab like we did. But the lack of other Muslims didn't stop me from finding friends and feeling right at home. My first and best friend was Amy.

Amy had big round brown eyes and long black hair that she always wore in two lopsided ponytails. I remember soon after we moved in, Amy crossed the street with her mother and came to say hello. Then while our mothers talked, Amy asked me if I had a bicycle.

"Yeah, I have a bicycle," I said. "It's purple and pink. Pink's my favorite color." After that, it didn't take Amy and me long to set up a routine. First, we'd grab our bikes and ride up and down our driveway, talking about all the things we were going to do that day, and when we grew bored of that, we'd head over to her back-yard and play until our moms called us in for dinner.

One time, not long after we moved in, Amy and I were sitting in the grass in her backyard and she asked me, "Ibtihaj, how come your mom always wears a scarf on her head?"

No one had ever asked me that before. All my friends in New-ark from my preschool and the masjid where we went to pray all had moms who wore hijab. In fact, I didn't have any friends except Amy who had a mother who let her hair out in public.

I had to stop and think for a minute before I could answer Amy's question. "My mom wears hijab because we're Muslim," I said as I pulled up a handful of grass and then tried to weave the blades together into some kind of tapestry.

"What's a Muslim?" Amy asked, a frown wrinkling her sun-tanned face.

I looked at my new friend and wondered why she didn't know what it meant to be Muslim. "It's our religion."

"When you grow up are you going to wear the same thing on your head like your mom does?" Amy asked.

I shrugged my shoulders. "Yeah, I guess so. Sometimes I wear a scarf now for special occasions."

"That's cool," Amy said, obviously satisfied with my answers.

In my room, I plopped down on the floor of the bedroom I shared with my sister Asiya. Asiya was only five, but she was a good listener. My mom always joked that Asiya was a good listener because I talked so much.

"What's the matter?" Asiya asked me as I picked up a Bar-bie doll from our stash. Playing with our Barbies was always my default method of passing time. I could lose myself play-ing with my dolls any day of the week, imagining a fabulous life for them with their cool clothes and ever-changing hairdos. As I found a new outfit for the honey-colored Barbie in my hand and combed her thick black hair, I recounted my tale of woe to my little sister.

"I hope Mommy can convince Abu to let me go to Amy's sleepover party," I said to Asiya. "Amy really wants me to be there. I'm her best friend."

"But we never sleep over anywhere," Asiya said, as if she hadn't heard a word I'd said.

I shook my head at my sister. What did she know? I turned back to my Barbie and continued dressing her. A short time later, I heard my mother calling me.

"Ibtihaj, come here, please."

Asiya looked at me, and I smiled. I hoped my mother had good news for me. I padded down the stairs and saw my mother waiting for me, still seated on the couch. Faizah was asleep in her rocking seat next to her. It appeared my father was gone.

"Where's Abu?" I asked, desperately scanning the first floor for him.

"He left for work," Mom said and told me to come sit with her. I leaped over to the couch and snuggled in close to her. I loved my baby sister Faizah, but she took up a lot of my mother's snuggle time, so when I got my chance, I took it. Mom was warm and soft and she smelled like comfort. I loved that we looked the most alike, with our matching golden skin and hazel-colored eyes.

My mother looked me in the eye. "Ibtihaj, you know your father and I make rules to keep you and your siblings safe. It's not safe for you to sleep over at other people's homes when we don't know who all is going to be there."

"But it's Amy's house. They live across the street. You know them," I said, trying not to whine.

"I know," she said, "but rules are rules."

I hung my head in defeat. Amy was going to be disappointed,

and I was going to continue to be the odd one out on Monday when everyone was talking about it at school.

"But"—she wasn't done—"I convinced your father that since we *do* know Amy and her family, and since they *do* live right across the street, you can go to the birthday party."

"Yes!" I shouted, jumping off the couch.

"Don't get too excited," she said. "I said you can go, but we will pick you up around eight-thirty, so no sleeping over."

To me this was still a win. I just wanted to be there.

I squealed, thanked her, and dashed over to Amy's to share the big news.

Amy's party was fun, but it wasn't as exciting as I'd expected. Most of the girls from our third-grade class were there, and we played in Amy's backyard until the sun set. Then Amy's mother called us all in for pizza and soda. After that, Amy's mother brought in a big sheet cake decorated with big pink-and-yellow flowers, and we all sang happy birthday and watched Amy open her presents. By the time my mom came to pick me up, the rest of the girls were changing into their pajamas and brushing their teeth because Amy's mom said the lights were going off in one hour. So the only thing about the sleepover I was going to miss was the sleeping part.

When I got home I told my sisters and my mom about the party as we sat around our big wooden kitchen table.

"Did you have fun?" Mom asked.

"Yeah," I replied honestly, "but they didn't actually do anything that special. We just played in the backyard and ate pizza."

"That's it?" Asiya asked, looking disappointed.

"Yeah," I said. "I guess I expected something more exciting."

"Well, now you know what goes on at sleepovers," Mom said. "I hope you're happy."

I shrugged. "I like sleeping over at Auntie's house better. She'd never make me sleep in the basement. That's where the girls are sleeping at Amy's house."

My mother laughed. "Ibtihaj, you are funny. All of this begging and pleading, and you're talking about girls having to sleep in the basement."

I laughed, too. "I'm perfectly happy sleeping at home in my own bed with my own family."

"Well, at least your dad will be happy about that," she chuckled.

CHAPTER 2

Just try new things. Don't be afraid. Step out of your comfort zones and soar.

—MICHELLE OBAMA

My childhood wouldn't have been full of adventure if it hadn't been for my brother. I'd follow Qareeb anywhere and everywhere. He was only eighteen months older than me and was the brains behind many of our heroic exploits and the person I most wanted to be like. I made it my life's mission to keep up with him, even if I knew it would land us in trouble and me sometimes in tears. Whether he was daring me to jump off the top bunk of our bunk beds or racing me down the block, I was always one step behind him, trying my best to keep pace. I even started school a year early because I saw my brother getting ready for school, and I really wanted to go with him. He wasn't going to leave me behind. I had the quiet determination of my mother, he had the boisterous nature of Abu and his brothers, but we were best friends. And even though our adventures almost always ended up with me getting bruises, bumps, scars, and even stitches, I wouldn't have wanted it any other way. Our older sister, Brandilyn, didn't try to keep up with Qareeb and me and knew to stay clear of Qareeb's rambunctious energy. Asiya was too small to keep up with us, so for a while it was Qareeb and me against the world.

"Can we do it one more time?" I asked Abu, as I wiped the water from my eyes during an evening pool race. I had almost beat Qareeb that last time, and I knew I could do it if I had one more chance. I was so close. I glanced up at the sky and could tell the sun wasn't going to be up much longer. Asiya had already gone inside to change, but I wasn't ready to give up just yet.

"I don't wanna race again," Qareeb said. "I'm tired."

"What? You're scared I'll beat you this time?" I asked, knowing Qareeb could never turn down a challenge.

"*Psst,*" Qareeb said, sucking his teeth as he adjusted his goggles.

Abu was laughing from his lawn chair on the side of the pool. "Let's see if you'll let your little sister beat you after all, Qareeb," Abu teased. Qareeb dog-paddled over next to me, and we both stood with our feet planted on the swimming pool floor waiting for Abu's signal. I fixed my gaze on the opposite end of the pool and put my foot against the pool's wall when Abu yelled, "Go!"

I moved my arms as fast as they could go, cutting through the water like chainsaws. My legs were like motors, up and down, up and down. I moved just like Abu had taught me. I kept my head down so I could glide faster through the water. I couldn't see where my brother was, if he was in front or behind me, but I didn't stop to find out. I just kept moving. When I slammed my hand on the edge of the pool at the deep end, I heard Abu screaming in triumph, and I knew I had done it. "You did it, girl! You beat Qareeb."

I paddled over to the ladder and hauled myself out of the pool and leaped into my father's open arms. Abu wrapped me up in my towel and patted me on the head. "Ibtihaj, you did just what I taught you," he said proudly. "You kept your head down and you used those long legs of yours."

I was ecstatic and spun my head to look for Qareeb. He was sitting at the edge of the pool, and he looked angry. Abu waved at him to come join us anyway. "You're going to have to work harder to beat Ibtihaj now, boy. She's tasted victory." Though Qareeb looked far from happy, I smiled anyway and bathed myself in Abu's praises.

Both my parents believed in sports almost as a way of life. Abu subscribed to the belief that playing sports would give us a competitive edge, making us winners on the field and in life. He taught all of his children how to swim and play baseball, basketball, and any other sport he could get us involved in. And he had us competing against each other as often as possible. Races across the swimming pool, free-throw contests, tossing around a football—it felt like there was never a day without sports or an ultimate challenge from Abu. First place was always up for grabs; usually it was Qareeb who claimed the title because he was a bit stronger and faster than the rest of us. And Qareeb was not the type of kid to let his sisters win just to be nice, so if we won, it was a true victory.

Mommy liked for us to play sports because they kept us active and engaged with kids from school and around the neighborhood. She saw keeping active as a halal, or kosher, way for us to interact with our friends. Rather than our hanging out after school and running the chance of getting into trouble, sports provided a space for us to grow athletically, develop our self-confidence, and learn to work well with others. In a nutshell, both of my parents believed that sports were the best way to keep all of us kids disciplined and continuing to learn outside of the classroom. I can't remember a single time in my life when we weren't expected to play a sport. Of course, the sport I loved the most wasn't one I played.

I loved football. Abu had played football in his younger years and was a huge Steelers fan. Abu's love and passion for football was passed down to my brother, with Qareeb playing football from a really young age in Pop Warner youth football programs, a local league for young boys. Every Sunday morning during football season, our family ventured out to Underhill Field in Maplewood to watch Qareeb and his team play or in front of the television watching NFL games. Even as a young girl I could talk football plays and strategy with the best of them. Hanging onto every word, I loved listening to Abu's commentary as we would watch the games, while Qareeb would yell at the television screen at every missed assignment or fumbled ball. Sometimes Abu would take Qareeb and me to the park and toss the football around.

"Get the rec book, Ibtihaj," my mother yelled from the kitchen. "You're next." It was a Saturday in early spring, and the new Maplewood Recreation booklet had just arrived in our mailbox. That meant it was time for all the kids in the family to pick sports programs for the summer. Qareeb was probably going to select baseball or basketball. He was also a part of the local youth track team, the Jaguars. Asiya, now seven, decided to try gymnastics.

I grabbed the booklet from the coffee table in the living room and walked into the kitchen. I plopped down at the table while my mother started making lunch. We had just moved Koocah's cage from the living room to the kitchen, where the family spent most of our time. As Koocah stretched her wings and soaked up the afternoon sun pouring in from the skylight, I flipped through the pages of the rec book. There were so many different programs to choose from, but I had already tried tee-ball and tennis. Both soccer and lacrosse were big sports in our town, but they didn't really pique my interest.

I pushed the booklet away with a sigh.

"What's the matter? You can't find anything that you like?" my mother asked.

"Nope," I said. "Can't I just swim and work in my garden this summer?" I had plans to try growing eggplant along with my tomatoes this summer. Even though I asked the question, I knew I was obligated to find a summer sport.

Mommy also taught summer school for the extra money, so she couldn't just leave five kids at home alone all day. She signed us up for the summer program at the Roseville Avenue mosque in Newark, which was a few blocks over from her school. Afterward, she would drop off us at practice.

"What about track?" she asked, looking over my shoulder at the rec book. "You could join the Jaguars with Qareeb."

I started to get nervous. Even though Qareeb really seemed to enjoy running track, I wasn't sure if I was fast enough to join the track program. But instead of admitting this concern, I opted for the obvious.

"I don't know, Mommy," I said. "It's going to be really hot." Although the Jaguars practiced at Underhill Field, the same place where Qareeb played football, that wasn't going to help me escape the scorching summer heat.

My mother tried to ease my worries. "Oh, you'll be fine," she said. "We'll pack you a water bottle. You'll be with your brother, it'll be great!" She turned back to finish preparing lunch.

"Um, I don't know," I tried again. I was already thinking about what I could wear. I remembered going to Qareeb's meets the year before. Everyone wore the same uniform, a tank top and shorts, with a yellowy gold stripe down either side. The girls wore black bottoms that looked more like underwear or bikini briefs.

"Mommy, what would I wear?" I asked, wondering how as a young Muslim girl the team uniform could ever suit me. "Have you noticed what the girls on the team run in?

My mom waved away that thought. "We'll find you some leggings and a t-shirt to run in. I'll talk to the coaches to see what colors they would want you to wear. Don't worry."

I wanted to point out that running in leggings would simply

make running in the heat even more unbearable, but I kept that thought to myself. Instead I asked, "What if I don't like it?"

She turned to look at me. "What if you don't like what? The uniform?" she asked.

"What if I don't like running?" I said again. "You know running isn't really my thing."

"You could have fooled me with the amount of time you and Qareeb spend running around this house," my mother huffed. "You might as well expend all that energy at track practice where it belongs." She walked over to the refrigerator and pulled out the rest of the food she needed. As she closed the fridge, I could tell there was no changing her mind. But she did have a point. Qareeb and I were a mess, constantly daring each other to do the craziest things. Clearly I didn't have an adequate defense about not liking running. And I knew my mother had already made up her mind. It was a done deal.

"I guess I could try it," I said, intentionally showing little enthusiasm.

"Good," my mom said. "I like the coaches over there. They're all Black and great role models for both you and Qareeb. I'm sure you'll make some good friends."

I didn't share my mother's excitement, but I knew I didn't really have a choice. A summer without a sport was not in the cards for me.

Because I was only ten and hadn't hit puberty, I didn't have to wear my hijab yet. My mom had me wear it to school sometimes, mostly on days when I didn't have gym class. Luckily, I didn't have to wear hijab to track practice. That would have been unbearable in the summer heat, especially with the spandex leggings I wore to cover my legs.

I knew I didn't want to run the long-distance events, and I

wasn't sure I was fast enough for the sprints, so I volunteered to run the 800 because it was a middle distance, not too fast and not too slow. The best part about track was the days when we had meets. Once I finished competing in my events, I would spend the rest of the day huddled in the bleachers with my friends chatting and laughing, or at the concession stand grabbing warm pretzels and nachos. The competitive part of me liked the feeling of winning, crossing the finish line, and coming home with a medal. Once I got a taste of winning, I could admit I liked the feeling, and it became a part of my being.

In the middle of July, we had our first away meet in northern New Jersey. The coaches told us the meet was really important and said to make sure we got plenty of rest and water the night before. The weatherman had forecasted a record high for the day of the meet. I knew I was going to be extra hot in my shimmery spandex leggings, and I knew someone was going to ask me about them and I was going to have to explain why I covered my legs. I also knew I was going to hate that whole part of the experience, even if I came home with a million medals. Qareeb was so lucky in that way. He didn't have to wear anything that made him stick out. He got to wear the same uniform as everyone else and didn't have to carry the burden of explaining our family's religious practices every time we went to an away meet. When people saw him in his uniform, he was just one more Jaguar. Me, I was different.

The night before the meet, Abu pulled me aside before I went to bed. He couldn't come to the meet because he had to go into work, but he wanted to give me some last-minute advice.

"Ibtihaj," he started, "it's going to be really hot tomorrow, and running in the heat can be dangerous. If you feel faint or like you can't breathe, it's okay to stop. The sun can be brutal."

I nodded and wrapped my arms around him in a hug, breathing in his familiar scent, a mixture of the sweet, musky oil he used in his beard and laundry detergent. Abu and I tended to bond the most when it came to sports, so when he offered this extra bit of advice I soaked it up.

On the day of the meet, the sun was bright, the sky blue, and the trees infinite as we drove down the highway. The ride to the meet was close to two hours. It felt like an eternity. Mommy drove as Qareeb and I stared out the window and Asiya and Faizah nodded in and out of sleep in their car seats.

My mom turned on the car radio to the only station she ever listened to, the one that played smooth jazz. Anita Baker's soothing voice filled the car, and my mom and I sang the lyrics together. When the song was over, I grinned at her. "I love that song."

"Me too," she said. "I love anything Anita Baker sings."

"Mommy, how come we can listen to smooth jazz in the car, but we can't listen to other music?" I asked. "Is smooth jazz halal?"

She turned the radio off and popped in a Quran recitation cassette. She didn't answer my question and kept her eyes on the road in front of us. I didn't ask again. I took a cue from my brother, settled back into my seat, and looked out the window for the rest of the ride.

When we got to the track, my mom told Qareeb and me to go find our coaches while she roused my sisters from their sleep. We both gave her a quick hug and then ran off to find our teammates. I had already worked up a sweat. It felt like it was 100 degrees.

As we started off, I told my brother I was worried about the heat.

"Don't be a baby. It's only like eighty-five degrees," he said.

I narrowed my eyes but didn't say anything. I trotted off to find my friends and left Qareeb to his own devices.

When it was my turn to race, I prayed that I'd survive the heat. I heard other girls talking about the heat, too, and they weren't even wearing long tights like I was. This did not bode well for me.

BANG! The gun went off, and I sprang out of the blocks. I

started off in the lead and felt good. I pumped my arms and length-
ened my stride. The first 200 done. But the sun was so strong I
could feel its rays on every inch of my body. The second 200 done.
I only had to make it around the track one more time, but my legs
had started to feel like they were made of lead. Two girls passed
me, and then another. I tried to sprint to regain my lead, but I
couldn't make my legs go any faster, and my breath started to come
in jagged heaves. Suddenly my father's voice popped into my head.
"If it hurts to breathe, you can stop." I tried to pull in a breath, but
there was growing pressure. So I slowed down, fell into a trot, and
then just started to walk. It was no use. I felt sick to my stomach.
Instead of heading to the finish line, I simply walked off the track.
I scanned the bleachers and found my mother and my two sisters
and slowly made my way over to them. I used the sleeves from my
t-shirt to wipe the sweat dripping from my forehead and kept my
head down to block the unforgiving sun.

As I got closer to my mom, I noticed she did not look happy.

"What are you doing?" she yelled before I even made it up to
their seats.

"Abu said if I couldn't breathe I could stop," I said, surprised
by her tone.

"No, no, no," she said. "You can't do that!"

"Ma, but I couldn't breathe!" I said.

"Look, the sun is strong, but you cannot stop in the middle
of the race," she insisted. "I don't expect you to always win, but I
expect you to give it your all. You have to give a hundred percent. I
didn't drive all the way out here to watch you give up."

"But Abu said that if I had trouble breathing…" I said, pleading my case.

Then Qareeb came over to us with a look of confusion on his
face. "Why'd you stop running, Ibtihaj? You were winning!"

I was now embarrassed and realized that maybe stopping

wasn't the best thing to do. I looked over at my teammates with tears in my eyes. The other girls had finished but I hadn't.

I couldn't look at Qareeb, so I turned back to my mom and said, "I'm sorry."

"Sorry isn't ever going to win the race, Ibtihaj," my mother said. "You have to work for the win," she said, "even if it hurts."

It was then that I realized that winning wasn't going to come easily; I never wanted to see that look of disappointment on my mother's face again. I never wanted to give her a reason to think I was wasting her time or that I didn't know how to work hard. I promised myself that next time I would do better and I would never give up. And that became my mantra as an athlete.

CHAPTER 3

My mission in life is not merely to survive, but to thrive.

—MAYA ANGELOU

Why are you wearing that tablecloth on your head?" Jack Bowman sneered.

I gritted my teeth and tried really hard not to let the tears that were pressing hard against my eyelids fall. I kept walking to my class and pretended not to hear Jack's irritating voice. Every time he passed me in the hallways at school, that kid would pick on me. I was always on high alert as I moved from class to class, praying I didn't cross paths with him. Middle school was hard enough without having to worry about this kid harassing me.

Now that I was wearing hijab to school every day since I'd officially hit puberty, and I was in seventh grade, my life had gotten complicated. Middle school is typically about fitting in, and that's all I wanted to do. On the one hand, I was a good student, I had a few close friends, and most of my teachers loved me, but on the other, it was impossible for me to ever blend in with the crowd. I'd never be just like everyone else. Because of my hijab, I was different. You wouldn't think a simple headscarf could cause so much commotion, and yet I'd frequently have to look over my shoulder to see if Jack or one of his friends was lurking nearby. Some days, I'd have to dodge insults being thrown at me walking down the hallway. Certain girls in the cool club acted like I didn't exist. And the thing was, I never knew if it was because they didn't like me, or they didn't like my hijab.

My hijab was part of me, though. I didn't see why it made me any different than the other kids. So I wore a scarf to cover my hair—*why was that such a big deal?* Other people projected that difference on me, because I didn't ask for any special considerations simply because of what I wore on my head. My hijab was a sign of my maturity and faithfulness to Allah, but I didn't need anyone at Maplewood Middle School to recognize that. I just wanted my hijab to be a nonissue.

One of the biggest issues Muslims in America face is that they often are misunderstood. People don't know that Islam is one of the three Abrahamic faiths, Christianity and Judaism being the other two. They don't know that Muslims recognize Moses, Abraham, and Jesus as prophets. They don't believe that we worship the same God as Christians and Jews do; we simply refer to that same God as Allah. The truth is, if people knew what it takes to be a Muslim— believe in one God, pray five times a day, give to the poor, make a pilgrimage to Mecca, and fast during Ramadan—they'd probably rethink their attitudes about my religion. Of course, there is far more to learn about Islam than the five pillars, as we call them, but those are the foundations of Islam. Those are the beliefs and practices on which we base our life. As a child, I understood we are to live our lives following the example of the prophet Muhammad. And as such, we do things a little differently than some people, but I never understood why that was justification for others to be cruel.

There was this one kid, Jeremy Jackson. For some reason, Jeremy wouldn't accept that I belonged at Maplewood Middle School just like all the other kids. He teased me whenever possible. My friends told me to ignore him, which I tried to do, but it was hard because I never knew where or when he'd show up.

One day I was in art class, and we were working with oil paints. I was excited to get started because I loved painting. I've always been considered the artistic one in my family, just like my dad. Abu taught me the basics of drawing, and from there I moved on to painting and sketching—I loved anything where I could be creative with colors. Sometimes I would sketch designs for new clothes for my Barbies to wear. Once I learned how to use a sewing machine in Ms. Deeds's home economics class, my imagination really took off. I started making clothes for my dolls and even patchwork pillowcases for everyone in my family. My creative expression also extended to my own personal fashion, often color-coordinating my hijab and sneakers.

Now that I was in seventh grade, art class had gotten far more sophisticated, and I looked forward to learning new creative skills. We had moved beyond Magic Markers and watercolors and were using oil paints on real canvas. I was trying to paint a bouquet of purple and orange flowers but the teacher, Ms. Murphy, wanted us to only use primary colors, so I blended the paints to get the colors I wanted. I had to really think about how to get the colors just right, so I didn't notice the shadow creeping up behind me. Suddenly I was blinded by a huge pain in my left arm.

"Ow," I cried out. Jeremy Jackson was standing next to me with a smirk on his face.

"Sorry," Jeremy said, but he obviously didn't mean it. He'd punched me as hard as he could in front of everyone, and I could barely see straight from the pain and the humiliation.

Jeremy had taken advantage of the fact that Ms. Murphy had stepped out into the hall to speak with another student.

I tried to hold back the tears, but they were already forming. My arm stung, but I was also seething. "I'm going to tell my brother you hit me," I said.

Jeremy shrugged and walked away. I had to force myself to

remain calm and try to breathe normally. How dare he hit me like that and then act like nothing had happened! I couldn't understand how kids could be so cruel for no reason. I tried my best to focus on my painting, but all I could see was red. I held my face down so no one could see the hot, angry tears running down my face. I tried to clear my mind of revenge. I wiped the tears off my face with my shirtsleeve and tried to pull myself together. "Deep breath, Ibtihaj," I told myself, remembering what my mom said to me the day I came home in the third grade after Delia Sanders and her brother Justin threw snowballs at me after school. She made me take a deep breath and reminded me that Allah rewards the kind. "So, let it go," she'd said. And I did, but I also told Qareeb what had happened, and he helped me ambush Delia and Justin with an arsenal of snowballs the following week after school.

As soon as the last bell rang, I found my brother.

"What's up?" he said when he saw me.

"I need your help," I said, pulling him away from his group of friends.

"What's wrong?" he said. "What happened?" Qareeb could tell by my voice and entire demeanor that I was upset. He knew that since I'd started wearing my hijab every day I was a target more than ever. And even though he was one of the cool kids at our school, his popularity didn't rub off on me.

I told Qareeb about Jeremy hitting me in the arm and calling me names. "And I said that I'd tell you what he did, but he said he didn't care, Qareeb. You have to talk to him and let him know he can't put his hands on me."

Qareeb looked angry. I was so grateful I had a brother who wasn't afraid to stick up for me. At home I spent a lot of time wishing Qareeb would calm down, because he was so hyperactive, but at times like this I appreciated my brother and all of his fearlessness.

"Which one is he?" Qareeb asked, already looking around the back lawn of the school where all of the students were dismissed.

I scanned the crowd of students pouring out of the middle school building and quickly spotted Jeremy. I had no idea how things were going to go down. I wasn't the type of person to engineer fights between seventh-grade bullies and my brother after school, but I was still mad. All I could think about was getting Jeremy to leave me alone, once and for all. I wasn't angry just for that day when he punched me, it was for every day he found a way to hurt or humiliate me in front of my classmates. I pointed Jeremy out to Qareeb. "That's him," I said, "the ugly one with the red shirt."

My brother gave me a look. "Are you sure he punched you on purpose?"

"Yeah, I'm sure," I said with confidence. "He teases me all the time."

"All right, come on," he said to me and started pushing through the crowd toward where Jeremy was standing with a bunch of his friends.

"Yo, Jeremy, why'd you punch my sister?" Qareeb said, getting straight to the point.

"I didn't punch her hard," Jeremy stammered. "I was just playing around and—"

Before Jeremy could finish his sentence, *KA-POW!* Qareeb punched Jeremy in the arm.

"Don't you ever touch my sister again," Qareeb said with extra grit in his voice.

I don't know if it was the pain, the embarrassment of being punched by an eighth-grader in front of his friends, or a combination of the two, but Jeremy started crying. Watching the boy cry didn't make me feel as good as I thought it would, but Jeremy never bothered me again.

But there were always others to take his place.

There was Jonathan Grady. He was a year older than me. He knew my brother, but that didn't stop him from finding ways to torture me. He followed me home from school on a day when I couldn't find Qareeb. I left the school grounds with a small group of my friends, but since I lived the farthest from school, I had to walk the last two blocks alone. I was only a block from home when I felt a kick from behind. Jonathan Grady had sneaked up on me and kicked my brand-new backpack so hard, he kicked a hole in it. He ran away laughing, and I cried the rest of the way home.

Looking back, I'd say middle school bullies got the best of my tears. My grandmother used to tell me, "Baby, if you keep crying so much, you're going to run out of tears." Everyone in my family, in fact, knew I cried a lot; it was usually because I was known as a bit of a drama queen around the house. But I didn't bring the troubles I had at school home with me. I tried to keep those tears to myself.

Usually when I got home, my father would be there. Because he worked the night shift, he would make sure we got busy doing our homework, and by the time he had to leave for work, my mother would be walking in the door. There was usually so much going on in our house after school with five kids running around that most of the time I didn't even have time to tell my parents about the problems I was having at school, and usually by the time I was safely ensconced in our family bubble, the problems didn't seem that bad. It didn't seem worth it to burden my parents with my middle-school issues. Qareeb told me to stand up for myself if I had to, but I didn't want to stand up or speak out or anything. I just wanted to be like my friends who could go to school and not have to worry about being harassed over their religion. They were free to be themselves, and that's all I wanted, too.

———————

"Mommy, do I have to wear my hijab today?" I asked once, early one morning after getting dressed.

My mother stopped what she was doing and gave me a look; I could not tell if it was pity or shame or disappointment.

"Yes, you have to wear it," my mother said. "It might be hard at times, but remember all of this is Allah's plan. And I know it feels hard for you now, but I promise you as you get older, you'll understand that wearing hijab is a gift, not a punishment."

Now I know my mother was right. But the kid in me who just wanted to fit in with her friends wasn't convinced. I guess a part of me knew that even without my hijab, there would still be other reasons people didn't like me. For instance, there was a group of girls who loved to tease me and tell me as often as they could that I wasn't "really Black" because I talked "white" and did well in school.

Maplewood tracked students by ability, and I was always in the track for advanced learners. By seventh grade, the tracks were well established, and the smart kids had all of their classes together. Usually I was one of a small number of Black kids in these classes. Maplewood is a diverse town, but in the classrooms, segregation was in full effect, and I was on the wrong side of the color line. I was quite well versed in being the odd girl out in every situation. The only Black girl, the only Muslim girl, the only hijabi.

So I put on my hijab that day and never asked if I could leave it at home again. I tolerated the teasing and tried to keep my attention on the things I loved about school, which were pretty much everything else. It wasn't always easy, but I would tell myself that if I got good grades and I was the smartest in the class, then people like Jonathan and Jeremy could eat each and every one of my perfect report cards.

As soon I turned eleven, my mother enrolled me in summer pre-college programs at places like the New Jersey Institute of Technology (NJIT) and the University of Medicine and Dentistry, specifically targeted to high-achieving Black and Latino children.

These summer courses were a soothing balm for the hits I'd taken during the school year. In these classes I was praised for being smart and hardworking. Everyone around me looked like me: brown. Even the teachers. There were even other Muslim students in the mix, so I didn't stand out at all. I could be myself and never worried that an ignorant person would say something mean to me.

My parents had already decided I would be a doctor because I did well in math and science at school, and these programs were to help me get on that path. Like many parents, especially those in the Muslim community, my parents demanded academic excellence from their children. If we didn't bring home all A's on our report cards it was understood we'd receive some sort of punishment. My parents ran a tight ship, and I had no reason to believe they weren't serious about their demands, so I didn't dare bring home any grade below an A-minus. My parents had high expectations about our professional future as well. They expected us to choose one of two prestigious career paths, doctor or lawyer. Even though I maintained an A average in all of my classes in middle school, I had a real aptitude for math and science, which is why my parents tried to steer me toward medicine. *ER* was one of my favorite TV shows.

The philosophy behind these pre-college summer programs was to get minority children on a college prep track as soon as possible. Not only did we have advanced academic classes, we were also taught time-management skills, essay writing, and public speaking. I loved it. The teachers taught us about how to apply for college admission and financial aid. They didn't promise us anything, but they told us if we worked hard and took advantage of every opportunity presented to us, we would succeed.

The first summer I attended the program I met a girl named Damaris. She lived in South Orange, a neighboring town to

Maplewood. Damaris's mother was Black and her father was Fili-pino. She had golden honey skin, almost the same color as mine, and a ready smile. Despite her biracial background, Damaris strongly identified as Black. She was always quoting famous Black writers and activists. We had almost every class together that sum-mer, and we managed to become close friends in a short time. I loved the fact that Damaris was Black like me, smart, and also reveled in spending her summer learning about cell reproduction and the best way to solve algebraic inequalities. She didn't care that I was a Muslim and didn't need me to catch her up on Muslim Basics 101 because she had a cousin who was Muslim. Damaris was the kind of friend I wished I had in middle school.

"I wish you could transfer to my school for eighth grade," I told Damaris on the phone one night.

"Yeah, that would be great," Damaris said. "But at least we'll be in high school together for four years," she said, always one to find the bright side of matters. "And when we are, you can also meet my friends Nicole and Ana. You'll like them, too."

If Damaris's friends were anything like her, I knew I'd like them. I still had one more year at Maplewood Middle School, and sometimes I couldn't help but wish I could skip the last year of middle school.

"You can do it, Ibtihaj," Damaris said, when I shared this thought with her. I'd told her about some of the bullying I'd faced. "You're stronger than you think, and you're crazy smart. As my mom always says, 'our ancestors fought too hard for us to give up now.'"

I smiled from the other end of the phone. Damaris was the best.

Even though I didn't tell my mother about every single time someone was mean to me at school, she wasn't unaware of my feel-ings of isolation. She knew I yearned to fit in with my classmates and on the school softball team. She had witnessed some of the cattiness at the mosque that I had to deal with, too. At the masjid we attended, there was a general sense that the kids who went to public school instead of a private Islamic school would probably be drinking, partying, and getting pregnant before they made it out of high school. As a public school kid, I had to fight against that stereotype. My mother shook her head in disappointment whenever she heard about "that nonsense," as she called it. "Those kids don't know what they're talking about, and their parents should be ashamed of themselves for letting them think that way," she said. I was told to ignore anyone who held such ridiculous beliefs.

At the end of the day, I had to put my trust in my parents and believe them when they said that if I just worked hard and focused on my studies, then everything would work itself out. That trust helped me survive my first years in hijab and middle school. My mom did her part, too. She was constantly on the lookout for activities and classes that would be good for me and my developing sense of identity.

One day, during the fall of my eighth-grade year, my mom and I were on our way to pick up Qareeb from school. He was a freshman now at Columbia High School, the same school I would be attending the following year. I soaked up every detail I could during those pickups, trying to get a sense of what high school would be like. At home Qareeb was a typical big brother, and when I pressed for information he gave me monosyllabic answers to my questions.

"Are the kids nice?" I'd ask.

"Yeah," he would say.

"Are the classes harder?"

"Sort of," Qareeb would tell me before banishing me from his room.

As we pulled up to the front of his school, my mom poked me on the arm and pointed toward the windows in front. "What do you think they're doing in there?" she said, craning her neck to get a better view of what looked like a bunch of kids sword fighting in the school cafeteria.

I rolled my window down to get a better view, but all I could see was a bunch of kids wearing white pants, white jackets, and what looked like masks, moving around with long, thin swords.

"I have no idea," I said, uninterested in whatever activity was taking place in there. My mind was busy with other things, like whether I'd still be the only kid wearing a hijab in high school and what classes I'd be able to take. My mom was looking at the kids in the cafeteria, but I was scanning the high school girls pouring out of the massive building.

"It looks like some kind of sports practice. And all the kids are covered up, Ibtihaj!" Mom said, still trying to see into the window. But then Qareeb jumped in the car, and we had to pull out of the schoolyard.

"Qareeb, do you know what they're practicing there in the cafeteria?" Mom asked. Her sports antennae were buzzing.

Qareeb gave a quick turn of his head to see what my mom was referring to and then said, "Oh, yeah. That's the fencing team. I don't know anything about it."

———

That night, my mom went online and discovered that Columbia High School had one of the best fencing programs in the state, which was a significant honor, because apparently New Jersey had the largest number of high school fencers in the country. The most intriguing information she found was that although many people claim that fencing originated in Europe—specifically in Italy and Germany—historians have found cave paintings depicting early sword fighting back in 1190 BC in Luxor, Egypt. Fencing didn't originate as a sport; it was a method of defense used by soldiers in the military and against enemies at war. Then in the fourteenth and fifteenth centuries Europeans began to consider learning swordplay to be a fashionable and necessary part of a gentleman's education; it became divorced from violence and transformed more into a show of athleticism. With the invention of the wire-mesh helmet and a sword with a blunted tip, accidental deaths and injuries became less common, and fencing was featured in the first modern Olympic Games in Athens, Greece, in 1896. It was originally a male-only sport; women's fencing was not introduced into the Olympic Games until the 1924 games in Paris.

The more my mother read about the Columbia High School team and the sport of fencing, the more boxes it checked off her list. A winning team? Check. A uniform where Ibtihaj would be totally covered without having to alter the uniform in any way? Check. An opportunity to participate in a sport that wouldn't require Mom and Dad to drive her to practice? Check. There was only one problem with fencing. No one in our family knew the first thing about the sport. Even though my father was the major sports fan, he told my mom that fencing was not in his repertoire. But this did not stop my mother. There was never a problem she couldn't solve. By the time I came down for breakfast the next day, Mommy had tracked down none other than the coach for the Columbia High School fencing team, and I had a private lesson scheduled for the following week.

———

I don't think my parents would normally send me to a strange man's house to learn how to fight with a sword, but Frank Mustilli wasn't exactly a strange man. He was more of a legend in the local fencing community. Coach Mustilli had been a college fencing champion at Montclair State College during his junior and senior years. Now, he was the president of a small bank in South Orange, but fencing was still his passion. What's more, both of his daughters were successful college fencers, and there was talk that the elder daughter might make it all the way to the Olympics. Clearly this man knew what he was doing.

My father and I went to see Coach Mustilli on a Saturday morning. On the short drive over, hardly a word was said in the car as both my father and I were lost in our thoughts. Neither one of us knew what to expect. We parked in the front of the coach's redbrick house, and before we could get to the front door, a short white man with thick, shiny black hair and wire-framed glasses wearing a t-shirt and sweatpants came out to greet us. "I'm Frank Mustilli," he said, extending a hand to my dad. And then he turned to me.

"How do you pronounce your name, young lady?"

"It's Ibtihaj," I said shyly.

"Ibtihaj," he repeated. "That's an interesting name. I like it. Now let's go get started."

The coach led us down his long driveway to the garage. "I have a whole setup in here," he said, pushing the button on a gadget to open the garage door. Inside, the garage looked like a mini gymnasium. There were a bunch of swords balanced in a rack that looked like an umbrella stand, a long narrow strip painted on the floor, and some bright red electrical boxes that I later found out were used to attach to the swords to track points.

"Come on over here, Ibtihaj," Coach Mustilli said, smiling. "We only have thirty minutes, so let's get right to it."

My dad found a chair in the corner and sat down.

"Ibtihaj, first lesson: fencing is like physical chess—you have to be strong and strategic," the coach said. I nodded and tried to keep the words "strong" and "strategic" in the forefront of my mind, but I was nervous. I think I was already sweating, and we hadn't even started moving yet. But this was my first one-on-one lesson, and I didn't feel comfortable in such close proximity to an adult male who wasn't related to me. I was used to learning sports with a group of kids on a field or a track—not in some garage with me as the center of attention.

"You have to be quick," the coach was saying. "Fencing is all about speed and agility. It's strategy, it's technique. And everything comes at you within a millionth of a second. You think you can handle that?" Before I could answer, Coach Mustilli grabbed a sword and was demonstrating what a fencer should look like in action.

"This is the strip," he said, pointing to the long, narrow, red rectangle on the floor. "All fencing takes place on this strip. If you step off the strip, or get pushed off, game over. Got that?" With his sword in the air, the coach proceeded to move back and forth on the strip in a series of lunges and quick steps, all the while moving his sword in jabbing and thrusting motions. I felt my eyes grow wide, and I snuck a peek at my dad, whose face was impassive. I turned back to watch the coach.

"Now before we have you get your hands on a sword and you poke me in the eye, let's show you how you have to move on the strip," Coach said. "Come stand over here with me."

I walked over to the strip and stood facing Coach Mustilli. I could barely look him in the eye. I felt incredibly self-conscious.

"Okay, Ibtihaj," Coach Mustilli started. "Here's what I want you to do. I want you put your right leg in front of you and then bend it, like you're doing a lunge."

I did what he said, but he wasn't satisfied.

"Straighten that back leg," he said.

The coach must have sensed my nervousness because before he put his hands on my back leg he announced, "I'm going to just adjust your leg here a little bit."

I think I flinched when he touched me.

I think my dad did, too. He definitely made some sort of noise in the back of his throat and shifted uncomfortably in his chair. Both of us were uncomfortable, but the coach seemed oblivious.

He continued on with his lesson, occasionally putting his hands on me to adjust my stance or to move my arm into the right position. He taught me how to lunge forward and then scoot right back. Lunge forward and scoot right back. It all felt very awkward and boring. There wasn't a lot of action happening. My body felt strange in the neutral fencing position with my knees bent and pointed outward. It felt like I was executing something in between a karate move and calypso dance. I could also feel Abu's thoughts. He kept shifting in his seat every time the coach put his hand on my leg or waist. I think it was pretty clear that my dad wasn't comfortable with what was going on. The frown on my father's face only added to my discomfort. When the coach finally said our time was up, I let out a sigh of relief. Abu thanked Coach Mustilli and paid him in cash. I almost ran back to the car.

When we got home, my mom could barely wait for us to walk through the front door.

"How was it, Ibtihaj?" she asked me, a look of giddy anticipation on her face.

I glanced at my father, who answered for the both of us. "Ibtihaj will not be fencing," he said.

My mom looked confused. "Why, what happened?"

"That man had his hands all over Ibtihaj," my dad said, the concern he'd been holding back now uncorked.

My mother turned to me for confirmation. "You didn't like it, baby?"

I shrugged my shoulders. "It was okay. I don't know," I said softly. "I didn't feel very comfortable in that garage, and it wasn't all that exciting."

Abu patted me on the back. "Don't worry, we'll find another sport for you," he said and told me to go upstairs to my room.

I didn't need to be told twice, and I headed for the stairs. I figured my dad was going to give my mom a blow-by-blow of the awkward fencing lesson and all the reasons I should never go back. I kind of felt bad for my mom because she was so sure this was going to be the perfect activity for me, but as far as I was concerned, fencing wasn't it. Like track and tennis, I was glad I tried it, but it wasn't for me.

CHAPTER 4

You can be the lead in your own life.

—KERRY WASHINGTON

I had to come up with a plan.

Even though it was hot in my attic bedroom, I had my own room now that Asiya had moved downstairs to share a room with Faizah. I could think in peace and escape into my own world when I needed to. Amy told me I was crazy to be worried about college before we even started high school, but I wasn't going to wait until it was too late. That's not who I am. I don't wait for things to happen to me, I go out and make them happen. When we finished our biology class at NJIT, Ms. Ramos had warned us about the student with a 4.0 GPA. He'd been accepted into five great colleges but ended up not going to any of them because his parents couldn't afford the tuition.

"Don't become the next cautionary tale," Ms. Ramos had said, giving a strong warning to us rising ninth-graders in the room. "It is never too early to figure out how you're going to pay for college. Don't automatically assume your parents are going to figure it out for you, either."

I knew Ms. Ramos was right, especially in my case. With four other kids to think about, there wasn't going to be a blank check from my parents for my college tuition. I had to focus on finding a way to pay for college. My parents would be there to help—my mom bought a giant book about college scholarships for me—but the work of earning that scholarship would fall to me. Ms. Ramos had already made us come up with our wish list of colleges we wanted to apply to, and I had chosen all eight schools in the Ivy League plus Duke, because I wanted to go to one of the best schools in the country. Earlier in the summer, we'd had a college fair, and representatives from the top colleges had been there to sell us on their institutions. I had collected their catalogs and completely bought into the dream they were selling. I wanted to go to one of the schools with the best reputation and that offered the best education. After all, if I was going to be a doctor, my future was riding on it.

I'd often pull out the collection of college catalogs I'd picked up and lay them out on my bed. I loved looking at the glossy pages of campus life, young people on their own and independent. I couldn't wait to get there. To college. To my future.

As I started to brainstorm how to get the most scholarship money for college, I again paged through my catalogs and I noticed something I hadn't noticed before. All these Ivy League institutions had fencing teams. I grabbed the Princeton catalog just to double-check and, sure enough, under sports teams, fencing was listed. I hopped off my bed and went over to my desk and turned on my computer. While I waited for it to boot up, I tried to remember what I'd learned at that lesson in that man's garage. I didn't remember much, only that it was rather uncomfortable and kind of boring. I started typing questions about fencing into the search bar on my computer, and one hour later realized I needed to give fencing another try. It was a practical decision. Ms. Ramos had told us to go after scholarships that we were uniquely qualified for instead of the ones that "everyone and their mama were going to try to get." I quickly devised my plan.

I had four years to become a good enough fencer to earn a scholarship. I could do that, I thought—maybe naively. I knew I'd put in the work. And I figured, even if I didn't get good enough for a scholarship, it would still make me stand out on my applications. I noticed that almost all of the fencers in the pictures I'd seen were white men, so a young Black woman who fenced, that would definitely make me an original. Like Serena and Venus Williams. And that's what Ms. Ramos said was the key: figure out how to make yourself stand out in the crowd. "Don't ever settle for being like everyone else," she'd said. I'd laughed a little inside when she said that, because "being like everyone else" wasn't even an option for me, the African-American girl wearing hijab.

I was so excited for high school. I devised this game plan that included taking all honors and advanced placement classes and I wanted to play three new sports, one for each season, of course, because I knew colleges wanted to see a diverse résumé. My parents did, too. Playing sports had become such an integral part of our family culture, and I saw no reason to move away from the status quo. I was going to do volleyball in the fall because Damaris played club volleyball and told me how much fun it was. Fencing would be my winter sport, and I would play softball in the spring. Now that I'd convinced my dad that fencing could possibly net me a scholarship and because I'd be fencing on a team instead of taking personal lessons in someone's garage, he was 100 percent in favor of my plan. It was perfect. Now all I had to do was convince my friends to try out for the fencing team with me. That way, if I still didn't like it, at least I'd be hanging with my girls.

After volleyball practice, I reminded Nicole and Ana that fencing tryouts were coming up. "All we have to do is show up for the first day of practice, and essentially we're on the team," I said, trying to make it sound easy.

"But do we really want to do this, Ibti?" Ana asked.

"Yeah," Nicole quipped. "Are we sure fencing is 'the thing'?"

Nicole's dad had fenced in college, so he was really keen on her checking it out. And Ana's mom wanted her to try out, too. So luckily for me, that left both Nicole and Ana with little choice in the matter.

But I wanted my friends to share in my enthusiasm. "Aren't you guys even just a bit curious to see what fencing is like?" I asked.

They shrugged. Nicole and Ana were on the volleyball team, and we'd become friendly at practice, plus Ana and I had a few classes together.

"Don't worry, Ibti," Ana said. "We'll be there. But if it's lame, I'm out."

"Yeah," Nicole said, nodding her head. "Me too."

On the day of tryouts, Ana, Nicole, and I met outside of the school cafeteria, where fencing practice was held. All of us were dressed in t-shirts and gym clothes. I had on my gray sweatpants, Nicole had on some cute purple Nike shorts, and Ana wore capris. We looked ready. Before we walked into the cafeteria, Ana asked me, "Ibti, aren't you hot in those baggy pants?" she said. "It still feels like summer outside."

"No, I'm fine," I said.

"I'd be sweating if I had to wear long pants all the time. I don't know how you do it," she said.

"I'm used to it," I said.

"Well, girl," Nicole said, "I could never be a Muslim because I swear to God I am always hot. Plus, I look too cute in tank tops." We all giggled, but I cringed on the inside. I hated feeling different, especially around my friends.

I forced myself to ignore their comments and kept a smile on my face. I had learned a long time ago how to assimilate, cover my discomfort, and just keep it moving.

"Come on, you guys, let's get in there," I said, hoping to get them interested.

I pushed the door open to the cafeteria, and the three of us peeked in. Most of the people milling around in the room were white and kind of dorky looking. At first glance, it didn't look like a welcoming space for three Black girls with something to prove. We pulled our heads out of the room and let the doors close.

Nicole and Ana looked at each other and almost in unison said, "No way!"

I laughed. "Come on, you guys," I said. "Let's just check it out."

"Sorry, Ibti, we've only been in high school for two months, and we are not going to kill any chance we have at having a normal social life by joining that team," Ana said.

I turned to Nicole. I couldn't believe she was going to just walk away. "Come on, it could be fun," I tried.

Nicole scowled. "You cannot make me go in there, Ibti."

"Are you kidding me?" I blurted out. I couldn't believe they were ditching me. But then again, lately, a lot of my friends were now more interested in boys and being popular than anything else. Me? I wasn't ready to give up my childhood. I still liked riding bikes, playing with my Barbies, and walking down to Main Street to get ice cream. Chasing boys and going to parties weren't even options in the Muhammad household anyway. My parents were consistent with their message of no parties. Maybe it was because I was only twelve years old when I started high school, but I could already feel some of my friends gravitating in a different direction. So I shouldn't have been so surprised when Nicole and Ana decided to back out. Even still, it hurt my feelings.

"Why don't we all try out for the track team instead?" Ana asked. "That way we won't be the only Black kids on the team.

And we wouldn't be associated with those guys in there," she said, gesturing toward the kids in the cafeteria.

At that moment, I had to make a choice: follow my friends or stick to my plan. I thought about trying out for the track team, and my mind immediately went to the uniform; what would I have to wear? Then I thought about the comments these girls had just made about my clothes and that clinched my decision. I was going to stick to my plan, because my plan was going to take me places.

"I'm going to try out, you guys. I'm sure it won't be that bad," I said.

"Suit yourself," Ana said. "We're leaving. Come on, Nicole."

They turned to collect their things.

"You guys are going to regret this," I said as they started to walk away.

"No, we won't," Ana responded without turning around.

I felt a mixture of anger and disappointment as I swiftly turned and marched into the cafeteria to find the sign-up sheet. I didn't have the luxury of worrying about my reputation as a potential cool kid. As one of the only kids in hijab and one of the only Black kids in honors classes, I would always be different. Being popular wasn't going to get me into college. If fencing was for nerds, I'd gladly fit right it. Besides, Columbia High School's fencing team was known for having the most state championship titles and the highest GPAs in the school. That sounded like my kind of crowd.

Coach Mustilli didn't say anything to me as I stood in line with the other kids as he walked up and down the length of the cafeteria examining us all. I figured he didn't remember me. There were at least 130 kids—boys and girls—and the coach and the team captains didn't waste any time trying to make nice. Within minutes of the official start time, we were running hall sprints, doing frog jumps and bear crawls until sweat was pouring from every inch of our bodies. I never knew I could work that hard, and these were just the warm-ups! After almost an hour, we finally got to the fencing part. After an explanation about the three different types of fencing weapons—épée, saber, and foil—we were told to select one we thought we'd like to try. "It doesn't matter to me what weapon you choose," Coach Mustilli said. I wasn't sure which weapon to select, but some of the other freshman girls I met earlier chose épée, so I did the same. When I picked up the sword, it was lighter than I expected. The blade was stiff and narrowed near the end. I was surprised to find what looked like a blunted smooth button at the tip of the sword instead of a sharp point. Clearly no one was going to draw blood with this weapon. I asked one of the older girls if she thought épée was a good choice for a beginner, and she said yes. Problem solved.

Then the coaches sent us over to the team storage shed, positioned in the back corner of the cafeteria, to find protective gear to wear—they called them fencing whites. Finding equipment that was my size and didn't smell like sweaty gym socks took time. I needed a jacket, half jacket, glove, and a chest protector. There were so many layers it was hard to figure out which piece to put on first. I had to watch the older kids demonstrate more than once. For the lower body, there were pants called knickers, long white socks, and special fencing sneakers. We were allowed to practice in our regular sweatpants so we didn't have to wear the knickers. The best part of the uniform was the mask. The special wire-mesh mask, which Coach promised would protect us from losing an eye, felt weird on my head at first, but I was so happy that it fit comfortably over my hijab. I didn't say anything because people probably would have thought I was crazy, but once we were all suited up, I looked like everyone else, covered from head to toe

Then the coaches divided us up by weapon. I followed the épée group into the adjacent cafeteria, where we were broken down into smaller groups of ten or so based on our ability.

The more experienced kids got started with their drills right away. I watched them moving back and forth on the strip the coaches had marked off on the floor using masking tape. I was blown away by their finesse; they could take the tip of their blade and hit their target with such precision. To me, those kids looked like they were fighting for real. It was impressive. Their moves looked choreographed, and with their faces hidden behind a mask, they weren't the same nerdy kids I saw in the hallways or sat next to in class, they were dueling opponents battling for victory.

It wasn't how I remembered my lesson the previous spring in Coach Mustilli's garage. If fencing had looked this interesting, I probably would have kept at it. I turned my attention back to the coach. I couldn't wait to get to the point where I looked like those kids and I could wield my sword with such precision. Coach Mustilli was working with the saber students, so those of us in the épée group worked with an assistant coach. His name was Jason, and he had recently graduated from New York University (NYU), where he had fenced for their team.

On that first day, we barely touched our weapons. First, we had to learn basic fencing footwork: how to advance, retreat, and lunge. What sounded really simple, moving forward and backward, was actually quite difficult. The legs had to be shoulder distance apart with the front foot facing forward and the back foot perpendicular to the front. Legs bent at the knee, along with the other beginners, I awkwardly advanced down the strip in this position over and over again. Toes up first and then land on my heels. It felt like I was learning how to walk all over again, trying to keep my balance in this awkward position, while simultaneously trying to forget how much pain my legs were in. Once we got a handle on the footwork, we finally got to pick up our weapons. Jason told us to hold our épées steady with the tip of the blade pointed out in front. Then we were to lower our left hand behind us and lower our stances even more. I tried to follow his directions to the letter, but I felt a shooting pain through the front of my right quadriceps and down the back of my left hamstring.

"It feels awkward, I know," Jason encouraged us. "But you'll get used to it. I promise."

I wondered if "awkward" was a synonym for "the most painful thing ever" in the fencing world, but I didn't say anything about my throbbing legs out loud.

I looked around at the other underclassmen on either side of me. Everyone had a look of serious concentration on their faces as they struggled to get the moves right. Some kids giggled nervously as they tried to maneuver their bodies into these "awkward" new positions, but no one was laughing at anyone else. No one was talking about anything but fencing. It was only the first day, but already we felt like a team.

Very quickly, fencing became a big part of my life. Coach Mustilli demanded it. In addition to practicing for almost three hours after school every day, Monday through Friday, we also had practice on Saturday mornings from nine a.m. to noon. Some kids on the team competed in the local and regional competitions as well, and those were held on Sundays! So there was no break from this sport. It felt like fencing was on 24/7. But Coach Mustilli always said that commitment and hard work were what separated champions from everyone else. He warned us that if we didn't want to put in the time, we didn't need to be on the team, because there were plenty of other students willing to put in the work. And Coach made sure we worked hard every day. Practice was methodical and intense. We usually started out with a warm-up run and group stretching led by the team captains. If anyone showed up late to practice, the whole team had to do sprints down the length of the hallway adjacent to the cafeteria. If ten students were late, we had to run ten sprints. No exceptions. We trained as a team, we won and lost as a team. I loved it because Coach Mustilli created a meritocracy. Everyone was treated equally, and you got out of the sport what you put in. We weren't Black or white or Muslim or Christian, we were athletes. I knew when I walked into practice every day, I'd just be one more Columbia High School fencer, not the Muslim girl or the Black girl. Even though I was the only Muslim on the team and one of only a handful of people of color, I always felt safe and that I was exactly where I belonged.

I didn't always feel that comfortable when we went to other schools to compete. Whenever we went to compete against other schools in New Jersey, I never knew what to expect. Fencing had a reputation for being an elite, white sport, and oftentimes that's what the other teams looked like when we made it to their schools. All white students, white coaches, and white parents watching from the bleachers.

Our team of more than a hundred fencers, with five Black kids and two Asians, was considered a model of diversity in the world of high school fencing. As the only hijabi, I often felt all eyes land on me when I walked into a gym for the first time. There were times I couldn't wait to fence just so I could hide behind my mask and blend in with the other athletes. The feeling of dozens of eyes on me made me uncomfortable. But at the beginning of my high school fencing career, I didn't get to fence all that much, because only the varsity team actually got to compete.

In a varsity match, only nine of the team's best fencers compete, three in épée, three in foil, and three in saber. Each fencer had to fence three bouts, one against each of the members of the other team in the same weapon. Whoever scored five points first won the bout. The first school to win fourteen bouts won the meet.

My first year on the team, I only fenced in the junior varsity matches. But not all teams were as large as Columbia's, so if there weren't any other underclassmen to fence, all of us JV kids would be left to cheer on our teammates. Coach Mustilli never made the kids who didn't get to fence feel like we weren't integral members of the team. While everyone knew who the top nine fencers on our team were, when the varsity team won, it was a win for all of us, not just the nine superstars who were on the strip that day. Coach Mustilli had a way of making each of us feel equally valuable, whether we fenced, cheered, or kept score. And if our team was winning by a sizable margin, which was more often than not, he would substitute a few of the junior varsity members in for a bout, so that's why we were always told we had to be ready to fence. That chance to be plucked off the sidelines and sent into action motivated everyone on the team to work hard, because you never knew when Coach might decide to throw you on the strip.

By the end of my first season, even though I hadn't quite distinguished myself as the world's best épée fencer, I was in great shape. I could see muscles in my thighs and stomach, where I had never seen muscles before. I could run four miles without even breaking a sweat. I felt confident and strong. I had a great new group of friends. And I had come to realize that while I enjoyed volleyball because I got to hang out with Damaris and my other friends, as an athlete, I much preferred fencing because it was an individual sport. I wanted to be in total control of the outcome of the game, so when I lost I was the only one to blame, and I could train harder to do better the next time.

By the end of my second year on the team, I still wasn't in the starting lineup, but I was a more confident fencer. I remember watching the newbies come in to practice and thinking how far I'd come since my days of learning how to hold my épée. When we had open fencing, where we were able to fence against each other at practice, Coach Jason didn't have to correct my fencing or footwork as much as he used to, and I could hold my own against some of the upperclassmen. Coach Mustilli was also letting me fence during varsity matches more often, especially when we were competing at larger matches against more than one school. Nicole and Ana still liked to poke fun at me for choosing to fence, but no one could deny the fencing team was Columbia High School's most accomplished sports team. And when my friends saw how hard I had to work to be a fencer, I know I earned their respect.

"I would never be trying to come to school on Saturdays for practice," Ana said on a Monday in the cafeteria after I told her and Nicole what my crazy weekend had entailed. Practice, matches, and then homework.

"Me either," Nicole quipped. "And I can't even imagine not being able to sleep in on Saturday mornings."

"I don't know how you do it," Damaris said, shaking her head. "And keep your grades up."

I shrugged. I wasn't about to tell my friends that I loved my team and couldn't imagine going through high school without them. I didn't feel like I could put into words how happy being part of the fencing team made me—not because I loved fencing so much, but because it felt good to be in that environment. Even when practice was hard, we still had fun. As a team, we were always winning, and, most important of all, I fit in without having to try. It was the only sport I had ever participated in where I didn't have to wear something different. I didn't stand out like I did on every other sports team I had been a part of. I could just be me, and for that reason alone, I was more than willing to practice six days a week and work harder than I ever had before. To me it was more than worth it.

"Are you still going to play softball this spring?" Damaris asked. She knew I wasn't having an easy time getting along with the girls on the softball team and I had confessed to her that I was thinking about quitting.

I still wasn't sure. My original plan was to play a sport each season for all four years of high school, but the softball team was tough. I was the only non-white person on the team, and the other girls generally weren't very friendly. When I compared playing softball with my experience on the fencing team, it was hard to find the enthusiasm to play a game I didn't love, with team members who made me feel like a third wheel on a bicycle, unnecessary and in the way. "I don't know," I finally said. "Maybe I'll play this year and see what happens.

"A very diplomatic Ibtihaj Muhammad answer." Damaris laughed.

I laughed, too. "Hey, I gotta make sure I'm doing the right thing for my future," I said. "I'm not as cute as you, Damaris, so I can't just depend on my looks."

Damaris, Ana, and Nicole all laughed. No matter what, it always felt good to have my girls.

CHAPTER 5

If you're going to do something, you're going to do it to be the best.

—COLIN KAEPERNICK

Who made that noise?" Coach Mustilli demanded as he ran into the épée and foil practice room.

No one answered. "I heard a roar, and I want to know who it was," he said, in his usual forceful tone.

I raised my hand, "It was me, Coach."

"Ibtihaj, get over here," he yelled. I dropped my weapon and mask and ran over to Coach Mustilli. I had been free fencing with my teammate and gotten really into it when I scored my last winning point. She'd attacked me like we were in a real competition instead of just practice, so I'd responded in kind. It wasn't often you heard épée fencers yell, especially at practice, so I figured I probably shouldn't have yelled so loud, but the instinct to open my mouth and scream as the point of my blade hit her square in the chest, scoring a perfect touch, was too much to resist.

The roar couldn't be contained within me.

"Yes, Coach?" I said on my approach. My friend Alex was standing nearby, and I stole a glance in her direction, looking for some guidance on what to expect, but she just shrugged.

For a minute, Coach Mustilli stood there looking at me and

then a funny smile appeared on his face. Then he spoke. "Ibtihaj, I didn't know you had it in you. That's the kind of fire we want to hear and see," he said, his face flushed with excitement.

I was confused, and Coach Mustilli must have seen it on my face.

"I heard that roar all the way from the other room," he said. "When I hear a sound like that, I come running, because that is the sound of a champion," he said, smiling like a man who had just unearthed a hidden treasure.

I smiled back. I didn't really know what to say, so I stood there awkwardly waiting for the coach to continue. So far, I'd distinguished myself on the team by being a hard worker and by being the one who always arrived to practice on time and ready to get to work. It's why I had been voted captain this year, even though I was only a junior. But it felt nice to have the coach call me a champion. Even though I hadn't earned the merit individually as of yet, the team had captured the state championship title two years in a row. This would be my first year in the coveted starting lineup on the varsity team, and I was really looking forward to contributing tangible wins for the team.

"I want you to come fence with the saber squad," Coach said.

That was not what I was expecting. At all. The last thing I wanted to do was switch weapons. I was finally one of the top épée fencers, and Coach wanted me to start all over from scratch? Saber was so different from épée. Not only would I have to learn an entirely new fencing technique, but the system of scoring was also totally different. In épée, you score a point by compressing the tip of the blade of the sword anywhere on your opponent's body, from the head to the toes. With saber, the target area is from the waist up, and saberists can use slashing motions to score with the side of their blades. I'd watched the saber fencers practice sometimes, and everything was a lot faster and way more aggressive than in épée. During competitions, the saber fencers were loud and screamed on almost every point, almost as if they were trying to convince the referee they deserved the point.

"No, thanks. I like épée," I said to the coach politely.

Coach Mustilli stopped smiling. "Then you're off the team," he said.

I couldn't tell if he was serious or joking. "I don't want to get kicked off the team, Coach," I said. "I just don't want to switch weapons."

"Look, Ibti," Coach Mustilli said, softening his tone. "All of our saber girls are graduating next year, so I need a new saber squad ready for next season. You'd be in our starting lineup."

"But I really *like* fencing épée." I tried again. I wouldn't dare say this aloud to him, but I also liked my épée friends. Over the last two years, practicing together, we had our own little group, and I didn't want to lose that.

Coach Mustilli rolled his eyes and took a deep breath. "Do you like winning?"

"Yes," I said.

"Well, the team needs you to win. We need a saber fencer, and you have what it takes to help this team repeat as state champions," he said.

I felt a wave of anxiety run over my body. He was putting a lot of sudden pressure on me. Of course I wanted to help the team win and defend our state championship title, but was I really the person to do that? Wasn't there someone already fencing saber who was better prepared than me?

"But why me?" I asked, giving the coach a chance to change his mind. Maybe if he thought this idea through he'd realize I wasn't his best option.

"Because I heard you roar," Coach said as if it were obvious. "Only a saber fencer roars like that. I thought you were a meek little person, but you obviously have something else going on in there."

I didn't know if I should be nervous or excited by coach's comment. But before I could say anything, Coach Mustilli added, "I know a star when I see one, Ibti, and you have the makings of a great saber fencer."

It was encouraging to hear. But did I really have the potential to be a great saberist? I kept coming back to all of the extra work I'd have to put in. I tried to imagine myself as one of the best on our team, but did I have the willpower and patience to learn a whole new weapon? I would have to start watching saber bouts more closely as soon as possible. Before I could ask any more questions, Coach Mustilli was explaining what made a great saber fencer and guiding me out of the épée and foil room. The decision had been made for me. When we got to the cafeteria where the saber fencers practiced, Coach Mustilli turned to me and said with a wicked grin, "Welcome to the dark side." Then we got right down to business.

***

Coach Mustilli began by telling me that fencing saber is all about speed and strategy. "It's controlled accuracy," he said. "To master saber, you've got to make quick decisions and execute them just as quickly," he said. This was very different from épée. "When you were fencing épée," he continued, "you were waiting around for just the right moment to make a move. You were reacting to your opponent. With saber, there is no waiting, Ibti. I need you to be a hunter and move like that," he said with a quick snap of his fingers.

I tried to keep up with Coach Mustilli's instructions, tried to grab on to some of his obvious passion for saber fencing, but I still didn't know if Coach had chosen the right person. I didn't see myself as a "hunter," and I didn't know if I was capable of the speed he was talking about. Was it possible Coach saw something in me that I hadn't seen in myself, I wondered.

"How will I know if I can do it?" I asked Coach Mustilli. What I really wanted to know was, what would happen if I failed, but I didn't dare utter the "f-word" out loud in front of Coach Mustilli.

"You don't have to know," Coach Mustilli said. "You just have to do what I tell you to do. And if I tell you to run through that wall"—he pointed to one—"you're going through it because you'll know that it is my job to tell you what to do and your job is to do it. No questions asked. Can you handle that?"

I nodded.

I didn't know if Coach Mustilli was crazy or just super enthusiastic, but something about what he said sent shivers of excitement up and down my spine. If the coach was right about me, that I could be a star, I was all in for that experience.

The first time I picked up the saber, it felt a bit awkward to hold. I had to get used to the grip—because it was different than the épée—but I loved how light the blade felt in my hand. I tried to imagine myself moving lightning fast on the strip with this new weapon that seemed engineered for speed. Coach Mustilli reminded me I could use the sides of my saber blade to score, not just the tip, and that if I missed the target, I should keep my blade out in front of me on defense to control my opponent's attack. He showed me the major defense moves—the parries—I would need as a saberist, and he gave me a handful of DVDs to take home to watch champion saberists and told me to pay attention to their footwork more than anything.

On my second day as a saberist, Coach Mustilli called one of my teammates over to fence with me. I tried not to freak out. Not only did he give me very few pointers before throwing me to the wolves, but he also called over Rachel Carlson, who was the best female saberist we had on the team.

"Okay, Ibti, let's see what you've got," Coach Mustilli said.

"But I don't know what I'm doing," I protested.

"That's how you learn," Coach said with a sly grin. "Sink or swim. But I think you're going to swim, Ibti."

Coach told Rachel to grab me a lamé, a conductive jacket that defined the scoring area on the fencer. He reminded me that the target area in saber was from the waist up. Once hooked up to the scoring machines using a body cord, points register when any part of the blade makes contact with either the metal mask or the lamé. This was much different than fencing épée, where the tip of the blade had to be compressed on the target to score.

Coach told us to get on guard, or starting position. "Ready," he said. "Fence!"

Before I even knew what was happening, Rachel rushed at me, her sword slashing. She hit me with the side of her blade and the coach yelled, "Point left." I don't even think I moved out of the ready position. Rachel quickly went back to her side of the strip, and out of habit, I did the same.

"Ready," Coach Mustilli said again. "Fence."

Rachel flew off of the guard line, and this time I had the where-withal to retreat. She didn't stop, and pretty soon she'd forced me to the far end of the strip until I literally fell backward to the floor. It happened so fast, I lay there on the ground while waves of embarrassment washed over me. As I struggled to stand up, I was relieved my mask hid my face as I fought back tears. Rachel was so fast; I had to figure out a way to stop her, but my mind was blank. I was totally overwhelmed, and I couldn't help but think that maybe switching swords had been a mistake.

Coach Mustilli gave us the signal to start again, but before anything could really happen he threw his hands up.

"Stop," Coach Mustilli yelled. "Ibtihaj, where's your fire? Where's the fight in you?"

I wanted to remind Coach Mustilli that he was the one who thought I was full of fire, not me, but I held my tongue.

"Get over here," Coach Mustilli yelled.

Rachel stayed on the strip, and I walked over to the coach. I pulled my mask off my face.

"Listen, Ibtihaj, I want to see that speed I see when you're running sprints. The next time Rachel attacks you, I want you to be faster than her in the box. If you miss, that's okay. Do you remember how to control your opponent when she runs at you? Control the distance and her speed. Keep that blade out! Remember to keep your blade out in front of you."

"Okay," I said, even though I wasn't sure. Rachel was being so aggressive, I thought perhaps the coach should have me fence someone else to start with, considering this weapon was so new to me. But I didn't say anything.

Once again, we were back on the strip. "Ready," Coach Mustilli said. "Fence!"

This time when Rachel launched her attack, I tried to remember her rhythm and speed from the previous points. I didn't think about scoring, but rather how to keep Rachel's blade from hitting me. I knew how fast she was coming, so I didn't have time to wait. But Rachel fooled me again, this time hitting me with a fast lunge underneath my right arm. I barely had time to think before she scored again, each time using a different tactic. Everything was so fast. In épée, I had time to feel my opponent out and was able to build my strategy during the bout. I knew there was a strategy to employ here, but I had no idea what it was.

"You're doing great, Ibtihaj," Coach Mustilli shouted.

I pulled off my mask in frustration. "Really? How am I doing great? I asked. "I haven't scored one point yet."

"Trust me. You're learning," Coach said with a grin. "Now, I want you to attack Rachel. I want you to do just what she did to you. Attack her and try to score a point."

"Don't take it easy on her," he said to Rachel, the two exchanging a glance. "Let's see if she has what it takes."

Once again, Rachel and I stepped to the on-guard lines, opposite sides of the strip, masks on. I had to think of a plan fast.

"Ready," Coach Mustilli said. "Fence!"

I hesitated as I tried to decide on my strategy.

"Move, Ibtihaj!" Coach Mustilli yelled. "Don't just stand there. Attack your opponent."

Before I could attack Rachel, though, she rushed at me and scored an easy touch on my arm.

I turned to Coach Mustilli. "Sorry, I wasn't ready."

He shook his head like he was disappointed. "Are you ready now?"

I shook my head yes. "Ready."

"Okay, you two," Coach Mustilli said again. "Ready. Fence!"

The sound of the coach's voice jolted me into action. I decided to trick Rachel. As soon as I heard the coach say "Fence," I made two advances with my blade extended, immediately followed by two quick retreats. Rachel made the same fast double advances, this time followed by a lunge, with her blade swiping only the air, narrowly missing me. I then lunged, throwing my arm out, and my blade hit the top of her mask. The green light on the machine went off. I had finally scored a point!

Coach Mustilli clapped slowly.

"Great action, Ibti," Rachel said from behind her mask.

"Thanks," I said, feeling a spark of pride.

"Now we're getting somewhere," Coach Mustilli said. "Let's do it again."

This time I tried to use my speed against Rachel, and it worked well. My double advance lunge was a tempo faster, but I hit her on the thigh, off target. I immediately realized my mistake.

"Darn it," I said under my breath.

"You're fencing saber not épée," Coach Mustilli shouted. "Remember you have to hit above the waist."

Coach Mustilli kept Rachel and me there fencing with each other for the next hour, and I began to get the hang of working with my new weapon. As I started to learn Rachel's go-to moves, I started scoring more and more. I may not have had the same amount of time under my belt as Rachel and the other saber fencers on the team, but I was a quick study, and there was no one on the team more competitive and determined to win than me.

This last time the coach yelled "Fence," Rachel and I both charged toward each other at maximum speed. I wasn't afraid of getting hurt; I was more concerned with accurately anticipating Rachel's moves. The rush of adrenaline coursing through my veins had all of my senses popping. For the first time, I actually felt like fencing itself was fun, not just the social aspect of hanging with my teammates but the sport itself.

Coach Mustilli worked with me one-on-one during practice for at least thirty minutes every day until he was confident he could turn me loose with the rest of the saber fencers. It only took about two weeks to feel like I'd been fencing saber all along. Saber came much more naturally to me than épée had, and I almost felt guilty that after two years of hard work on the épée squad, I abandoned it with no regrets.

———

Within a month, Coach Mustilli was adding me to the varsity starting lineup during our matches against other schools. The coaching staff said I was a natural with the saber, and I soaked up the praise. It felt great to finally contribute to our wins and help the team capture the coveted state championship title. As team captain, I wanted to do more than lead warm-ups and keep morale up. Now I got to contribute in a more tangible way.

Since I was doing so well with the saber, Coach Mustilli mentioned the idea of me entering some of the local and regional fencing competitions. Some of my teammates did the local competition circuit, but I wasn't sure I was ready so soon after switching to saber.

"Ibtihaj, let me be very clear," Coach Mustilli said. "I never, ever send a kid to a competition if she's not ready. And I'm not going to tell your parents to shell out their hard-earned cash to pay for the fees if I don't think you're ready to compete at that level. And you, my dear, are ready."

"But there's no way I'm going to win anything," I said.

"It's not always about winning," Coach said. "The more bouts you fence and more experience you get, the better you'll be. We need you at your best, Ibti and you can't be the best without more experience on the strip. You need to compete against fencers from other clubs."

That night I went home and over dinner told my parents about the coach's plans for me.

"Coach Mustilli said he wants me to start going to some local fencing competitions," I announced. It was one of the rare nights when everyone was actually seated around the dinner table. No one had a game, and Abu had the night off.

"Local competitions? What does that mean?" my mom asked.

"It means that I would sign up for fencing tournaments here in New Jersey on the weekends. Coach Mustilli said that doing well at certain local competitions could qualify me for the Junior Olympics at the end of the season."

Abu finished chewing his mouthful of salad and asked pointedly, "How much does it cost?"

"It's not that much," I said. "The entry fees are only like thirty dollars per competition."

"And how many of these competitions would you be doing?" Abu asked.

I didn't actually know the answer to that question because I didn't know how many competitions Coach Mustilli had in mind for me. "I'm not sure," I said. "I think there's like one competition every weekend, but I don't have to go to all of them," I added, not wanting to make it seem like fencing was going to cost even more than it already did.

"That could really add up, Ibtihaj," Mom said, exchanging glances with Abu across the table. "But we see how hard you've been working. If it's something you and the coach think is important, we'll figure out some way to pay for it. And you can talk to Auntie and Uncle Bernard. Maybe they'll help out with the extra fees or some of these other costs, like your new uniform. You know Auntie thinks of you like her own kids."

"Don't worry about the money," Abu interrupted. "You let us handle that, and you focus on winning."

I smiled and wiggled in my seat from excitement. I couldn't wait to try competing outside of our school meets, but I didn't take for granted that my parents had to pay for all of my sports activities. I knew we weren't rich by any definition of the word, but my mom worked summer school and Abu often picked up additional security jobs to help pay for all of our "extras," like summer academic enrichment programs, Asiya's gymnastics, Qareeb's football camps, and now my competitive fencing fees. My parents never acted like all of our extracurriculars were a financial burden, but they were also very clear that they were only going to put their money where they saw us putting forth our best effort. If we weren't giving 100 percent, they weren't going to invest either their time or money supporting us. Ever since I started fencing, though, both of my parents could tell I was serious. I was all in and, true to their word, they were, too. They made it clear they were willing to financially support my fencing career, which was a commitment in itself, because fencing was not cheap.

Even without the extra competitions, fencing was expensive, even at the high school level.

Historically, fencing was a sport for society's elite, which meant it was a predominantly white sport. Following tradition, most of New Jersey's fencing programs were clustered in wealthy neighborhoods or private schools. To help alleviate the costs for beginners or for kids whose parents weren't willing or able to purchase fencing equipment, our high school had equipment for rent, like jackets, knickers, and lamés. In addition to uniform costs, we had to pay a fee to be on the team, which covered the cost of supplying and maintaining all of the equipment, like the scoring machines and reels, as well as the eight heavy fencing strips the team had invested in over the years. Fencing was no small sacrifice for my family, so I promised myself to put my entire heart and soul into my efforts.

My first regional competition was in Hackensack, New Jersey. It was only forty minutes away from Maplewood. I caught a ride with one of my teammates who was also going. Coach Mustilli also planned to attend the competition. The tournament was held at a fencing club, and when we walked in the door there were already tons of people inside. I could feel the butterflies in my stomach furiously beating their wings like they wanted out. I wanted out, too.

"Ibtihaj! Claire!" Coach Mustilli had spotted us and was heading our way. He pointed out where the girls' locker rooms were and urged us to hurry and change. Claire had been to several local competitions before and just missed qualifying for the Junior Olympics the year before. We were in pre-calculus together, too. We weren't exactly friends, but we were friendly. I decided to stick to Claire's side like there was Velcro on her uniform.

"Relax," Claire told me as we walked out of the locker room

searching for the coach again. "You're going to do fine. I promise you. Everything is going to go by so fast you won't even have time to be nervous."

"I hope you're right," I said.

We spotted Coach Mustilli and walked over to where he was standing on the floor. Claire and I started warming up, mimicking our team stretches we'd done a thousand times before at practice. I stole looks at the other fencers around the floor, and if I looked closely, I saw some nervous energy throughout the room. Girls fidgeted with their hair, tied and retied the laces on their shoes. It gave me a small sense of relief to see that I wasn't the only one who was nervous.

Once we were warmed up, Coach Mustilli gave us some drills to practice with each other. Claire was to attack me, and I was to only practice my parries. And then we were to switch. When he was satisfied that we were warmed up enough, Coach took me over to the table to see if pools had been posted.

Unlike fencing in school, these tournaments were all about the individual. Each fencer was put into a randomly selected pool with other fencers based on ranking. Because this was my first local tournament, and I didn't have a ranking of any sort, I was randomly placed in a tough pool with the number one seed. Each pool had seven fencers, so that meant I would fence six bouts, each to five points. The fencers who advanced from this preliminary round were determined by the number of wins and losses in the pools. The more bouts you won and the larger the margin you won by, the higher your ranking post-pools. Once pools were over and the bracket was set, the goal was to keep winning and advancing through ever-shrinking rounds of fencers. First there was a round of thirty-two, then sixteen, then eight. After the round of eight came the semifinal rounds, and eventually the finals, where the last two fencers would fight for first and second place in the entire tournament. Coach Mustilli had registered me weeks ago, so all we had to do was find my pool and head over to my assigned strip.

"Here you are, Ibtihaj," Coach said once he found my name. "You're in the first pool, and you're going to be fencing another girl with no ranking. She's from Millburn. Her name is Melinda Grady. Do you know her?"

I racked my brain to see if Melinda from Millburn High School rang any bells, but it didn't. "No, Coach," I said.

"Good. Because you don't want to go up against someone you know. When it's your turn, I want you to let that tiger out and attack Melinda so fast she won't know what happened. If you get that first point in fast, you'll blow her confidence and then you can just take those other points away from her."

The butterflies in my stomach started up again. I had to remind myself not to waste time being nervous and that the bout would be over in an instant. Five points was nothing. It'd be a breeze.

"Okay, Coach," I said. "I'll try that."

Coach Mustilli shook his head and pointed his finger in my face. "Don't try. Do! Do exactly what I said and you'll win! Got it?"

"Got it, Coach," I said.

That day I came home with a twelfth place finish. Considering there were sixty other girls in the competition, I was pretty happy with twelfth place. Claire had finished in second place, so she took home the silver medal. Coach Mustilli was ecstatic. I was really happy for her and knew she was that much closer to qualifying for the Junior Olympics. With my twelfth place finish, theoretically I could think about the Junior Olympics, too, but I knew that wasn't something I should be focusing on so early in my career as a saberist. The fact that I'd competed and placed in the top sixteen was a great start.

When I got home from the competition that evening, both of my parents were waiting for me. "How did you do?" Mommy asked.

"I came in twelfth," I said triumphantly. "Out of sixty other kids," I added to ensure they understood what that meant.

"Not bad. So, who won?" Abu asked.

I felt my triumph deflate. "I don't know her name, but she was from Hackensack. She was really good," I said.

"Well, did you learn something from this girl from Hackensack? Maybe you could use some of the same techniques she did the next time you compete," Abu said, always trying to figure out how to coach us from the sidelines. "Remember, always pay attention to the winners," Abu said, and I promised I would.

Abu was right. I began to pay more attention to the fencers who were better than me. At practice and at the local competitions I watched all of the fencers who consistently did well and took note of what techniques they employed on the strip so I could try to do the same. I watched their footwork, their attacks, and their defensive moves. Meanwhile Coach Mustilli worked me harder at practice than before and was now having me fence against the boys, because he said if I could hold my own against the guys in practice, I could handle any girl in competition. And he was right. I quickly became the best saber fencer on the Columbia High School team, and I watched my ranking rise at the local competitions, often coming home with medals in my hand.

In January, after winter break, Coach Mustilli told me he wanted to talk to me in his office after I finished leading warm-ups. As I led everyone through thirty minutes of intense warm-up exercises and stretching, making sure I saw sweat on every forehead, I was racking my brain trying to think of what the coach might want to talk to me about. I tried to figure out if I had done anything wrong, but I couldn't think of anything. Even though I could have made the team do more wind sprints, I wrapped up warm-ups and turned everyone over to the assistant coach and then I ran over to the coach's office.

"Ibtihaj, sit down," Coach Mustilli said.

I sat and tried not to let my nerves show.

"I'm sitting here looking at your rankings. Did you know you're only one result away from qualifying for the Junior Olympics next month?"

"I am?" I said, incredulous. I knew I'd been doing well at the local tournaments, but I didn't realize I was anywhere near qualifying status for JOs. I knew a bunch of the seniors had already qualified, but it never occurred to me that I was in the running.

Coach Mustilli smiled. "Yes, you are. All you have to do is finish in the top eight in one more competition. And I think you're more than able to do that. There's two competitions this month. If you don't do it in the first one, you can try the following weekend."

I couldn't believe it. All the other kids talked about qualifying for the Junior Olympics like it was the pinnacle of their fencing career. And here I was about to make it to that pinnacle when I'd only been fencing saber for three months. It was crazy. I left the coach's office and went back to practice in a daze. I couldn't wait to tell my parents. *Work hard, see results* had always been their formula, so I was happy to report that they hadn't wasted their time or money on me.

———————

One month later, my mother was driving me to Cleveland, Ohio, for my first ever Junior Olympics. With Coach Mustilli cheering me on, I had cinched my spot at the last qualifying event in January, finishing in fifth place. Now I was on my way to compete against the best youth fencers in the country at the biggest tournament I had ever been to. I was so excited I could barely contain myself. It felt like just yesterday I was trying to convince Nicole and Ana to try out for the team with me, and now, here I was en route to the biggest national competition for fencers ages twenty and under. Coach Mustilli was going to meet us at the competition because there were at least ten other fencers from my school team who had also qualified.

"I'm nervous, Mommy," I said somewhere between western Pennsylvania and Ohio.

"I know you are," she said. "I'm nervous for you. I still can't believe you're going to the Olympics already."

"First of all, Mom, it's not *the* Olympics. It's the Junior Olympics," I said, laughing. I still had to pinch myself every time I stopped to think about how quickly all of this had gone down. But I didn't dwell too much on that because I knew I needed to keep up my confidence, think about the future, meaning the competition coming up. Coach Mustilli had warned me that there were going to be the best of the best at this competition and that since I was still so new at the sport I shouldn't expect to walk away with any medals, but I was feeling pretty confident. At least I was until I walked into the convention center on the first day of competition.

I looked around the room overwhelmed by the sea of white before me. I was used to going to smaller, local competitions and being the only Black fencer in the room, or the only Muslim fencer in the room, but there were thousands of fencers in the convention center that day, almost all of them white, it seemed, dressed in all white. Even the majority of the referees were white. The feeling of otherness settled upon me, and I couldn't help but wonder if people were staring at me, wondering what I was doing there in their world. "Snap out of it, Ibtihaj," I said to myself. "Don't psych yourself out." I had to remind myself that once my mask was on, I had the opportunity to show everyone how good an athlete I was, and if people were surprised to see someone who looked like me on the strip, let them be surprised and then amazed when they saw that I could hold my own. I just had to stay focused on my goal and ignore any haters—both real and imagined—that I might perceive.

Once I found out who was in my first pool and what strip I'd be fencing on for my first bout, I found a seat and sat down and tried to calm my nerves. I had twin urges to throw up and jet as far from Ohio as my legs would take me. My mom was standing a few yards away with some of the other parents from our school. Coach Mustilli was running all over advising all of his athletes attending this competition.

Because there were so many fencers competing at the Junior Olympics, the tournament was more than four days long. As with every other tournament I'd been to, we started with the pool rounds and then progressed to direct elimination bouts. The first two days' worth of competition was to whittle those two thousand plus fencers down to a manageable sixty-four when the elimination bouts began. For my first Junior Olympics, I had a goal for myself to make it into the top sixteen. For my last few tournaments in New Jersey, I'd been finishing in the top sixteen consistently and sometimes I was even finishing in the top ten. I didn't think my expectations were too high.

But they were.

I didn't even make it out of the first round of pools. Basically, I was finished with the whole competition before things even really got started. I fenced my first six bouts and lost five, so I didn't even advance to the direct elimination bouts. It was embarrassing and humiliating. I couldn't even hold the tears in. They started to fall before I took my mask off. I felt so demoralized. I practically ran to find my mother, who was now, thankfully, sitting away from the other parents. I threw myself into her arms and bawled.

She was talking to me, trying to console me, but I couldn't hear her over my own inner monologue beating myself up for doing so badly. Finally, I sat there with my face in my palms, covered in tears, replaying each bout and rehashing where I could have done things differently.

"Ibtihaj, you tried your hardest," my mom kept saying. "There's no reason to beat yourself up like this."

"You drove me all the way here..." I cried, unable to finish my sentence. "I have been practicing. A lot."

My mother pulled my head up and forced me to look at her. "Ibtihaj, you've been practicing for only a couple months with saber. Knowing you, if you just keep working at it, you'll do better next time."

"There might not even be a next time considering how badly I fenced today," I said, which brought a fresh batch of tears to my eyes. Was my fencing career over? I wondered.

"Ibtihaj, you don't have to be a has-been already," Mom consoled me. "I just think you might need some extra help."

I wiped my eyes and looked at my mom. "You think I should get a fencing tutor?" I asked.

Mom shrugged. "I don't know what you would call it. I'm just saying when you need to get better at something, you need to find someone who can help you. Clearly your father and I can't help you be a better fencer, but we could probably find someone who can help," she said, always the one to find a solution.

The idea didn't sound too bad, but I couldn't even think about my fencing future after my dreadful performance out there. I just wanted to melt into the floor and disappear. I let out a deep sigh.

"Do you want to get back on the road early and call it a day?" Mom asked.

Part of me wanted to say yes. I wanted to put as much distance as possible between me and this soul-crushing experience. I didn't want to talk to my teammates and have to tell them that I'd done so poorly that I didn't even make it out of the first pool. But I also didn't want to leave right away. I'd never been to a Junior Olympics, and I wanted to see the best of the best go at each other. I wanted to see what the best junior fencers looked like on the strip.

I also didn't want my mom to think she'd wasted her time bringing me all the way out here.

"Let's stay a little while longer," I said softly, while wiping my nose on a tissue. "Is that okay?"

"It's fine," my mother answered, and we both settled into our seats and tried to find a bout to focus our attention on. I was scanning the floor when a flash of color caught my eye. I don't know why I hadn't seen them before, but on the far end of the convention center there was a group of African-American kids in matching uniforms. I followed their line of black-and-yellow sweatshirts to find that they were cheering on a Black fencer I hadn't noticed before. They were screaming and yelling with such passion, I knew they had to be a team of some sort. Usually the only sounds you heard at fencing tournaments were the primal grunts and yells from the fencers themselves on the strip. Fencing fans tend to be a subdued crowd, but this group of fans was anything but subdued. There were only a handful of them, but they had enough energy to fill the entire hall.

I nudged my mother. "Look over there at all those Black people. Who do you think they are?"

My mom turned her head to look. "I don't know, but it's nice to see them here. I was starting to think we were the only ones here."

"Well, we are in Ohio," I reminded her.

"Yeah, but this is a national competition. There should be some diversity up in here."

I shrugged my shoulders. My mom was right, but I didn't want to have a conversation about diversity in fencing at that moment. I just wanted to watch the competition.

CHAPTER 6

I just never give up. I fight to the end.

—SERENA WILLIAMS

We heard about this place in New York City specifically for Black fencers. Since I'd started fencing, other parents had casually mentioned it to my mom when she was in the stands at my competitions, thinking she might be interested in checking it out since we were Black. After my disappointing performance at the Junior Olympics, my mother decided it was the perfect time to try to find some more information about this club people kept talking about. We both thought this might be the place where I could get some extra help and training.

With only a little bit of digging, my mother discovered the name of the organization was the Peter Westbrook Foundation. Through sheer coincidence, around the same time Mom was doing her research on the club, a documentary film about Peter Westbrook himself was premiering in New York City. My mother took that as a good sign and decided to take Faizah and me into the city to go see the film.

Peter Westbrook's story was a fencing fairy tale that unfolded right in our backyard of Newark, New Jersey. The child of a Japanese mother and an African-American father, Peter and his younger sister were raised by his mother alone in a housing project in Newark during the 1950s and '60s. As a child of mixed race heritage and during a time when race relations were tense due to the burgeoning civil rights movement, Peter struggled with his racial identity, and his mother worried that without a father figure in his life, he would turn to the streets for answers. In Japan, his mother's paternal heritage included a long line of men of the sword—samurai—and these men held an honorable role in society. Peter's mother wanted the same for her son and thought fencing could provide a similar sense of honor and pride. More importantly, she felt it would provide an outlet for his energy and a safe space from the Newark streets. Once Peter's mom found out there was a fencing team at his high school, she begged her son to try out for the team. As a high school freshman, Peter had already discovered the importance of the street hustle, so legend has it that he struck a deal with his mother. He agreed to try fencing if his mother paid him five dollars. His mother agreed, so Peter went to the team practice after school. Secretly Peter enjoyed the sport, but he didn't tell his mom that. Instead he told her he wasn't yet convinced. She offered him another five dollars if he went back, and he built a small bankroll until he couldn't deny he had found a true passion. As a saber fencer, Peter excelled on his high school's fencing team and was recruited with a fencing scholarship to attend New York University, one of the best collegiate fencing schools in the country.

Peter's stardom only continued to soar from there. In his first year in college, he won the NCAA title for a saber fencer. By the time he was a college senior, he had become the national champion, an honor he would repeat twelve more times over the course of his career. In 1976, he attended his first Olympics. By his retirement from competitive fencing, he had been to five Olympic competitions, winning a bronze individual medal in 1984. During his last Olympics, in 1992, he was selected to carry the torch for Team

USA. It wasn't just his success as a fencer that made Peter Westbrook so remarkable, though; it was also the fact that he came from such humble beginnings and still managed to dominate a sport that had previously been reserved for the white and wealthy. He battled opponents on the strip and was forced to fight racism and classism in order to claim his spot among the annals of fencing greats, which he did on his own terms. Peter claimed the title of being the first ever African-American to win a national gold medal in saber fencing.

Once he retired from competition, Peter Westbrook didn't hang up his saber. Knowing how fencing had saved him from a life of dead ends, he decided he wanted to help other young kids without a lot of advantages. At the urging of a friend, Peter created the Peter Westbrook Foundation in 1991 in midtown Manhattan. The idea was to use fencing to not only teach a remarkable full-body sport, but also to teach life skills to underserved children from the New York City area. What started as a small program for fewer than a dozen kids ballooned into a powerhouse operation serving more than 250 kids from the community, plus an elite athletic program created to train young athletes with potential to fence on the national and international circuit. Pretty soon, the Peter Westbrook Foundation had developed an international reputation as the place where good fencers of color go to become great.

When the film was over, I had tears in my eyes. Our stories were similar. We were both born in Newark. We were both rarities in fencing—Peter for his race and me because I wore hijab. Peter had reached a level of success I could only dream about at the time, but I still felt an instant kinship with this bald-headed, brown-skinned, petite, wiry fencing elder. There was a reception after the film, and we had a chance to meet Peter and some of his coaches. I was so nervous I didn't know what to say when it was our turn to shake his hand. Luckily my mother didn't have the same problem. She knew exactly what to say. She told Peter that I was a saber fencer, that I attended Columbia High School, and I was looking for a way to improve my game. My mom may have been unsure of the differences between saber and épée, but she knew how to help her children get ahead. And sure enough, Peter told my mom to bring me to the foundation on any Saturday morning, and they'd be happy to see what I could do.

_____

Mom and I took the train into New York City's Penn Station on an unseasonably cool day in May. It was toward the end of my junior year of high school. We then walked down to 28th Street and Seventh Avenue. The Peter Westbrook Foundation was housed on the second floor of a nondescript building not too far from the Fashion Institute of Technology. The foundation shared the space with the New York Fencers Club where elite athletes from around the city also practice. We took the elevator up and entered into a huge space dominated by hues of blue. Bright blue walls and pillars extended down the floor. The smell of sweat and metal hit us as soon as we entered. The sound of fencing blades clashing and loud chatter filled the room. Mom and I paused in amazement as we entered the space. This was the largest fencing club I'd ever been in, and almost *everyone* there was some shade of brown. And there were a lot of people. Dozens of little brown kids were getting fencing lessons from coaches who were also brown. There were some white, Latino, and Asian kids on the floor as well, but the overwhelming majority of students seemed to be African American. My mother and I stood there for a moment taking it all in. We turned to each other at the same time and grinned.

"Can you believe this?" I whispered to my mom.

Seeing all of those Black people in the room was such a contrast to what we were used to seeing in the world of fencing. I felt like a five-year-old at Disneyland. Everything around me seemed like a dream. Fencers that looked like me. Coaches that looked like me. I could feel the tension in my shoulders release as an immediate sense of belonging settled over me. To walk into a room full of fencers and not feel like the odd one out, to not feel eyes surveying my body, pausing at my hijab, wondering if my race or religion would prove an impediment to my success on the strip, felt like freedom.

"I know," my mom whispered back. "This is going to be great, Ibtihaj," she said squeezing my arm. "I can just feel it."

I recognized some of the Olympic fencers I'd seen in documentaries and videos we'd watched during practice. And they were standing only ten feet away from me. Coming from Columbia High School where we were always state champions, suddenly I felt a cold dose of reality hit me. These were the real champions.

"You must be Ms. Ibtihaj Muhammad," a man said as he walked over to us from the center of the floor. "Welcome to the Peter Westbrook Foundation. My name is Jerry."

My mother stepped forward to make the introductions.

"Hello, Jerry, I'm Ibtihaj's mother. We're here to get Ibtihaj some extra training, and we've heard great things about your program here."

"Thank you," Jerry said. "And we've heard some good things about you, Ms. Muhammad," he said, looking at me. "Your coach, Frank Mustilli, goes way back with Peter, and he said we should check you out. So, come on in, Ibtihaj," he said. "Mom, you can have a seat," he added, gesturing toward a row of folding chairs near the door, but within perfect view of all the action.

"Thank you," I said as I followed him across the floor. I wondered what Coach Mustilli had said about me.

Jerry instructed me to get changed, pointing out the girls' locker rooms, and then told me to meet him back outside. I went into the locker room and came back out in my full fencing kit, holding my mask in one hand, my saber in the other. My parents had bought me my own fencing equipment after my first year on the team. When I switched weapons, they also had to buy me a saber lamé—the special Kevlar jacket all saber fencers are required to wear—which ran another $150. A near seven-hundred-dollar investment wasn't a small sacrifice in our home, so I wore it with pride, like armor. In my uniform, I was transformed into a warrior, and I was intent on showing everyone at the Peter Westbrook Foundation what I could do.

"Come on over here," Jerry said, beckoning me over to an empty strip. After a quick warm-up, another girl who appeared to be my age and height trotted over. "This is Angela," Jerry said. "We're going to have you fence with her and see how you do."

"Okay," I said, excited to see another Black female fencing saber. I was trying to size Angela up, wondering how good she was but also wondering if we would become friends. But first we had to fence, and only one of us could win—and that was going to be me.

Angela and I assumed our positions on opposite sides of the strip. Knees bent. Sabers up. When Jerry yelled, "Fence!" I didn't wait for a second. I exploded out of the box toward Angela. I moved so fast she didn't have time to react. I scored a point, finishing quickly, underneath her right arm.

"Point left!" Jerry cried gesturing toward me. He smiled at me. "Good work," he said.

"Thank you," I replied from behind my mask.

"Ready," Jerry said, telling us to take our positions. "Fence!" Jerry yelled again and this time I let Angela rush me, which I knew she would, but I blocked her blade with a parry, then hit her with a swift motion to her mask.

"Point left," Jerry yelled again. I smiled, knowing no one could see my face behind the mask.

After a quick match with me scoring all five points, Jerry dismissed Angela, and another girl took her place. She was obviously a better fencer than Angela, but Jerry yelled, "Point"—"Point"—"Point," all in my favor as I easily took her out, winning all five points again. Jerry said he had one more girl he wanted me to fence—again, me scoring all of the points and the girl walking from the strip just as fast as she'd walked on. Finally, I took my mask off and allowed myself to breathe. Sweat was pouring from my forehead, but I wasn't tired. I was just getting warmed up. And Jerry wasn't done with me, either.

"Brandon, come over here," he called, and a kid who looked like he could be a high school junior or senior came running over. He was my height and kind of lanky. I sized him up and figured I could take him. I was used to fencing against boys during our school practices so I didn't even blink. I put my mask back on and assumed my starting position. A small crowd of other coaches had now gathered around to watch me fence with Brandon. Before we could start, though, Jerry called Peter Westbrook himself over, and suddenly my knees felt weak. I was going to fence in front of the legend himself. I didn't let myself panic, though. I knew I could do this. I waited for the command, and when Jerry yelled, "Fence!" I didn't wait to see what Brandon was going to do. I started off fast from the on-guard line, accelerating to a fast lunge around Brandon's premeditated parry. Coach Mustilli called that a number twenty-one. He had numbers for all of the different tactical move he had taught us, so when we were at a match he could shout a number to us and we'd know what to do. I now planned my bouts in numbers, and used that to my advantage to stay focused. Brandon was a decent opponent but I still bested him, scoring the final winning point. I felt triumphant, but Peter Westbrook wasn't smiling at my win. He seemed unconvinced of my talents. He had me fight two other boys before taking a break. I beat them both, too. All of the other coaches clapped for me, patted me on the back, and commended me on my skills. But I wanted to hear it from Peter Westbrook himself.

"Ms. Ibtihaj, I can see Frank Mustilli has taught you well," Peter said and then, finally, he rewarded me with a smile.

"Thank you," I said, panting. I could admit now, I was tired. But I felt good about my performance.

Peter told me to go back and change and then meet him over by the front desk. When I came from the dressing room, I could feel the strain in my leg muscles, and my right arm ached from the effort. I walked slowly over to where my mother was sitting. Peter was already over there talking with her.

"So, I was just telling your mother how talented you are," Peter said.

"Thank you," I said. I couldn't believe Peter Westbrook was calling *me* talented.

"Here's what we're going to do," he said. "We have about two hundred students coming in here every Saturday for fencing lessons, but Ibtihaj here is beyond that. Frank's doing well with her. We'd like to have her join our elite group of students who come in to train after school. You have to promise to work hard, and in exchange we'll waive your membership fee, we'll give you your own locker, and when we think you're ready, we can help with the funding for tournament expenses. How does that sound to you all?"

"That sounds good," my mom said. "But will she be working with you directly, Mr. Westbrook?"

"Ms. Muhammad," Peter Westbrook said, focusing all of his attention on my mom. "I'm here every single day on the floor with all the kids. Ibtihaj will have her own special coach, but yes, I will be overseeing everything that goes on here. Nothing happens here without my say-so."

My mom seemed satisfied with that answer, and I was, too. The energy that filled that room was palpable, and I wanted to be a part of it, to fence with other athletes of color and learn from Olympians and Olympic hopefuls alike.

"That sounds like a good deal," mom said, and then she turned to me. "What do you think?"

"I think it sounds great," I said. I felt like I'd just won a prize. I knew joining the Peter Westbrook Foundation could help me achieve my goal of landing a fencing scholarship for college, but also, it would help me develop into a better fencer, ensuring better results during competitions. The memory of my Junior Olympics performance still made me cringe. That was an experience I never wanted to repeat. So I shook Peter's hand and officially became a Foundation fencer.

I started training at the Westbrook Foundation during the summer before my senior year. At the foundation, we were treated like athletes, not students. There was no babying or hand-holding. From the moment we walked inside the door, we were expected to be respectful athletes, and we could expect the same respect from the coaches.

Every day the routine was pretty standard. Upon arrival, I would join the group class where we would do footwork and drills. We would spend a lot of time working on our technique, practicing a series of footwork or a particular move over and over again, so at game time, we would instinctively be able to execute. Once class ended, after about an hour and a half, we would have open or free fencing, during which time everyone would also take individual lessons with their personal coach. Every once in a while, mostly on Wednesday nights, Peter would come and watch us fence.

Peter was a manic ball of energy and would walk around praising a well-executed attack or correcting a failed attempt to score. Sometimes he'd interrupt a bout and push one fencer to the side so he could demonstrate exactly how an action was done. Even at fifty years old, Peter was still an exceptional fencer, exhibiting the fastest hand work I had ever seen. And he loved to deliver lectures or sermons about life while he was with us. Peter always had a Bible verse or life lesson to apply to fencing, and his loud, booming voice could always be heard above the sounds in the cavernous fencing club.

I loved the atmosphere at the foundation. I felt like I was spending time with my family when I was there. I quickly made friends with the other fencers, and when we weren't fencing against each other, we would be laughing, enjoying one another's company, and making fun of each other in jest. Sometimes I fantasized about going to college at New York University, just so I could keep fencing at the foundation and maybe even work there on Saturdays as an instructor, to give back to the community and follow in Peter's footsteps.

When school started back up in the fall, however, my affection for the foundation grew harder to maintain. My schedule was brutal. College applications were due. The pressures to perform at the highest level in sports and academics were higher. In addition to maintaining an A average, taking all honors and AP classes, and playing on the volleyball and fencing teams, I had to go to the foundation three days a week, plus Saturdays. My schedule was nonstop.

During the fall when I played volleyball, I still had fencing practice in New York City at the foundation. My mom was like superwoman, able to work a full-time job, get home in time to make dinner, then pick me up from practice a bit early, just in time to take the 5:40 p.m. train into Manhattan. Mom would also pack my meal in a Tupperware container so I could eat my dinner on the train, and once I got to the club, I would take a lesson, free fence for a bit, then catch the 8:50 p.m. train back home. Even though I'd want to do nothing more than fall asleep on that train, usually I'd take advantage of the forty-minute ride to study.

It was a nutty schedule, but I'd made a commitment to myself to become a better fencer. That didn't mean I was willing to give up anything else in my life to achieve that goal. Not when I was so close to graduation. I knew my hectic schedule wasn't going to last forever, and playing volleyball had its purpose in my plans to get into college just as much as fencing did. I didn't expect or want a volleyball scholarship, I simply wanted to prove to colleges that I was well rounded and could handle sports and academics year-round. Plus, I really enjoyed volleyball. Not only were some of my closest friends on the team, I had made a commitment to my teammates, and I wasn't going to quit on them. I told my parents if my grades dropped or it felt like too much I would slow down, but it never got to that point for me. I maintained my A average, and my fast-paced lifestyle became the norm.

Even when Ramadan arrived during the season and I had to play volleyball and fence while fasting from sunrise to sunset, abstaining from food and water, I still didn't want to quit. The truth was, I really enjoyed playing sports, and I liked the opportunity they provided to spend time with my friends. Not only did we practice after school, but even during the summers we were together for camps and tournaments. The way I looked at it, giving up either volleyball or fencing would mean giving up not only an opportunity to develop my athletic abilities, but also my primary opportunity to socialize. I didn't go to parties or have time in my schedule to "hang out," so playing team sports was not going to get cut from my agenda. I was willing to put in the hard work and executive-level time management skills in order to fit it all in.

As a senior, for the second year in a row I was captain of the fencing team, and we continued defending our state champion status. Fall sports previews had us repeat state champions and as Coach Mustilli had predicted, I was now one of the best saber fencers in the state. In February, I qualified for the Junior Olympics. This time the competition was in Colorado, and I had much higher hopes than how I fared the year before. I flew to the competition with fencing friends from other local high schools and the foundation. It was the first time I had been out of the state on my own, and it felt like I was really part of something important. I finished in the top thirty-two, but a blizzard hit the same day we were due to fly home, so we were stuck in Colorado for three days. While I knew my family was worried about me back in New Jersey, my friends and I loved living in a five-star hotel watching the winter wonderland from our windows and pretending school and fencing practice and college applications weren't going to be waiting for us when we returned.

The craziness of my life as a top student-athlete became my new normal. My day-to-day life indeed felt like a car ride where my foot always had to be firmly pressed down on the gas, but I had gotten used to the speed. My parents had instilled in me a strong work ethic and a nothing-but-the-best mentality. They had me convinced that if I was willing to work for it, anything was possible. For me, that "anything" meant getting an acceptance letter to an Ivy League university.

My mom and dad were good as their word, too. They demanded excellence, but they created a life for us where we could focus 100 percent on our studies and sports. They didn't make us get after-school jobs. Other than our chores in the house, we had all the time we needed for our homework and sports practice. And my mom was a soccer mom times ten, always picking up someone from practice, dropping someone else off, fixing a uniform, or cheering someone on from the sidelines. I would have felt guilty if I didn't give maximum effort, considering how hard my parents worked for us. And it wasn't only me that needed my parents' support.

Even though my brother Qareeb was the apple of my eye, watching him begin the college application process was a lesson for me in what *not* to do. If it weren't for my mom, he would have missed a bunch of deadlines and fallen behind in the whole process. My mom had to help him get up to speed.

"Mom, isn't Qareeb supposed to be doing this by himself?" I asked as the two of them sat at the kitchen table, heads bent over a piece of paper I assumed was an application.

My brother shot me a look across the room.

Getting straight A's wasn't on Qareeb's bucket list, despite my parents' best efforts. He was super smart, but he wanted to live his life on his own terms. I turned to leave the kitchen knowing I wasn't needed, but I couldn't help offering my mom a small bit of consolation on my way out of the room. "Just so you know, Mom, I'll do all of my college and scholarship applications by myself."

"I know you will, Ibtihaj," my mom called after me. "I know I can always count on you to do the right thing."

———

"She only got into Duke because she's Black." I heard Heather Clark and her two best friends talking about me as I walked behind the three of them in the hallway. I knew they were talking about me, because I was the only person from my graduating class—Black or white—going to Duke University in the fall. Jenny Murphy had been waitlisted. The guidance counselor put my name and Duke together on the bulletin board outside her office with the other students who were on their way to college. Ultimately, Duke beat out NYU and Columbia as my top choice because Duke offered me the most money in academic scholarship funding and they recruited me to be on their fencing team. I wasn't sold on going so far away from home for college—living in New Jersey, I just assumed I'd land somewhere in the Northeast—but I couldn't turn down an amazing opportunity even if it did mean going to school below the Mason-Dixon line, a line I was a little bit hesitant to cross as an African-American hijabi. I didn't know what kind of welcome I'd receive in North Carolina, but I figured on Duke's campus I'd be in a safe environment where I would surely be able to find my "people." After hearing what Heather and her friends were saying about me, I felt a twinge of anger. My scholarship wasn't a handout. I'd worked my butt off to get good grades and become a nationally ranked fencer. I'd sacrificed a social life, free time, and my summers to make myself a well-rounded student who would be accepted into an elite university. And yet Heather and her friends wanted to make me seem inferior, like somehow I wasn't actually qualified to gain admittance into a prestigious university.

As I walked up and down the hallway that week, I was full of fire inside. I debated whether it would be worth it to let Heather and her friends know that I had earned the right to go to Duke with excellent grades in honors and advanced placement classes and being the captain of the fencing team. My admittance essay was about how I didn't let my race or religion stop me from getting ahead in a world that wasn't kind to people who looked or worshipped like me. As much as I wanted to educate those girls about my reality, I knew it wasn't worth arguing with ignorance. No matter what I said to Heather and her entourage, they would still walk away thinking it was my race and not my high school record that got me into college.

Heather Clark wasn't the only person who gave me grief about going to Duke. My fencing family at the Westbrook Foundation had their own plans for me. They wanted me to stay in the tri-state area for college so I could continue training at the club. Even though I had gotten into NYU, Peter's alma mater, the financial aid they offered wasn't enough to compete with Duke. I promised Peter that I would keep up my training at Duke and planned to come home during all of my school breaks to train at the foundation. I'd continue to take as many classes as they wanted me to, but they still weren't thrilled with my decision.

The truth was, I was looking forward to taking a break from the foundation for a bit, because things weren't as perfect as they originally seemed.

When I first heard that Sam was going to be my coach, I was excited. Not only was Sam a United States Olympian around the same age as Peter, he was also Black and a Muslim like me. I thought we would have a lot in common and hoped we'd have a real connection, but from day one, something was off. I'd met him briefly at the movie premiere of Peter's documentary and he'd been drinking a beer at the time. As a sixteen-year-old, I didn't understand how Sam could consider himself a Muslim and drink alcohol. It made me uneasy, which might have made me seem hesitant at first when I was around him. Whatever it was, we definitely got off on the wrong foot. Maybe Sam felt uncomfortable around me because I wore hijab and he was a less conservative Muslim. Maybe he just didn't like my personality. Whatever the reason, I never knew what type of mood he'd be in when I came to practice. He was the one dark spot in my experience at the foundation.

I remember one day I walked into practice, and apparently I had upset Sam before I could even open my mouth. I came out of the locker room ready to work, and Sam gave me an irritated look.

"You didn't say hi to me when you came in, so you can go home and try again tomorrow," he said. "Go home," he repeated, turning his back on me.

I was shocked and confused. I knew from past experiences not to question Sam because that would make him more upset. So I went back into the locker room, got dressed and headed for the door. When Peter saw me in my street clothes he stopped me.

"Where are you going, Ibtihaj?" he asked.

I told him what Sam had said.

"Go get changed. You're staying right here for your lesson. I'll talk to Sam." And so, for the second time in less than fifteen minutes, I headed back to the locker room and got ready for practice.

These kinds of bizarre mind games were commonplace working with Sam. I wasn't the only one who dealt with his erratic behavior. One day Sam sent two girls home from practice, telling them they had gained weight and not to come back until they lost ten pounds. Another time he told me not to come to practice unless I brought him a fifty-dollar box of Titleist golf balls. When I complained to some of the other coaches at the foundation about Sam's behavior, nothing seemed to change, so I stopped complaining. I just did my best not to provoke his ire. My parents had some idea about Sam's odd behavior, but I didn't tell them everything because I didn't want to give them any reason to stop sending me to the foundation. I was confused. I was young and inexperienced, and my coach was an Olympic medalist. I didn't have any power in our coach-pupil dynamic. I knew at the foundation I was part of one of the best fencing programs in the tri-state area and receiving excellent training in a sport I had grown to love. I always told myself that since my lessons with Sam were usually only thirty minutes out of a two-hour practice, I could suck up the abuse. My teammates at the foundation had turned into family, and Peter Westbrook himself had become a mentor to me. I didn't want to lose all of that. But most days after working with Sam, now that college was in sight, I found myself planning my escape.

Even though it was never my intention to travel so far away to go to college, being recruited to fence at one of the country's most prestigious universities with the added benefit of being five hundred miles away from Sam felt like an unexpected gift. I was ready to continue my fencing career somewhere I didn't have to deal with people like Sam Jones. And I looked forward to pursuing my career in medicine. The way I looked at it, it was my time to close the door on this chapter of my life, and start a new page.

CHAPTER 7

Women are intersectional human beings who live multi-issued lives.

—LINDA SARSOUR

Ibtihaj Muhammad, 2005 Junior Olympics National Champion."
I ran my fingers over the inscription on the trophy and tried to
dredge up a small amount of the elation I had felt just two days
ago when I scored the winning point and secured the gold at the
Junior Olympics tournament in Ohio. It was an amazing moment.
A marked contrast to my first Junior Olympics in high school. The
pinnacle of my fencing career so far. But I couldn't muster up that
feeling anymore. All that was left of that day was the trophy sitting on the windowsill in my dorm room.

"What's the matter, girl?" my roommate, Kendall, asked.
"You're over there moping like you lost your best friend and you
just won that big ol' trophy. Why aren't you out celebrating or
something with your team?"

I sighed and tried to plaster a smile on my face. The Junior
Olympics was an individual event and had nothing to do with my
membership on Duke's fencing team. But even still, I wouldn't
have anyone to celebrate my win with from the Duke team anyway. The sad, lonely truth was that after a year and half on the
fencing team at Duke, I could only call one teammate—Josh—my

friend. He was the only other Black person on the entire squad, and we immediately bonded over that commonality. Josh could make me laugh and tried to get me to not take fencing so seriously, but I didn't know how to be anything but serious when it came to sports. I came to every practice on time and to every tournament ready to win. When it came to sport, I had an unapologetic intensity that not everyone understood, and because I already had a winning record to show for it, most of the other women on the team didn't seem interested in getting to know me. Whether it was jealousy since I was the best saber fencer on the squad, because I looked different than the rest of the squad, or something else, I'll never know. Unfortunately, I knew at that point I'd never have the family feeling at Duke that I had on my high school team or at the foundation, which was unfortunate because the majority of my time as a college athlete was spent with my team.

I didn't think Kendall needed to hear all of that, so I said the first thing that popped into my head.

"I don't have time to celebrate, Kendall," I said, which was actually true. "I have that chem test on Monday and I didn't get a lot of studying done on the plane ride back from the competition."

"Well, I guess that means you don't want go to Central Campus. Me and Tesia and Sandra are going to a step show," Kendall said.

"Thanks, but I can't," popped out of my mouth on autopilot. As much as I would have liked to go hang with my roommate and the other girls from our dorm, I knew there wasn't enough time. There never seemed to be enough time to fit a social life into my schedule. The only reason I was barely able to keep up in my classes and fence was because I had eliminated all of the extras from my life. Socializing was the first thing cut—just like it had been in high school. Only now, I wasn't socializing with my fencing teammates.

"You sure?" Kendall said. "You know you need to have a little fun once in a while."

Before I could figure out another nice way to say "thanks but no thanks," someone knocked on our door.

"Who is it?" Kendall called, although we could tell from the giggling coming from the other side of the door.

"Bitch, open the door," someone said, and more giggling.

Kendall jumped off her bed and flung open the door. Tesia and Sandra stumbled into the room laughing. They were both dressed for a night out. Tesia wore black leather leggings, a red belly-button-baring midriff shirt, and a tapered denim jacket. On her feet she wore high-heeled, black strappy sandals. Sandra wore dark denim jeans and a purple blouse with a plunging V-neck, and she had similar strappy sandals, only hers were gold. Even though they had invaded my dorm room, I suddenly felt incredibly underdressed in my bulky blue sweatshirt.

Sandra came over to my bed. "Ibtihaj, why don't you come with us? You need to get out, girl."

I smiled. "First of all, I wouldn't even know what to wear to hang out with you three," I joked.

"Well, it's not going to be that tired Duke hoodie," Tesia said, and everyone laughed. Even though I didn't hang out with these girls on the weekends, we were a tight bunch of Black women who lived in the dorm together. Duke had decided for us that all the Black women should have Black roommates and live on the same floor. They weren't very subtle with their attempts to segregate us or at making a safe space for people of color, but the truth was, I appreciated the sisterhood we'd formed. It was nice to have women who looked like me in close proximity on a campus that was overwhelmingly white. The culture shock I'd felt when I first got to campus was real. Duke, unlike anything I'd ever experienced in Maplewood, was truly a majority white environment.

"I'm making an executive decision," Kendall said. "You're coming with us, and I don't want to hear any more excuses. Even if you only stay for one hour, you're going to have a little bit of fun tonight."

I looked at the chemistry book on my desk and then back at my friends, who were all looking at me expectantly. It wasn't a hard choice: my friends won.

———

Two hours later, I was standing in a fraternity house in Central Campus wondering why I had agreed to come out. The evening had started out so well, too. We'd gone to a step show and watched a bunch of guys from the Black fraternities compete for bragging rights as the best steppers on campus. I didn't get into the craziness of Greek life, but step shows were fun to watch. The choreography these guys came up with was really intricate. It was like they were having a conversation with their bodies. Then after the step show, Sandra swore she knew about a small party that was happening that was going to be "totally low-key." If low-key meant pumping music, throngs of people sipping on beer or mixed drinks, and clouds of smoke hanging in the air, then that's exactly what it was.

"Really, Sandra," I screeched when I saw what type of party she'd brought us to, "this is not low-key in any way."

"Oh, Ibtihaj, you needed this," she said. "Trust me. You are going to thank me in the morning." And with that she slipped off to look for something to drink.

Pretty soon Tesia and Kendall also went off making small talk with people they had met around campus. Meanwhile, I stood in the hallway and tried to figure out where to train my eyes, how to stand so I wouldn't attract attention, and what to do with my hands since I wasn't holding a drink or gripping a cigarette.

"Hey, Ibtihaj!" a guy named Mark from my dorm came up to me. He was one of the handful of African-American guys who still lived in our dorm. Most of the African-American students liked to live around Central Campus. "I didn't know you partied. Someone told me Muslims didn't drink."

"I don't drink," I said, holding up my empty hands.

"Well, you wanna dance then?" he asked.

I felt my face flush but knew Mark wouldn't be able to see the color in my cheeks because it was so dark in the room. I didn't want to tell Mark that I couldn't and didn't dance. Part of that was because of my religion and part of that was just my unfortunate lack of rhythm. So I just said, "No thank you," as politely as I could.

Mark simply shrugged and moved on. I was grateful he didn't press the issue. After Mark, a couple other guys came over to talk to me; one offered me a drink to see if I was "really a Muslim" and one just wanted to tell me he'd never seen a Muslim at a frat party before.

"What am I doing here?" I groaned out loud. I couldn't feel any more out of place. I did a quick check to see if anyone was staring at me. I squinted my eyes and scanned the room, looking for a familiar face. I decided I'd put in enough time at this party, and it was time to leave. I brought my phone up to my face. It was 10:30 p.m. I figured if I left right away, I could still get some studying in back at the dorm. I started moving through the crowds of people. I saw my roommate close to the door.

"Hey, Kendall," I shouted, "I'm going to head home."

Kendall's brow furrowed in concern. "Are you sure? We just got here."

I shook my head. "No, I'm okay. I just have to go home and study."

Kendall cocked an eyebrow, and her hand went on her hip. "Really, Ibti. You're going to study? Now?"

I couldn't help but laugh. I was going to force myself to get in an hour of chemistry, but that wasn't what was making me high-tail it out of that party. I didn't feel comfortable, and I was clearly making other people uncomfortable as they walked past me in my hijab, doing double takes and then whispering to their friends.

"Kendall, I am going to go study, but I also don't need to be here. You guys have fun. Tell me if I miss anything good." And with that I left the building and headed to the bus stop where I would catch the free shuttle back to my dorm. I promised myself that would be the last frat party I'd ever go to.

Back in our room, I wouldn't allow myself to feel bad for trying out the "normal" college student experience for one night. Sometimes I just wanted to fit in, hang out, and be like all of the other girls in my dorm, but I could never quite get it right. I wanted to do well in my classes. I wanted to qualify for the National Collegiate Fencing Championships or the NCAAs and I wanted to spend time with my friends. But I couldn't fit academics, fencing, and socializing into my schedule. And I was still struggling to figure out how to be social in a way that aligned with my faith. Frat parties clearly weren't it.

I changed out of my jeans and cashmere sweater back into my sweats. I unwrapped my hair and forced myself to sit at my desk with my chemistry book in front of me. I willed myself to read. After only five minutes, I felt my eyelids grow heavy, and my bed started calling my name. I tried to refocus, but it was no use. I stood up and did ten jumping jacks, my go-to method to boost my energy levels. Then I walked over to the bookshelf Kendall and I shared. I looked at the books we'd accumulated in the last six months. Between the two of us, we'd amassed an impressive collection of books written by twentieth century Black female authors. Toni Morrison, Alice Walker, Octavia Butler, and Zora Neale Hurston were all represented. I pulled out a copy of Morrison's *Song of Solomon* and flipped through the pages. I loved the African-American literature class I'd taken my freshman year where we had read fiction to try to understand American history in the nineteenth century. I learned so much in that one class. Just thinking about that class made me wish I could just stop and read Alice Walker instead of memorizing formulas and definitions. I went back to my desk and tried to dive back into chemistry, but I was getting nowhere. I kept rereading the same sentence over and over again to make the information stick in my brain.

I slammed the book shut. "This sucks," I said to the empty room. "Why can't I study something that I'm actually interested in?" Saying that sentence aloud made me pause. And then I realized something fundamental. I didn't really want to study chemistry. Not only that, I didn't want to take any more math and science classes. I wanted to read more Toni Morrison books and learn more about African-American history. I wanted to learn more about where my people came from, where I came from, and all the great contributions Black people had made to American civilization and society. There was a giant hole in my knowledge bank about these fundamental parts of history that had been skipped over in all of my education up until now. But I couldn't just drop my plans to be a doctor, could I? I had been working toward a medical career for my entire life.

I got up from my desk and fell into bed. I tried to figure out what options I had. I still hadn't officially declared my major, so there was still time to decide. If I majored in African and African-American studies, what would I do upon graduation? There wasn't a clear career path associated with African-American studies majors. I could be a lawyer, or a teacher, or my worst fear, unemployable. I fell asleep thinking about the potential look of disappointment on my parents' faces when I told them I didn't want to be a doctor anymore.

The next morning, I woke up feeling uneasy about dropping my medical school plans, but I didn't have time to dwell on it, because there was little room in my schedule for indecision. I was the girl who always had a plan, and I attributed most of the successes in my life to staying faithful to those plans. Now wasn't the time to switch things up, I told myself, because there was too much going on.

If I thought balancing academics and athletics in high school was challenging, college was ten times more intense. Every morning I started with weight training, then I had my academic classes, followed by fencing practice, which ran from three p.m. to seven p.m. in the evenings. Competitions generally fell on the weekends, and we usually had to travel out of state for those. I'd return to campus sometime between late Sunday evening and early Monday. After spending the entire bus ride home from competitions studying and doing homework, I'd stumble to my room and fall asleep as soon as my head hit the pillow. The whole process would then start all over again when I awoke. I also had a part-time work-study job at the Duke Annual Fund where I would call alumni to ask them for donations.

Most of the time I functioned on autopilot and moved through my schedule with practiced determination. The fact that after nearly two years on campus I hadn't found a social group to call my own was disappointing, but most of the time I was too busy to even think about it. Lately, I found myself looking forward more and more to my daily prayers. Those precious moments were the only time in my day when I required myself to slow down, reflect, and remind myself of what was important.

———————

A few weeks later I made two critically important decisions in my life. Despite my best efforts to convince myself that being a doctor was my destiny, I decided to double major in African and

African-American Studies and International Relations with a focus on the Middle East. I also chose to add a minor in Arabic. These were the subjects I was truly interested in studying on a deeper level. These were the issues that whetted my intellectual appetites. Becoming a doctor had really been my parents' dream, not mine, and now I was ready to deep-dive into my own identity politics, from race to religion. When I told my parents that I was ditching my plans to be a doctor, they were surprised because I'd always been so career focused, but they still said they would support me in whatever path I chose.

"If there's one thing we know about you, Ibtihaj," my father said to me over the phone when I told my parents the news, "it's that you always come out on top."

"Yeah, we're not worried," my mother added. "We trust you."

The other major decision I made had to do with my social life. I was losing my connection to Islam, and I realized how much I missed my Muslim community back home. Even though there weren't many Muslims in my high school, we had a diverse Muslim community in New Jersey that formed such a large part of my childhood and teen years. At Duke, I was literally the only hijabi on campus, and I found myself mostly practicing my faith alone. My first interaction with the Muslim Students Association (MSA) as a freshman hadn't resulted in the warm welcome I'd expected. As the only hijabi and one of only two Black Muslims in the group, yet again, I felt like an outsider where I should have found an immediate connection. The female upperclassmen did not approach me or make any real efforts to be my friend, so I only went to the meetings sporadically my first year. I'd convinced myself I didn't need to be involved with the MSA to be a devout Muslim on campus, only it turned out I did.

Lately, I'd found myself praying mostly in times of distress, when classes felt too hard, when the members of my fencing team were giving me a hard time, or when I was homesick. But I didn't want to be a Muslim who only turned to Allah when I needed something. I knew that wasn't right. I needed to center my faith, and I knew having a community could help me do that.

Even though the MSA was a group with way more men than women and still had zero other hijabis in the organization, I decided to officially join the MSA and get from the group what I could. It wasn't about what other people could bring to my life, it was what I wanted for myself. And what I wanted was a Muslim community that I could pray with and also have fun with. I was looking for a safe space where I could be social but I didn't want "being social" to involve anything that would compromise my faith. I knew how easy it was to make mistakes with drinking and drugs a normal part of campus life. And I knew if I kept hanging with my non-Muslim friends, those vices would always be around to tempt me.

That wasn't what I wanted from my time at Duke.

By joining the MSA, I promised myself from now on—even with my fencing schedule—I'd make an effort to attend Friday *Jumu'ah* services as often as possible. The MSA would be my community. I didn't have to be best friends with all of the members in the group, but I wanted the MSA to be a source of light for me on campus.

———

One year later, just a few weeks into junior year, my life at Duke was still a whirlwind of activity, but I finally had a social routine that revolved around my Muslim friends. Every Thursday, Friday, and Saturday night, when I wasn't at practice or a competition, I spent time with members of the MSA. We'd do everything from bowling to volunteer work in the community. I made peace with the fact that my hijab made some of my fellow Muslim women uncomfortable. I became friends with the other members of the MSA, both male and female, who didn't have an issue with it. If I had competitions, or if practice ran late, I'd have to take a rain check on the MSA. More and more I found myself wishing it were the other way around, though. I wanted to skip practice so I could hang out with my friends. For the first time in my life, fencing had become a source of stress. But it wasn't the sport itself, it was the team.

Every year since joining the Duke fencing team, I'd been to the NCAAs and named All-American. I was almost undefeated on the collegiate circuit. There were only one or two other people on the team who shared the same work ethic. Many would have no problem missing practice if they had to study for a test, for example. At Duke, missing practice to study for a test was an acceptable excuse. But I never made those excuses, and I still managed to get it all in. Maybe that's why my female teammates weren't interested in being friends with me. I can't say for sure. All I know is that the fencing team at Duke did not provide me with a feeling of team spirit. In fact, it mostly caused undue levels of anxiety.

If the only problems on the fencing team were about certain girls not wanting to be my friends, I wouldn't have minded that much, but the real issues at play were laced with racial undertones. My friend Josh and I were the only Black fencers on Duke's team, and we both were on the receiving end of endless numbers of "harmless jokes" and offhand comments that permeated our team culture. Our teammates thought it was funny, for example, to ask Josh and me if we really liked to eat fried chicken and watermelon for dinner. They weren't even original with their racism. Josh fumed at their ignorance and eventually decided fencing wasn't worth subjecting himself to that type of abuse. He quit the team before my junior year, leaving me as the only Black person on Duke's fencing team. At that point, my feelings of isolation only intensified.

One time the team was traveling by bus to a competition at Notre Dame. Our coach hated to fly, so we always had to drive to our meets. We made a pit stop to eat at a Cracker Barrel restaurant about three hours into the trip, and everyone piled off of the bus. As we stood in the entranceway of the restaurant waiting for a table, the hostess came over and offered to find a table for two— for me and my friend. Because I happened to be standing next to the bus driver, who was Black, she assumed the two of us were together and not part of the Duke fencing team. Everyone on the team burst out laughing. No one spoke up to correct the woman's mistake. Of course, the hostess wasn't to blame for her error, yet the experience perfectly exemplified how I felt about the team in general. Like an outsider. Separate. Different. Out of place.

"I'm going to quit," I said to Josh, who was telling me for the eleventh time how great his life had been since he'd left the fencing team. He had time to socialize, to join all kinds of clubs, and even take weekend road trips around North Carolina with his friends. It sounded like heaven. A freedom of time I'd never had.

"You? Quit fencing?" Josh said, while stuffing a French fry in his mouth. "I'll believe it when I see it."

I gave my friend a look across the table. "What? Isn't it possible I want what you have? I'm ready for a real life. Being a college athlete eats up all of your time and energy."

Josh carefully dipped a fry in a pool of ketchup before responding. "You're not like regular people, Ibti. You have some kind of superhuman ability to work two hundred times harder than anyone I know. Win on the strip and somehow still manage to get good grades while double majoring. You wouldn't know what to do with yourself if you stopped fencing."

I laughed. "Yes, I would."

"Oh, yeah, like what? "Josh said. "What would you do to burn up all that energy you use to run around the golf course every day, lift weights, and train for three hours? You'd be going stir crazy."

I didn't want to tell Josh that he was probably right. I didn't know what I would do. That unknown was the only reason I continued to fence. Fencing had been a part of my life for so long now. It was true, I couldn't imagine it not being a central part of my life. But I also couldn't imagine another year with people who made me feel uncomfortable in my own skin. It wasn't worth it. I shrugged my shoulders and fiddled with the paper from my straw. "I'd find something. I mean I have three years of lost time to make up for," I said.

"Like I said," Josh repeated. "I'll believe it when I see it."

Josh's words haunted me because he had identified the real reason I was still on the team. I didn't know what I would do or who I would be if I quit the fencing team. If I wasn't Ibtihaj Muhammad the fencer, who was I? Luckily my financial aid package didn't require me to fence, so I was free to make this decision without worrying about my tuition. The real problem was, I didn't really have anyone to talk to about it who could truly understand all of my issues. I didn't want to call anyone back at the foundation because they would say, "We told you so," if I brought up the idea of leaving the team. There was no one on the fencing team at Duke who had my best interests at heart, and Josh didn't believe I was serious. I understood where he was coming from. I always came to practice ready to work, and my results on the strip reflected my efforts. Even I wondered, from a practical standpoint, if leaving the team was a good idea. And yet lately, every day I woke up and headed to the gym for weight training, I found myself wishing I were heading anywhere but there. I fantasized about leaving the fencing team and embarking on some other adventure. There were parts of the college experience I yearned to have, but that were impossible as a college athlete. Finally I decided to do something most college athletes can never contemplate: leaving campus to study abroad.

I called my parents and asked them if they would help fund a summer study abroad trip in Morocco where I could further my North African studies and practice my Arabic. I knew it was a bit drastic, but I decided I could kill two birds with one stone: put some distance between me and the fencing team *and* spend time in a new country while fulfilling credits for my major and minor. I emphasized the latter with my parents, and they agreed to cover the costs for the program. I didn't know what would be waiting for me back at Duke when I returned, but I figured no matter what, I'd be better able to deal with it after this time away.

In Morocco, I lived with a Moroccan host family in the capital city of Rabat and took classes at the Center for Cross Cultural Learning situated in the old city or medina. I immediately felt a connection to the Moroccan people. It was a good feeling not to be stared at everywhere I went and to easily blend into the crowds. To not have to explain myself to anyone. I was another Muslim in a Muslim country. For the first time in my life, I wasn't a minority. I probably experienced less culture shock in Morocco than I had when I first arrived at Duke. But even I felt completely overwhelmed at times by the foreign sights, smells, and sounds of this ancient coastal city. All five senses were bombarded by the frenetic activity of the shopkeepers in the medina as I walked to school every morning through the winding streets of the old city. The smell of baking bread and sweet spices mixed with the pungent coppery scent of raw animal flesh being chopped by seasoned butchers filled my nostrils. There was the constant background noise of motorbikes roaring in the near distance and the sound of voices communicating in a language I was desperately trying to learn but had yet to master.

After spending the morning in our intensive Arabic and Moroccan culture classes, my American classmates and I would play volleyball at the beach until the sun went down. On the weekends our Moroccan friends would take us surfing, and we would go on train trips up and down the coast. The people were so nice and the food was delicious and, of course, halal. I felt truly carefree that summer. For the first time in a long time, I allowed myself to enjoy and experience life without a timetable and rigid commitments. It was such a big difference from my life back at Duke, from the life I'd been leading since I was thirteen. In Rabat I was immersed in a culture that had only been accessible through words in a book or pictures on a screen. My major in international relations with a focus on North Africa was no longer an abstract area of study, it was what I was living, eating, and breathing every day for three months. My mind was stimulated, my spirit was full, and I seriously woke up every single day excited to learn something new. Fencing rarely crossed my mind.

One day toward the end of my time in Rabat, as I sat on the beach looking out over the crashing waves of the Atlantic Ocean, as the sun painted the sky a startling display of pinks and purples, I thought about what I wanted my life to look like when I returned to college. I made a mental list of what I wanted to prioritize in my life—things like community service and charitable work were on the top. Even though my time in Morocco had been better than I could have ever imagined, many times I had come face-to-face with extreme poverty and suffering and I realized how much privilege I had living in the United States. How much privilege I enjoyed despite the obstacles I faced as a woman. As an African-American woman. As a Muslim African-American woman. I knew I wanted to make time for helping other people when I returned home. I also knew I wanted to continue studying the Arabic language and find ways to practice so I didn't lose the momentum I'd acquired in Morocco. The list went on, and as I rolled through what I truly wanted in life, I realized fencing hadn't even made the list. When I thought about fencing at Duke, my stomach clenched, and a wave of dread passed over me. I curled my toes into the sand. I closed my eyes and tried to imagine my life at Duke without fencing. Rather than the blank canvas I feared during my conversation with Josh, I saw myself volunteering with the MSA, shining in my classes, and having time for myself. I felt relaxed instead of pressed for time. I opened my eyes and knew I had made a decision.

When I returned to the United States and to Duke, I immediately informed my fencing coach that I would be leaving the team for my senior year. He took it pretty well, considering I was a standout on the team. He understood my desire to have at least one year of college where I could focus on something besides fencing and my classes. But the truth was, my coach really couldn't do anything to stop me from leaving even if he wanted to. I hadn't signed a contract, and I wasn't fencing on any scholarship, so I was free to go, just like Josh had before me. I don't know if he figured something must be amiss if the only two Black fencers on his team both quit, but I wasn't interested in sticking around to help him figure it out. I had my own dreams to pursue, and making Duke's fencing team a more inclusive space wasn't one of them.

As I had imagined on that beach in Rabat, my senior year was full of activity, activities that I chose for myself instead of following a never-ending to-do list. I played pool with the members from the MSA after Friday prayers, I went to the mall in Durham with my friends, and sometimes I would just hang out in my dorm room listening to music. It wasn't all official business, and that suited me just fine. For the first time at Duke, I prioritized my personal happiness. My senior year at Duke was the year I started to really figure out who I was and what was important to me.

By the time I hit graduation, I felt confident and comfortable with who I was, as a Black American woman and as a Muslim American woman. I had a deep and appreciative understanding of African-American history, and my faith had evolved and expanded to include the things in life I deemed important and acceptable. I'd moved beyond a childhood relationship with Allah, and my faith no longer required my parents' supervision or interpretation. There were things I decided I could do as a Muslim woman that my parents might have frowned upon, like listening to popular music and having male friends, but I had proven to myself that these things did not alter my steadfastness or obedience to Islam. Although the MSA had been a critical part of keeping me focused while at Duke, I had now developed my own routines that reminded me of and kept me close to God.

All told, I felt like Duke had given me an excellent education in mind, body, and spirit. I graduated knowing so much more about myself and my history. I left Duke with a sense of pride and appreciation for my identity that I didn't have before. By the time graduation rolled around, I'd decided I wanted to go to law school, with a specific focus in international law. I planned to work for one year while I studied for the LSAT, then I would apply to law school. I didn't know exactly where I would land career wise, but with all things in my life, I knew taking things one step at a time was the way to go. I was confident that once I got into law school I would find the right path for me.

As soon as my diploma was in my hands, we packed my parents' car with all of the stuff I'd accumulated over four years and headed home. One thing I didn't love about Duke was its location.

I was too far from my family, and I missed the diversity of New York City. And like most successful college graduates, I was ready for real life to start. As for fencing, I figured that part of my life was over. I hadn't fenced competitively or trained for almost a year, and I had no intention of hopping back on the strip. Fencing had gotten me all the way to an elite university, just like I had planned. Now it was time to move on.

CHAPTER 8

If you have no critics, you'll likely have no success.

—MALCOLM X

I took the elevator to the twenty-third floor and smoothed the pleats on my pants. I'd selected my go-to interview suit, black trousers and blazer with a gray pinstripe blouse and black kitten heels. I felt and looked the part of a corporate executive. My makeup was minimal, and I carried a black leather briefcase with copies of my résumé. When the elevator doors opened, I put on my corporate smile and walked over to the woman sitting at the reception desk.

I was interviewing for a paralegal position in the mergers and acquisitions department of a prestigious multi-national corporate law firm. I was excited for this opportunity because this firm did a lot of international business in the Middle East and Europe. They had offices all over the world, and I could already imagine myself being transferred to the office in Abu Dhabi and using my Arabic language skills. I was getting way ahead of myself, but I knew I could kill it at this job if given the chance.

"May I help you?" the woman said to me, barely glancing up.

"Yes, I have an appointment at ten-thirty with Craig Finch in human resources," I said.

"Name, please?" she asked.

"Ibtihaj Muhammad," I said slowly.

Now the receptionist looked up at me. "Can you repeat that, please?"

I did.

"Just a minute." She then picked up her phone and called who I presumed was Craig. "There's a woman with the last name Muhammad here to see you. She says she has an appointment at ten-thirty."

Without making eye contact, the woman told me that Mr. Finch would be out in a moment, and then she pointed to a bank of seats where I could sit and wait. I thanked her and sat down. I tried to not take her frosty demeanor as a bad omen. This was New York, my home city. People were notorious for not being overtly friendly. I reminded myself that I wouldn't have been called in for an interview if the people weren't interested in hiring me. As I sat there in a stiff, stately upholstered chair and tried not to sweat, I reviewed my talking points, reminded myself that I was more than qualified for the position, and sent a quick prayer to Allah that this time would be different. This time I would get the job. *"Bismillah,"* I said under my breath.

For three months after graduating, between studying for the LSAT, I had dutifully sent off dozens of résumés and applied for jobs at law firms and major corporations in New York and New Jersey that seemed like a good fit. The summer before graduation I'd completed an internship at a money management firm in New York, so I added financial institutions to my list, too. So far, I wasn't having any luck, though. No one was even calling me back. Most of my friends were in grad school or had found great jobs already, working at prestigious firms like Goldman Sachs and Morgan Stanley. But not me. Everyone said it wasn't my fault; it was the economy. We were in the Great Recession. College students couldn't find jobs, and thousands of people were being laid off from long-term careers. While I knew this was all true, it didn't make me feel any better. I simply wanted my life to start already.

Finally, a tall blond man who looked to be in his mid-thirties came through the glass doors into the reception area where I was waiting. He wore crisp khaki pants, a light blue oxford shirt, and a navy-blue tie and blazer. He might as well have stepped out of a Brooks Brothers catalog. Except for his designer glasses and brown leather Italian loafers, he oozed corporate respectability. He walked right over to me and held out his hand.

"Ms. Muhammad, I'm Craig Finch. Thanks for coming in today."

I stood up and took his hand. "Thank you."

"Why don't you follow me and we can get started."

I grabbed my briefcase and followed him as he led me back to his office. To get there we had to walk through a maze of cubicles and offices. I tried not to be obvious as I scanned the faces around me to find anyone who looked like me, but I didn't see more than two people of color and absolutely no other women in hijab. My heart sank just a little. This wasn't the rainbow coalition work force I'd expected to see given the company's global profile.

Craig led me into a separate department where the hum of activity felt different from the area where we'd been before.

"Welcome to human resources," Craig said as he led me to his corner office with views that showed off the impressive New York City skyline. He gestured to the seat in front of his desk, and we both sat down.

"So, Ms. Muhammad," Craig said, "tell me a little bit about yourself."

I was ready for this open-ended question. I launched into my abbreviated life story where I highlighted my academic achievements and my success in fencing. I emphasized my ability to work independently, that I was a self-starter and had excellent time management skills. I finished talking about my desire to work in international law and how a job at this firm would be the perfect gateway into that field. I told Craig how I'd studied Arabic at Duke and in Morocco.

"That's all impressive," Craig said. "And I have to say you have a lot of the skills and attributes that we're looking for in our paralegal candidates."

"Thank you," I said, smiling. I tried not to sound too excited, but inside I was feeling very confident.

"Now, as I'm sure you are aware, Ms. Muhammad, this position will be in our mergers and acquisitions department, which is a very demanding department to work in. Everything is always an emergency or high stakes. There is no room for mistakes or accidents."

"Of course," I said.

"And the lawyers you'd be working for are very demanding, and if they need you to stay at the office to work until two a.m., then you have to stay on until two a.m., or come in on weekends if need be. Would you be comfortable with that?"

"Absolutely," I said. "I am known for my work ethic. I am not afraid of working hard or staying late if that's what's required of me."

"Okay," Craig said, but there was an odd note of doubt in his voice. He paused and cleared his throat before continuing. "I'm just wondering if there would be any conflict with your, um, lifestyle choices that might interfere with the work we do here."

I didn't know how to respond. It was illegal for an employer to ask someone about their religion in a job interview. My religion was evident in my name and it sat obviously covering my head, so I knew Craig was referring to my religion. But I didn't understand what he was trying to get at circuitously.

"I'm sorry, I don't know what you mean," I said.

"Well, I'm just thinking that there are certain things about your, um, lifestyle that would prevent you from giving one hundred percent here in the office."

Now I was really confused and, honestly, I was angered, too. Before I could take a minute to consider it, I just blurted out, "Are you saying because I'm a Muslim I won't be able to do the work here?"

Craig immediately threw his hands up as if to block the words that had just come out of my mouth.

"No, no, no. I would never say something like that. I'm just thinking that maybe some of the late nights here or working with certain people might be uncomfortable or interfere with some of the things we do here. For example, I'm wondering if your head wrap is something you wear all the time, because we do have a company dress code policy that is really strict and you might feel out of place."

I was shocked. Why would I feel out of place? Why would being a Muslim prevent me from doing the work at a law firm? But this wasn't a moment to get indignant if I wanted this job. I simply needed to explain what being a Muslim meant and what it didn't. At this point in my life, I should have been used to explaining myself, and yet it always felt like an unfortunate burden.

"Mr. Finch," I said in a reassuring tone, "I have lived and worked and gone to school with non-Muslim people my whole life. I don't feel uncomfortable in those situations."

"Right," he said, nodding, but I could tell he didn't believe me. Actually, he probably wasn't worried that I'd be uncomfortable, I'm sure he was thinking that his other employees would be uncomfortable around me.

After that, Craig Finch asked me more banal questions, like where I lived in New Jersey and what my favorite class at Duke had been and why. I knew my answers didn't matter. It was obvious that he only saw my hijab, not me. I continued to answer his questions and kept a smile on my face, but I knew the interview was over. As we walked back to the elevator, I knew that would be the last time I ever saw Craig Finch, and it was.

———

Following that interview, I continued applying for jobs. Now seven months since I graduated, my phone had stopped ringing. The whole experience was unsettling and completely demoralizing. I started to feel desperate. I wasn't used to this level of powerlessness. As an athlete, I knew if I worked a little harder I would find the success that was eluding me. As a student, I knew if I struggled, I could find a tutor or take an extra class, and eventually I would catch on. But here we were in real life, and for all of my smarts and skills I couldn't think of one single way to get what I wanted, a good job in corporate America. I even applied to Teach for America—the national teacher placement organization that places college graduates in needy schools in underserved communities. I hoped to have more luck outside of the corporate world, but I was turned away after the third round of interviews. I didn't want to assume that my frustration finding a job was because of my religion, my last name, or because I wore hijab, but I wasn't naïve. It was at least part of the problem.

Ever since the September 11 attacks, Muslims in America were looked at differently. On the morning the terrorists struck the Twin Towers in New York, I was in the eleventh grade. The teachers turned the television sets on in our high school in Maplewood to watch the horror unfold, and all of the Muslim boys, including my brother, were rounded up and isolated in one single classroom for the rest of the day. School officials said it was for their own protection, but it sounded like punishment and discrimination to me when Qareeb came home and told us what had happened to him. I had no idea they had treated him that way because I was left in class to watch the carnage with the rest of the students in my grade. From that day forward, it was apparent that Muslims had become the boogeyman in America. Hate crimes against Muslims in America have more than quadrupled since 2001, and everyday activities like traveling through airports are fraught with tension. It was 2008, and I had been lucky enough to avoid any direct threats of violence, but now I had to wonder if the reason I wasn't able to land a job was because of people's prejudice against Muslims. At worst, I was a potential terrorist; at best, I was an outsider who wouldn't fit into corporate culture.

The day after the interview with Craig Finch I found myself back in New York City. I wasn't looking for a job, though—I was going to visit the Peter Westbrook Foundation. After I left Craig Finch's office, my mind swirling with conflicting emotions, I had walked around midtown trying to figure out my next steps, but with everything in my life dangling in limbo, nothing was clear and everything seemed out of my control. I couldn't force anyone to give me a job. At least I could come back to the one thing in my life that had always been a constant: fencing.

Standing outside of the foundation building, my limbs tingled with a sense of familiarity, like they longed to get back on the strip. Fencing felt like the one thing in my life that I could actually control. I didn't have a plan or a goal, I just wanted to be in a space where I knew what the rules were and where I didn't have to prove myself. If there was even just a small part of the day where I was doing something for myself, instead of waiting for someone or something to make my life make sense, I was ready to give fencing another chance.

Soon enough, I fell back into my old routine of going to the foundation four days a week. Not only was it nice to reconnect with my friends at the foundation, but it brought back some sense of regularity to my life. Now I didn't just have to sit home and wait for my phone to ring.

Most of the other students in my classes were in high school or still in college, and I was twenty-one, but I didn't care. I liked losing myself in the physicality of sport where I didn't have to think or plan for what was next. I just had to show up and work. On my worst days, fencing was my therapy. If I'd wake up feeling aimless or uncertain about where my life was headed I'd train harder to be certain I was at least the best fencer that day. With all of my emotions charged up in the saber, I'd attack without mercy. I'm sure some of the younger fencers didn't understand my tenacity or competitive nature during practice, but fencing was my only way to seek revenge on an enemy with no name. I couldn't pounce on Craig Finch or others like him in their midtown offices. But on the strip, I ruled. I could slash and hit the target of my opponent. I could name my enemy and fight her. On the strip winners and losers, enemy and friends were clearly defined. In the real world, nothing was that clear. Nothing was that easy.

It only took me a little while to get back in shape, and the physical exertion required during my training kept my mind off my failing job search. Soon, fencing became my number one diversion, so I did it as much as possible. When I wasn't at the foundation, I would go to the gym close to our house and work out. I even went back to competing at some local and regional tournaments. But there was one small problem with my new lifestyle; fencing wasn't free or cheap. The Peter Westbrook Foundation was no longer investing in me, because I had aged out of their training program without reaching the national or international circuit. The foundation only waived their fees when young athletes showed potential to distinguish themselves on the national and international stage. I hadn't attained that level of status in my career and at my age, I was already considered a has-been. Peter and his coaches were happy to have me around, but mostly so I could serve as a training partner for everyone else. I was just another paying customer. I had to pay for my own club membership now. I had to pay for my lessons, competition entry fees, and travel. I also had to pay for my equipment. My parents were happy to let me live at home rent-free—my father expected all of his daughters to live at home until they got married anyway—but they made it perfectly clear that they would not be footing my bills when I had a college degree. In their minds, fencing was my new hobby, and they were not in the business of bankrolling hobbies, not when they still had to get Asiya and Faizah through the rest of high school and college.

One day in a fit of desperation, or maybe it was just perverse frustration, I put in an application at the Dollar Store. I'd seen a help wanted sign in the window and applied right there in the store. I was hungry for a regular paycheck. Even the temp agency I had signed with had been unable to find me any type of consistent assignments, so I had no dependable income coming in. When I got the call from the Dollar Store that I had been selected for a part-time job as cashier, I actually felt a moment of elation simply because *someone* had been willing to hire me. But those feelings didn't last long. Working at the Dollar Store was mind-numbing and humbling work. Customers were rude and dismissive and treated employees like we were insignificant beings to be tolerated. Sometimes I found myself cackling on the verge of hysteria when I was stacking bottles of no-name brands of dishwashing liquid. I would wonder why I had stressed over that research paper I'd written at Duke on the economic effects of Reconstruction if working at the Dollar Store was to be my life's work.

At home, I pulled the light-green Dollar Store uniform shirt off over my head, balled it up, and threw it in the corner of my room. I changed into a t-shirt and sweatpants and went downstairs so I could sit on the couch and watch television for the rest of the afternoon. I should have been scouring the want ads looking for a job that paid more than the Dollar Store or studying for the LSATs, but I couldn't summon the energy to do anything except watch daytime talk shows until my mind went numb. I didn't know who to talk to or ask for advice. I'd never been in a rut like this before. I felt so far from those days in Morocco when I felt I had a clear direction and plan for my future. Now I was adrift. Even Qareeb and Brandilyn hadn't struggled like this to find work after college. Brandilyn had been independent since graduating from high school, and Qareeb's job had recently transferred him to California.

Two hours later I was still on the couch when my mom and Faizah came home. When they walked in the front door and saw me there, they both exchanged a look. I knew what it meant. It was the "poor Ibtihaj" look that I seemed to be getting more and more these days. I hated it. I hated being the object of pity in my own home. I pulled myself up into a sitting position so I didn't look so pathetic. I rearranged my disheveled ponytail.

"Hey, you guys," I said, forcing myself to sound cheery. "How was school, Faizah?"

My little sister came to sit next to me. "It was good. I had a fencing lesson with Coach Mustilli today. He said to tell you hi."

Faizah was only in eighth grade but was already taking private fencing lessons with Coach Mustilli in anticipation of being on the high school team. After watching my success in the sport and knowing her girls would be covered, my mother had practically begged Asiya and Faizah to try it. Asiya had refused and took up basketball instead, but Faizah was fencing and excelling at the sport. I was really proud of her.

"Did he ask anything else about me?" I blurted out, worried my sister might have told my former coach that I was working at the Dollar Store. For some reason, it mattered to me that Coach Mustilli thought of me as successful. He'd made me believe I could do anything. I was the captain of the fencing team for two years; I went off to fence at Duke. I didn't want him to see me as a failure now.

My little sister gave me a look. "No. He just said, 'Hi.'"

I smiled, relieved. "Oh, good. Well tell him I said 'hi' back."

"You could go tell him yourself and see his new club," Faizah said. "It's so much nicer than when you had to fence in the cafeteria," Faizah added with a grin.

I had to smile back. Faizah was so sweet, and I knew she just wanted to get me out of my depression, but I didn't think I could face Coach Mustilli until I had a job. I pretty much felt that way about everyone. I didn't want anyone who knew me or knew my family to know about my current circumstances. That's why I was happy I was working at the Dollar Store in Irvington: I was less likely to be seen there.

I hauled myself off the couch and padded behind my mother into the kitchen. She told Faizah to go upstairs because she needed to talk to me. I figured another pep talk was imminent. My mother was a doer. She hardly ever sat still, and I knew seeing me on the couch every afternoon was making her crazy.

"Have you fed the bird?" Mom asked. Before I even had a chance to respond, she was already grabbing the birdseed from the cabinet and filling Koocah's bowl. Koocah rewarded her with a hearty screech.

"Sorry, I forgot to feed her," I mumbled, but my mom acted like she didn't even hear me.

"Ibtihaj, I was talking to some of my colleagues at work, and they all think you should apply to be a substitute teacher," she said, while pulling pots and pans out for the evening meal. "You're so smart and you're good with kids, and it will pay you a lot more than the Dollar Store."

I scrunched up my face because of the way she said "Dollar

Store." "Substitute teacher? I don't think that's what I want to do," I said.

My mother stopped what she was doing. "Excuse me. The last time I checked you were working at the Dollar Store, and last month you still needed to borrow money for your phone bill, so I wouldn't be turning my nose up at substitute teaching."

"I wasn't turning my nose up at anything," I cried. "I just don't really see myself as a teacher."

"Do you see yourself as a cashier at the Dollar Store?" mom retorted.

"No," I said and crumpled into my chair. "I didn't see myself not being able to find a job with a degree from Duke," I said sadly. "I don't know what to do."

"What you can't do is give up," Mom said. "You have to keep trying things until a job turns up."

"I've been trying," I said, bordering on tears. "And nothing is working. As soon as they see my name on that résumé—"

My mother made a soothing noise in the back of her throat. "Baby, you're going to be okay. I promise."

"I don't just want to be okay. I don't want to be a substitute teacher or a cashier. I didn't work that hard in school and college to just be okay."

My mom turned away from me and went back to preparing dinner. "It's your life, Ibtihaj, and you're going to have to live it. I left the paperwork to apply for substituting on the dining room table."

I sat up and wiped my eyes. I could tell my mother didn't have time for a big baby. She had two other kids to take care of besides me. She didn't need any more of my moping around the house bringing everyone down. I quietly left the kitchen and went back to the living room. I plopped back down on the couch and turned the volume up on the TV. My favorite show was about to come on.

A few weeks later, I found myself at Coach Mustilli's new club, the New Jersey Fencing Alliance. Coach Mustilli had grown his program and his footprint in the fencing world. He now had his own fencing club where he gave private lessons and where he trained the Columbia High School team. The high school team now got bused to his club after school, a short five-minute ride away. The new club was also only about ten minutes from our home. Ever since Faizah had told me that Coach Mustilli had said hi, I'd been nostalgic about how simple things were in high school. That was a time in my life when I knew what I was doing and why I was doing it. I felt invincible and self-assured. I felt appreciated and supported. I would have given anything to feel like that again.

I quietly slipped into the club and was thankful that it was mostly empty on this particular weekday evening. There was a coach giving a lesson on the strip. I could immediately tell it was Coach Mustilli. His unmistakable compact frame and booming voice yelling commands at his opponent immediately made me feel at home. I sat down at one of the tables in the waiting area and watched Coach finish up the lesson he was giving. When he was done and the kid ran off the floor to the locker room to change, I stood up and gave a nervous wave. "Hey, Coach," I said with a small smile.

"Ibti, good to see you," Coach Mustilli said, walking toward me with his helmet in his hand. When he got closer to me, he reached for his glasses, which were lying on a nearby table. We exchanged small talk, but neither of us were really good at it. Soon there was an awkward pause in the conversation, and Coach Mustilli stared at me expectantly.

"What can I do for you, Ibtihaj?" he finally asked.

I wanted to say, *Can you help me makes sense of my life?* Instead I settled for, "Do you think you could give me a lesson?"

Coach gave me a funny look, but he said okay. "Get your gear on," he said and went into his office. I already had on sweats and a long-sleeved shirt, so I walked over to the equipment area to find what I needed. I pulled a saber out of the rack of weapons and found a spare mask and glove.

"Do some warm-ups," Coach yelled from his office. I ran around the court a few times, and stretched out my legs and arms. Part of me felt like I was wasting the coach's time with my request for a lesson, but I pushed those feelings aside, because I needed to be in this safe space again.

We set up on strip number one—there were twelve different strips on the floor—and Coach took me back through all of my best high school moves. It felt like coming home. I easily parried and lunged and landed the most fluid attacks on my former coach.

Thirty minutes later, Coach Mustilli was panting, but I was just getting warmed up.

"Coach," I said half laughing but still serious, "can you give me a harder lesson?"

Coach raised his thick, bushy eyebrows. "Okay, Ibtihaj, let's see what you've got," he said. And then he let me have it. It was the first time Coach Mustilli treated me like an equal opponent. He didn't hold back. He ran me up and down the strip, giving me the hardest lesson I'd ever had. I met him lunge for lunge, attack for attack. I was quick on my toes, and my saber sliced through the air. The sounds of our blades clashing and an occasional roar filled the room. I could feel the electricity coursing through the air like I was coming alive for the first time in months, and I loved it. I was in control, and no one could take that feeling away.

Finally, Coach Mustilli yelled, "Time!" We were both out of breath now. I took off my mask, taking in big gulps of air, and smiled at Coach Mustilli. "That was awesome, Coach."

He walked slowly off the strip and over to the tables. He got two bottles of water from his cooler and beckoned me over to sit down. The sweat was pouring off his face now, and his black hair, now lightly streaked with gray, was plastered across his forehead. He took a healthy swig of water before asking, "Ibtihaj, what are you doing here? What do you really want?"

I was unprepared for this question. What did I want?

"What I saw out there," Coach continued, still trying to catch his breath, "was something I didn't know you had."

My eyes grew wide in surprise. "Really. You think I still have talent?"

"Talent? Ibti, I don't think you've even hit your peak yet. I think if you want to go all the way with fencing you can."

I couldn't believe what I was hearing. No one had ever said this to me before. Not at Duke and not even at the foundation. And I never really imagined anything beyond college fencing.

"What do you mean go all the way, Coach?" I asked nervously.

"I mean that you should think about competing on the international circuit and maybe even think about the Olympics," Coach Mustilli said. "I'm serious. I saw something out there today that I honestly didn't know you had."

I beamed from inside and out. After all of the recent rejections, this assessment of my potential ignited a spark that I thought had long since been extinguished.

"Don't thank me, Ibti," Coach Mustilli said with a warning in his tone. "If you decide to actually take up the challenge, it won't be easy. In fact, it'll be the hardest thing you'll probably ever do. Being a champion is a long, lonely road. You'll have to get up every morning hungry, and you can't go to bed until you've exhausted yourself. Every single day. And there won't be anyone on this path with you. It's you, and that's it."

Even though I trusted Coach Mustilli with all of my fencing aspirations, I didn't think he wanted to hear about the existential life crisis I was currently living in, questioning my very purpose in the world. I didn't think he needed to hear that his words were literally feeding my soul at that moment.

"Do you think you can do it?" Coach Mustilli asked, interrupting the jumble of thoughts and emotions running through my mind. But what I heard then in his question wasn't *could I handle the hard work as a full-time athlete?* What I heard was *would you like some purpose in your life again?*

"Yes. I'm up for it," I said to Coach Mustilli, quietly at first, and then I repeated it again to convince the coach, but also myself.

"Okay, Ibti," Coach Mustilli said with a smile, "if there's anyone I know who has the strength and determination to do this, it's you."

"Thanks, Coach," I said, returning his smile.

"Don't thank me, Ibtihaj, until you win. Until then, your life is going to be harder than it's ever been before."

CHAPTER 9

Don't let the hand you hold hold you down.

—JULIA DE BURGOS

Once I committed myself to fencing again, my life became a nonstop hustle to support my training. Now that I had found a purpose, I had to figure out how to make money. Unlike a regular career where a person earned money, I had to *spend* money to support my fencing pursuits. More specifically, I needed a high-paying, flexible source of income. I knew it was time to rethink substitute teaching.

Being a substitute teacher not only paid relatively well, but it also allowed me to pick and choose assignments that worked with my training and travel schedule. Originally, I registered to teach in my own school district, but my mom informed me that I could make more money in the Newark public schools, despite its record number of failing and struggling institutions. I quickly landed a long-term sub position teaching art history at the Malcolm X Shabazz High School in Newark. This school had recently been assessed as "one of the country's most troubled high schools," but I was willing to give it a try.

On my first day on the job, I walked into my classroom and tried to present myself as an authority figure, someone confident and intelligent, but inside I was a nervous wreck. The thirty kids in the classroom—all juniors and seniors—were only a few years younger than me, and I was afraid they wouldn't respect me. I had precisely one minute to prove my worth. After taking attendance, I asked the students to read in their textbooks, per the instructions that their teacher had left. Half of the students didn't even bother to open their books and simply took up the conversations they were previously having. When I asked one girl to please take out her book, she snapped, "I'm not reading anything in this class, and don't ask me again!"

I was shocked by the student's blatant disrespect and, honestly, I was a little bit worried too by the naked hostility emanating from these teens. I knew this job was going to be challenging, but I don't think anyone could have prepared me for what I confronted in the classroom. No one wanted to do any work. The students wouldn't listen to me, and I felt like I didn't have the tools to make anything better. But I was committed to making it work. Teaching was a means to an end, and I *had* to figure it out. I talked to the principal, and I talked to my mom. I consulted with other teachers and quickly realized that I wasn't going to be teaching as much as I would be making sure the students stayed in the classroom for the forty-five minutes they were supposed to be learning art history with me. Sometimes I called my job glorified babysitting. Sometimes I felt like I was letting everyone down, but this was what I was given, and I didn't have a whole lot of other options.

My parents bought my sister Asiya and me a car to share so that we could get ourselves to our respective jobs and school without having to rely on public transportation. I went to work at my teaching job, then hopped on a train to Manhattan to work out at the foundation. Three days a week I'd train from five to nine p.m. On the days I wasn't at the foundation, I'd be at the gym, doing exercises to improve my speed and agility. On Saturday mornings, I would teach young kids at the foundation, and

Saturday afternoons were dedicated to more training and private lessons. I was hustling like a pro, but the only problem was that I didn't exactly know what I was hustling for. I couldn't visualize the prize because I didn't exactly know what the prize was. A spot on the national fencing team? Qualifying for the Olympic Games in 2012? These were ideas I got from random conversations with the coaches at the foundation, but I didn't really understand how it all was supposed to work, and no one stepped up to lead the way.

Even though Coach Mustilli told me he believed I had what it took to make it all the way to the Olympics, my path to becoming a world-class athlete didn't suddenly materialize. I felt like I did my part in that I gave myself over to fencing 100 percent. I stopped looking for corporate jobs, and I put law school farther down on my list of priorities. I arranged my life so that I could afford to travel and compete on the fencing circuit, but there was a key detail missing. I didn't know what part of my training or fencing to change in order to get better.

I'd been grinding like a workhorse for months but didn't have much to show for it. I hadn't broken through on the domestic circuit yet, so my national ranking was barely worth mentioning. And my family and friends all thought I was crazy for focusing so much on fencing when I had a degree from one of the nation's top universities. I was beginning to doubt my plans, too. And having Sam as my coach again at the foundation wasn't helping. Sam had me doing the same workouts I'd been doing in high school. He barely changed my training schedule. I asked Peter if there was another coach I could train with, but he said Sam was the only saber coach with Olympic experience. He was *the* saber coach at the foundation.

"But I need something more," I said to Peter as we sat in his office. "I want to go all the way with this."

"There's no one standing in your way. If you want to go all the way that's on you," Peter replied.

"But I've been working with Sam for almost six months now, and every lesson is the same," I said. "I just feel like I'm stagnating, and it's pretty obvious Sam isn't interested in my development."

"How old are you?" Peter asked, squinting at me as if he were seeing me for the first time.

"I'm twenty-three," I said, trying to keep the defensive tone out of my voice. By my age, most athletes who were considered to have any real Olympic potential already had cadet, junior, or even senior national teams under their belts. Meanwhile, I knew my name wasn't even on the radar for the foundation coaches. But Peter had never let age stop him from competing.

He pursed his lips and tented his fingers in front of him. "Ibtihaj, you do remember that we urged you to stay here instead of going off to Duke. I'm not saying you can't do it, but you've made it hard on yourself. No one here is going to stop you from chasing your dreams, but I don't know if it's a realistic goal for you."

My heart sank. My hero was telling me that it might be too late to follow my dreams. The truth was out. He didn't believe in me. The foundation didn't believe I could make it. They looked at this pursuit as a joke. Here I was doing everything I knew how to do, but I needed something else. I needed someone else to be able to look at what I was doing and then tell me how to do it differently or better. Part of me felt angry at Peter and Sam because they knew I wanted to get ahead, yet they wouldn't take the time to focus on me. Maybe I *was* too old? If I really had the talent to be successful in the sport like Coach Mustilli said, why wasn't the foundation taking my effort more seriously by helping me get to the top? I considered leaving the foundation in search of a new coach, but I felt a deep loyalty to the foundation and to my teammates there who had become more like family. Leaving the foundation would have repercussions beyond losing the support, camaraderie, and good will of my friends—I felt like I'd be considered a traitor to the unspoken brother/sisterhood of Black fencers. When participating in a sport that is so overwhelmingly white like fencing, it did make a difference to have a strong support system made up of Black fencers who understood the rules and nuances of the sport and could help a younger fencer navigate the game both on and off the strip. So I wasn't going to leave my fencing home. But I knew something was going to have to change in my life, because I felt like I was putting in all of the work and only getting grief in return.

The grief wasn't only happening at the foundation.

———

"You talk white!" The accusation was hurled like an insult, and that's exactly what it felt like. Even though I was standing in the front of the classroom as the teacher, a student named Deliah Jones had taken me all the way back to the hell I'd experienced as a kid.

"Yeah, Ms. Muhammad, you sound all proper when you talk," a boy named Terrance, who actually looked mixed race to me, said. "Is your daddy white?"

I closed my eyes and drew in a deep breath. "No," I said through gritted teeth. "The fact that I speak grammatically correct English doesn't make me white."

"Dang, she do talk white!" another kid called out, and then the room erupted in laughter. They didn't have much to say about their schoolwork, but just about everyone in the classroom had something to say about me and how "white" I really was. I so desperately wanted them to know that I wasn't their enemy, that we had a shared history in common, that they had descended from greatness and didn't have to shun their education, but every attempt I'd made to get them to really listen to me had failed.

"Okay, you guys, when you're finished having your fun and you're ready to get back to work, let me know," I said and I retreated to my sanctuary behind my desk. There I plopped down, took my book out of my bag, and tried to read while my students tried their best not to read. I scanned the words on the page, but couldn't drown out the sound of the students' giggles and snide remarks. I wouldn't give them the satisfaction of seeing me upset, but it took a lot to do so. For probably the hundredth time in less than a week I had to remind myself that working at this school served a purpose besides a paycheck.

One of the main reasons I continued to show up every day to Malcolm X Shabazz High School was because my father's mother, Louella, had moved back to Newark, and her home was only a five-minute drive from the school. At the urging of my father, sometimes on my lunch break, I would drive over to check up on her, make sure she was doing okay, because she was now in her eighties. On the days I didn't have to go into New York after work for fencing practice, I'd sometimes stop in then, too. Soon, I grew to look forward to those visits as the highlights of my day. My grandmother was beautiful and full of life. People always said we looked alike, which always made me feel like we shared a special bond.

My grandmother always had wonderful stories to tell me about her childhood and what it was like raising twelve children alone. Abu rarely spoke about his childhood, so these stories were all new to me, and I loved hearing about where I came from and what my father was like as a child. For instance, even though my grandmother wasn't Muslim, she told me that Abu had actually first become intrigued by Islam, not by his brothers joining the Nation of Islam, but from watching his favorite childhood movie, *Sinbad: Legend of the Seven Seas*! I never knew that, and it made me feel even closer to my dad.

Unfortunately, my grandmother got really sick during this time and refused to go to the hospital. She was from a generation of Black people who avoided hospitals like the plague—she birthed all twelve of her children at home—and nothing I said or did would convince her to seek medical treatment beyond visiting her primary care doctor, who could only offer palliative care. I supported her the best way that I knew how, by continuing and even increasing my visits. It was crushing to watch my grandmother slowly die, and yet it felt like I had been divinely placed there by Allah to take care of her. I was so grateful I had the privilege of being nearby so we could spend her last days together.

On some of my weakest days, when I wanted to give up on those loud, rambunctious kids, or when Sam pressed all of my buttons and I just wanted to quit everything, I would witness firsthand my grandmother's resilience and strength, and it made me dig deeper into my own reserves of strength. Watching her struggle inspired me to press on with my own challenges. It put everything I was going through in perspective. I didn't like to complain to my grandmother, thinking she didn't need to worry about my problems on top of her own, but she knew I was having a hard time. She could see it on my face, she said. Sometimes I'd tell her a bit about what was going on in my life, including the temptation to quit everything.

"You're going to be okay," she'd say. "But you can't give up, because the minute you do, it all comes crashing down. I promise you, if you get up every day and put one foot in front of the other, and don't give up, that's the answer. How do you think I managed by myself all these years, with all those kids? Did I know everything was going to work out? No, I just never stopped."

I smiled. "You're so strong, Grandma."

"And you have my same spirit, Ibtihaj. You just keep moving forward and don't take any mess from anyone who tries to tell you different."

Visiting my grandmother's house every day and watching the strength she carried even when she was in pain made me take her words to heart. If she could carry on, so could I. I just had to remind myself that all the work I was doing to become a better fencer would eventually come to fruition.

The problem was, whether I wanted to admit it or not, what other people thought bothered me. No one thinks a career in sports is a "real thing" unless it involves the NBA, NFL, or a big paycheck. People thought I was crazy for choosing an obscure sport like fencing in the first place and then crazier for sticking with it. I could ration off some of the blame to my parents or my religion about why I'd picked up fencing in high school, but the decision to keep going at twenty-three years of age was my weight to carry alone.

The average person doesn't understand that a professional athlete isn't born, she's made. It takes relentless, all-consuming training and untold personal sacrifices before any of the glory is seen. Sometimes even I questioned this path I'd chosen, but I had to shift my thinking and convince myself that the struggles I was experiencing served a purpose. Most of my family didn't understand why I was working so hard for a still unnamed goal, and I knew it was a struggle for my parents to sign on to my dream because there was no precedent in our family for what I was doing. I wasn't in graduate school. I wasn't married. I didn't have a real job. There was no easy reference point for my decision to pursue sport.

My parents smiled through it all, though, and never tried to move me away from fencing. I loved them for not giving up on me because charting this unknown territory on a leap of faith at times was paralyzing. Every day I had to silence my internal voices of doubt, and I would still be left wondering if this was the right path for me. I feared the unknown. I couldn't guarantee success was coming. Would I ever make the national team, much less an Olympic team? I heard judgment in the innocent questions people would ask. "How long are you going to be doing this?" "Are you still going to law school?" "What's your plan if things don't work out?" "When are you getting married?" That's when I would think about my grandmother Louella, her strength and her convictions as a woman, and I would renew my promise to continue on my quest to be the best, with nothing but faith in my pockets and courage in my heart.

———

One day in early 2009, almost a year to the day since I'd committed myself to fencing, something happened that would completely change the trajectory of my career. More people were joining the Fencers Club, so we were in desperate need of another saber coach. There had been some talk about a former foundation fencer, moving from Texas back to New York, who would take the new job. His name was Akhnaten Spencer-El, and he had been on a few national teams as a kid and even qualified for the Olympics in Sydney back in 2000. I had met Akhi at the New Jersey Fencing Alliance back in Maplewood, when he briefly worked for Coach Mustilli before joining the foundation. He'd towered over Coach Mustilli. With his golden skin, permanent five o'clock shadow, and eyes that crinkled like crescent moons when he smiled, I found him to be easily approachable and always very encouraging when I'd stop in for a secret lesson unbeknownst to Sam. I didn't know much about Akhi, but he seemed really nice and invested in the development of his students, so I didn't hesitate to tell Peter that I wanted to switch coaches. I had grown tired of walking on eggshells around Sam and dealing with his unpredictable behavior. Lately Sam had been showing up to my competitions late, if at all, and dressed like he was going out clubbing in Harlem in the 1920s. Instead of wearing sweatpants and sneakers like most coaches, one day Sam showed up in what looked like a pink zoot suit—pink slacks, pink shirt, pink fedora, and pink alligator shoes. His choice of attire showed just how uninterested he was in coaching or in helping his athletes during competition. He proved to be more of a distraction than an asset. Even though I really didn't know if Akhi would be the right coach for me, I figured he had to be an improvement over Sam. At that point, anyone would have been an improvement over Sam.

"Ibtihaj, I think you could be one of the best fencers in the world!" Akhi said to me after our first lesson together.

"Really? Me?" I asked, my disbelief clear. Since it had been a year since that meeting with Coach Mustilli, I was now holding on to my confidence by a thread. It felt wonderful to hear someone else verbally acknowledge my potential.

"Yes, you," he said, chuckling. "Who else am I talking to?"

"Okay," I said, grinning like a fool.

"You have a really good sense of timing and you're really fast," he said. "You have a natural counterattack and that's a strength we can exploit. I'm going to have fun turning you into a champion, Ibtihaj."

I wasn't used to being praised by the coaches at the foundation for my skill or potential. More often than not, they seemed to see the potential only in the male saber fencers. But here was a former Olympian telling me that he could turn me into a top fencer. I relished the idea and couldn't wait to get started. I could already feel my spirits starting to rise.

"So, when do we start?" I asked, the smile still plastered on my face.

"Actually, our training is going to have to be put on hold for a minute because I have to take care of something," he said.

"What do you mean?" I asked.

"I want to be a certified fencing Maestro so I have to go through a certification course in Hungary, and it's about to get started," he said. "I don't want to be an assistant coach forever."

My world crumpled at the thought. "Hungary? Like the country, Hungary?" I asked, unable to hide the disappointment in my voice. "How long will you be gone?"

"Three months," he said, grimacing, "but I'll give you some exercises you can do while I'm gone, and I'm sure Sam can continue to work with you until I come back."

A cold ball of dread formed in my stomach at the thought. If only Akhi knew what I'd been going through with Sam. Here I'd mustered up the courage to let go of Sam, and now I had to work with him again for three more months, with the added burden of him knowing that I no longer wanted to work with him. The unselfish part of me was happy for Akhi and knew it was a necessary step for him to take in order to be a respected coach in our club, but the selfish part of me wanted him to stay in New York. That night as I rode the train home, I had to try to psych myself up for working with Sam again for another three months. I prayed that he wouldn't hold it against me that I'd dared to finally cut our ties.

Apparently, Sam wasn't up to the task. He was either unwilling or unable to take the high road. Instead, Sam made it his mission to make the next three months unbearable for me. I was convinced he wanted to break me or see me quit, but I wouldn't give him the satisfaction. On the contrary, he just fueled my desire to succeed even more. He would never see me quit.

It was obvious Sam didn't want to work with me, either, but Peter hadn't given him a choice. In response, Sam routinely came to my lessons late or would cut my lesson time short. I knew better than to ask for any more than he was willing to give, because it would have fallen on deaf ears. He was passive-aggressive in his treatment of me, but the worst part was his refusal to acknowledge my talent and ambition. He treated me like a chore or, worse, like a waste of his time. Sometimes I just wanted to scream and yell, "What did I ever do to you? I can be better if you'd just help me, if you'd just do your job and coach me!" But it wouldn't have mattered.

I'll never know why Sam was so dismissive of me. My only guess is that he had a general lack of respect for women. When I was younger, he always seemed to favor the boys in class, always allowing them to stand in the front line as examples to the rest of us, or hand-selecting male students for special activities that girls were never chosen for. As an adult I saw the way he treated other girls and young women in the program, often with the same disregard for their potential. I told myself it wasn't me, it was my gender that Sam had a problem with, but it still made me so angry. Deep down I sensed he wanted to see me to give up, like many of the other female fencers unfortunate enough to be coached by Sam, but walking away from fencing would have proven him right, that I wouldn't amount to anything. So I showed up early to every lesson, gritted my teeth through the arduous group classes, and was always the last one to head home. I was literally counting down the days until Akhi's return, but I would never give Sam the satisfaction of seeing my pain. My negative feelings about Sam were finally confirmed when he was fired from the foundation some months later. Although it didn't take away from all the suffering he had caused, I did feel vindicated.

Akhi was back by the summer, and we started training right away. Most fencers take a break from training in the summer since the fencing season runs from October through June, but when Akhi came back in early June, we got right down to business.

Working with Akhi felt like having a gourmet meal after eating a steady diet of gruel. He was as hungry as I was for success. As a new coach at the foundation, Akhi needed to prove he had what it took to turn regular athletes into champions. I was hoping to be his first success. My spirit came alive under his tutelage. We were the first people in the gym every morning and the last ones to leave at night because we had a goal we were working toward, and that was to make me one of the best fencers in the world. Finally, I had a coach who was willing to climb on board my crazy workhorse train, to put in the hours and grind. It was such a welcome relief to have someone who not only rooted for me, but also believed in me as well. It wasn't only his positive attitude and willingness to put in the time that made working with Akhi so different, he was also showing me a whole new approach to the sport of fencing.

Until this point, I had always been taught to fence defensively by reacting to my opponents. I was given methods and approaches to attack or defend and was told to execute these moves with speed and strength. Akhi had a different approach. He told me fencing was a mind game, so instead of focusing on the physical, he taught me to think tactically. We spent a lot of time watching videos of some of the world's best female saberists—some from Russia, others from Ukraine—and Akhi would break the matches down for me point by point.

"You have to realize that it's human nature to want to score," Akhi explained. "Even the best trained athlete is vulnerable to a strong tactical game, so you have to figure out how to get into your opponent's mind. Let them think there's an opportunity, but really you've devised a plan to score using that false action that your opponent has fallen for."

I nodded my head to show Akhi that I was listening. I felt like I was being given the secret keys to the kingdom. Akhi's face was animated and his eyes were lit with enthusiasm when he spoke. He had a love for this sport that could not be denied.

"You have to use your strengths, Ibtihaj," Akhi continued. "Your sense of timing and explosive speed have to be used to your advantage. And you must have a plan A, a plan B, and a plan C. Before every competition, you have to know your opponent's strengths and weaknesses and how you plan to beat them. Just like a football coach has a plan of attack, you need one, too."

I devoured everything Akhi said and tried to faithfully execute everything he told me through the weeks and months of practicing together. I had never had someone put that much time and thought into helping me develop as an athlete. Throughout my journey, I had been given advice, but nothing compared to Akhi teaching me that my opponents' strengths and weaknesses were as important as, if not more important than, my own. Akhi's style of coaching was brand-new to me, allowing me to discover an entirely new approach to fencing. I shook my head at the time I had wasted with Sam. Maybe Sam's approach to fencing had worked back in the day when he used to compete, but it had never worked for me. He was probably ten years older than Akhi, and things do change, the sport evolves, so maybe that was it. It didn't help that Sam genuinely had no interest in coaching female athletes, either. I was just grateful I had been brave enough to switch coaches. Deciding to work with Akhi had required a wild leap of faith on my part, but it was one of the best decisions I ever made in my life.

To say things changed dramatically after I started working with Akhi would be an understatement. Even though I had performed well at Duke on the college circuit, competing at domestic and international competitions was a whole different experience. It was like the difference between playing college basketball and being drafted into the NBA. Yes, college competition was tough, but domestic competitions meant competing against a much larger field of competitors, fencers of all ages from across the United States. It's a separate universe entirely. I had to pinch myself as I started to walk away from these domestic competitions with gold medals around my neck after training with Akhi over the summer. Akhi had helped me perfect my craft and develop my natural talents of timing and speed. Most importantly, Akhi showed me that with a good tactical plan, I could beat anyone on the strip.

———————

Just a few months into the season, I had fenced well enough in the domestic competitions that I now had a high enough national ranking to compete on the international circuit. In my wildest dreams, I couldn't imagine that happening so quickly.

This World Cup competition was to take place right outside of London. Even though I'd traveled to Morocco in college, this was my first international fencing competition. My parents were worried about me traveling alone, but the coaches at the Westbrook Foundation assured them that I would be well cared for. They also reassured my parents that I'd never be alone because there was another young female fencer, Candace, who was also competing. Candace also fenced saber and was one of my favorite people at the foundation. She was always the face of calm, which is good company for any competitor.

Candace and I flew into London's Heathrow Airport together, and took a taxi to our hotel. It was my first time in London, but I was so nervous about the competition, I hardly paid attention to the world speeding by outside the taxi window. Once in our hotel, both Candace and I quickly unpacked and headed out to find a grocery store where we could buy some healthy snacks and bottled water to take with us to the competition the next day.

The competition was to take place on the outskirts of London at a private boys' school in an area called South Croydon. Pulling up to the Whitgift School on the first of the two days of competition, I decided the school looked more like a prestigious college campus than any primary school I'd ever seen before. The imposing brick buildings on the campus looked like castles. Candace and I found our way to the school's gymnasium, which had obviously been modernized, as it stood in stark contrast to the gothic buildings surrounding it. Once inside, the distinctive sound of metal hitting metal and the fierce yells of the competitors permeated the room.

My face must have shown the fear and apprehension I was feeling because Candace smiled and said, "Don't worry, Ibtihaj. You're going to do fine."

Candace had been fencing saber from an early age and was a better fencer than me. Everyone at the foundation, including me, was waiting for Candace to qualify for the United States National Team. In order for that to happen, she would have to be one of the top four saber fencers in the country at the end of the season. I knew she was close, and I was praying for her to succeed.

"I'm so nervous," I said.

"Of course you're nervous," Candace said with a grin. "If you weren't, you'd be overconfident, and that's a surefire way to lose."

"Well, I have enough nerves right now, I must be on my way to win the gold," I joked, trying to make light of my current situation.

"You're going to be fine, Ibti," Candace said. "We both are. We're going to show these people what two beautiful brown girls from the USA can do with a saber on the strip." I laughed. I was so happy to be here with Candace. I tried to capture some of her enthusiasm, bottle it up, and carry it with me on the strip.

There are usually two days to a competition. The first day is used to whittle down two hundred fencers to forty-eight. The second day those forty-eight fencers from the first day join the top sixteen seeded fencers in the world to complete the elimination rounds of the tableau of sixty-four. I likened the top sixteen fencers in the world to superheroes, insanely fast, mesmerizing to watch, and lucky enough to not even have to fence the first day of World Cup competition. I clearly wasn't there yet, so I had to fence in the preliminary rounds and hope I made it to the second day of competition.

When I walked into the gymnasium on the first day, the talent I saw on the floor overwhelmed me. I watched women seemingly fill every available space, running, stretching, fencing, warming up for this, the first World Cup of the season. These were the world's best fencers, and I was about to join their ranks. After finding my pool number and strip assignment, I looked at which women from which country I was slated to fence and tried not to psych myself out. After warming up with Candace, we sat together as long as we could before wishing each other luck and heading over to our respective strips. Unfortunately, it didn't go well for me or Candace.

I had thought after all of those wins in the United States on the national circuit that I had proven that I could handle a major competition. And here I was, my first international competition, and I was out before the fun even started. Neither Candace nor I made it to the second day of competition.

Back at the hotel Candace tried to cheer me up, but nothing was more devastating to my pride than going out so early. I started down a steep slope of feeling bad for myself. Candace stopped me.

"Ibtihaj, you can't let every loss destroy you. There are going to be way more losses if you're trying to do this full-time, so you have to get used to this. Why don't we go to watch the competition tomorrow?"

"Why, so I can feel horrible all over again?" I said.

"No, so we can watch the fencers that we lost to. Let's take detailed notes, so we can work on those moves back in New York. We'll never get better if we don't learn from our mistakes."

I stopped packing and sat down on my narrow hotel bed.

"I guess you're right," I said, remembering Akhi's instructions to know my competition. I couldn't go back to him without some sort of feedback, so I agreed to go.

"Remember, our coaches always say that fencing requires smarts and strength. We know we have the strength, so we have to be smart, too."

I knew Candace was right. I knew that I had been outmaneuvered and that I needed to figure out why and how. Sulking on a transatlantic flight back home wasn't going to help me any.

So, the next day, Candace and I got up early and headed back to the Whitgift School. Because we weren't competing, we had to pay our own entrance fees to the competition. We came armed with notebooks and pens and were ready to spend the entire day transcribing every match and studying as many fencers as we could. For each athlete I watched, I made two columns, one for strengths and one for weaknesses. These were the same women I'd inevitably see at the next competition—women from Russia and China, Tunisia and Hungary—so I would be ready when I faced them on the strip. As I watched, it became clear to me that everyone had their own styles and techniques. I liked how all of the French fencers had strong parries and could easily score after successfully blocking their opponent. I admired the speed the entire Korean team seemed to have and how fearless the Russians were no matter who was on the other side of the strip. It was inspiring. As the day wore on and my notebook pages became filled with my frantic handwriting, I found myself eager and fired up to get on the strip again to apply what I was learning sitting in the stands. Candace was right: I knew I was fast and strong; now I had to learn how to fence a smarter match even under pressure.

CHAPTER 10

Just believe in yourself. Even if you don't, pretend that you do and at some point, you will.

—VENUS WILLIAMS

Ms. Muhammad, can I go to the bathroom?" I looked up from my desk where I was reviewing the lesson plan I knew I'd never actually get to teach, and considered my answer. Obviously, I should say no because class had only started five minutes ago, but if I denied her request, Tiffany was going to go to the bathroom anyway and probably curse me out in the process. It wasn't worth the fight.

"Yes, Tiffany, you can go." I sighed. I had less than a minute before the copycats began.

"Can I go, too, Ms. Muhammad?" two other girls called out, not even bothering to raise their hands. I tried not to let the frustration show as I excused them, too.

I told the students that as long as they were reading and/or sitting quietly at their desks, I wouldn't force them to actually do the work they had been assigned. It hurt my heart to see that for most of the kids in the classroom, reading meant playing with their cell phones or sleeping on their desks.

I would always bring in a couple of books by African and African-American authors that I hoped some of the students might

Training for my Olympics qualifier, wearing an ankle brace for support with an injury. *(Ezra Shaw—Getty)*

Eighteen months old. *(Courtesy of Ibtihaj Muhammad)*

Now all grown up. Wearing Louella by Ibtihaj Muhammad. *(Courtesy of Ibtihaj Muhammad)*

Qareeb's pre-K and my preschool moving-on celebration. *(Courtesy of Ibtihaj Muhammad)*

Abu, Qareeb, and me enjoying the warm weather while vacationing in Orlando, Florida (1993). *(Courtesy of Ibtihaj Muhammad)*

Semi-final match during the team event at the Olympics, fencing Yekaterina Dyachenko of Russia. *(Vaughn Ridley—Getty)*

With one of my best friends, Paola Pliego, waiting for the next round of matches to begin in Panama City, Panama. *(Courtesy of Ibtihaj Muhammad)*

My family taking in the sights during the Olympic Games in Rio de Janeiro. *(Courtesy of Ibtihaj Muhammad)*

A surprise party hosted by my family after my return from Rio. *(Courtesy of Ibtihaj Muhammad)*

Enjoying the sunset after a desert tour on the outskirts of Dubai, United Arab Emirates (December 2017). *(Courtesy of Ibtihaj Muhammad)*

Quick selfie with my sister, Faizah, at the Global Village in Dubai, United Arab Emirates. *(Courtesy of Ibtihaj Muhammad)*

Visiting Sheikh Zayed Mosque in Abu Dhabi, United Arab Emirates (December 2017). *(Courtesy of Ibtihaj Muhammad)*

On the podium at the Olympic Games, embracing one of the most surreal moments of my life. *(Tom Pennington—Getty)*

be interested in, or I would make photocopies from the art history textbook hoping to entice them with short, digestible pieces of information. There were maybe three students, out of thirty, who eagerly devoured the materials I brought in, and they were the reason I was able to come back every day. Those few kids and the fact that I wanted to fence kept me teaching.

Now that my fencing career was on an upward swing, I wanted to dedicate the majority of my time to training, but *aspiring world-class athlete* doesn't come with a paycheck, so I had to keep my teaching job. The fact was, now that I was training and competing internationally full-time, I needed even more money than before. Between tournament fees, airplane tickets, hotel costs, and food, the average cost to compete in one World Cup competition was around $2,000, and there were eight World Cups a season. What a disaster it would have been not to be able to compete because I couldn't afford the fees. That would have killed me, so I continued to hustle, working at the school and I also picked up a second job coaching the fencing team at Columbia High School. Sometimes I wanted to tell Tiffany and her classmates about my fencing aspirations, but I held back. The one time I'd started to talk about fencing, one of the boys interrupted me and said, "Wait, you build fences?" Everyone thought that was funny and laughed, and I didn't bother to correct him. Since most of my students seemed profoundly uninterested anyway, I felt guilty sharing my good news because I knew my main motivation for working at their school was to feed my own passions, not because I had aspirations to be a teacher.

It was hard not to compare what I was witnessing every day in Newark with what I observed back at Maplewood's Columbia High School where I was coaching. Granted, coaching suburban kids in a sport that they enjoyed was a completely different animal than teaching art history in a struggling inner city high school, but the difference between the students was glaring. And this wasn't just a case of Black and white. Most of the kids at Columbia were white, but they were still rambunctious and silly, and I had to repeat myself over and over and over again to get them to do what I asked on the strip, but they were eager to learn. They wanted my advice and directions. They didn't roll their eyes at me when I demanded more from them. I wished I knew how to inspire the students in Newark, to get that kind of hunger from them, but I didn't know where to begin. So I did my best and hoped that by showing up, at minimum they knew I cared.

As a coach, I could give my fencers all of my knowledge, energy, and enthusiasm. I knew what tools to equip them with because I'd been exactly where they were. I could use my personal experiences as an athlete to train and inspire this younger generation, truly making a difference in their lives, including in the life of my sister Faizah.

Even though she was six years younger than me, Faizah had closely followed in my fencing footsteps. She admitted she had initially resisted fencing because she really didn't want to fight in my shadow, but Coach Mustilli helped develop her talents and made her a fierce saber fencer. Before I left for college, Faizah had been a little girl of twelve. I loved her and I just thought of her as my baby sister. Now, she was seventeen and dominating on the high school fencing circuit. As a high school fencer, my little sister was already better than I had ever been. She had an almost undefeated record and frequently found herself in the folds of the New Jersey *Star-Ledger*, identified as the best female saber fencer in the state. Of course, I didn't play favorites while I was coaching, but she really made me proud, and it was through fencing that Faizah and I morphed from sisters to best friends. Now I had someone to talk to who could understand my world. And she had someone to talk to who could guide her in the sport.

Even though I felt like I had broken through so many color barriers while I was in high school, seven years later my little sister was still facing pushback and discrimination as a successful Black female fencer. Whether it was comments from other fencers or their parents or being given a hard time by coaches or referees, Faizah had to deal with it all.

———————

"Ibtihaj, they say I can't fence because of my hijab?" Faizah came up to me breathless, her large brown eyes wide with emotion. She was supposed to fence in ten minutes, but a referee was questioning her paperwork. I had been in the middle of a pep talk with the foil fencers, but I turned my back on them to deal with my sister. We were at the Santelli Tournament, the largest high school fencing completion in the nation, where all of the state's teams competed for a chance at the coveted championship title.

"What's going on?" I asked. "I already filed the paperwork for your hijab." Every time Faizah fenced, we had to have official paperwork from the New Jersey Board of Education with us, which stated her hijab was for religious reasons·and she was eligible to compete. Knowing this from my own days of being a hijabi high school athlete, I always made sure to submit Faizah's paperwork early, at the start of the season. There must have been some mistake.

Sadly, this wasn't the first time something like this had happened to her. This was her senior year, and she was legendary in New Jersey fencing circles. Most people applauded her wins, but there was always someone lurking in the wings who didn't want to see her succeed. "They said they don't have my paperwork, and if they don't have it, I can't fence," she said again, panic creeping into her voice.

"Don't worry, Faizah," I said. "Go over to your strip and just get ready to fence. I'll take care of it," I said, and I meant it. After witnessing this type of behavior before, I always came prepared to our competitions. I had an extra copy of Faizah's paperwork in my bag, so I grabbed it and tracked down the referee in question. Sometimes the refs gave me a hard time as well, for reasons I can only assume had to do with me being only one of two non-white female fencing coaches in the state.

I approached the bout committee with the warmest smile I could manage. "My athlete says you don't have her paperwork," I said, with my hand outstretched with Faizah's documents.

The man, who looked to be in his early fifties, took the paper and put on his glasses before studying the paper carefully. Even though it was a standard letter of only about ten lines, it took him an extraordinary amount of time going over it. Finally, fearing he was going to make Faizah miss her bout, I interjected, "Is everything okay? It's the same letter we've been using for the last three and half years without any problems."

Finally the referee looked up at me. He didn't smile. "Okay, she's good. But make sure you get this stuff in before we start next time. We need to have it in early."

I wanted to argue but I held my tongue. I didn't want any confrontation to affect Faizah's outcome on the strip. Since saber fencing is so subjective—the referee ultimately decides every contested point—I didn't want to give him any added reason not to award points to my sister during her bouts. So I just smiled, said thank you, and ran over to tell Faizah that everything was okay and she could fence. My sister thanked me profusely.

"Don't thank me," I told her. "Just win."

And of course, she did.

When I look back at the hectic schedule I was leading—teaching, coaching, and training—it is a wonder I didn't burn out from exhaustion. But I was on a winning streak, and the better my results, the more I wanted to try for even better results. I looked at every competition as an opportunity for the unmatched feeling of exhilaration when I scored the perfect touch. Akhi was right there with me, continuing to meet me at the foundation every day, working with me, fine-tuning my technique, and pushing me to work even harder than I already was. I felt like I had finally found the missing piece of the puzzle to help me chase my dreams.

Because all of my wins thus far had been at domestic competitions, Akhi now wanted to see how competitive I could be on the world stage under his tutelage. We both had our sights on the upcoming World Cup event, a Grand Prix in Tunisia. My London showing earlier in the season had been disappointing, but the last six months of training had made a difference. I was getting stronger, and I had stepped into my confidence and belief in my own abilities. Akhi and I were working hard to bring his goal of turning me into one of the best fencers in the world to fruition. A solid performance in Tunisia was the next part of our strategy.

Besides the World Championships, a Grand Prix was worth double the points of a World Cup, and therefore a valuable opportunity to improve one's world ranking. It's basic math: the better a competitor's result, the more points she's awarded, and the higher her ranking becomes. The national points standing list included points accumulated at both domestic and international competitions. My national ranking was steadily climbing, but I had yet to really break through on the international World Cup circuit. I'd become more consistent in winning my pool matches and a few direct elimination bouts, but nothing to brag about. The Tunisia Grand Prix felt like an unofficial debut for me. If I could remain consistent and advance to the second day of competition and win my first few direct elimination bouts, I'd have my first major international result.

Unlike my trip to London with Candace, this time I traveled

with Akhi, and I wasn't nervous. I was excited. I felt confident in my abilities. Akhi kept reminding me that believing in myself and being in the right head space when stepping on that strip was just as important as being in prime physical shape. "You can do this" looped through my mind repeatedly, serving as a mantra for any challenge during competition. It helped we were competing in a Muslim country surrounded by people who looked like me, so I didn't have to worry about how I would be received.

After a fifteen-hour journey, which included a three-hour layover in Istanbul, we landed in Tunis. Despite the long travel time, Akhi insisted that I stay awake when we arrived. "You have to try to acclimate as soon as possible to the time difference so you can be at your best when you compete," he said.

While stifling a yawn I said, "Okay."

Akhi didn't look convinced. "Look, put your stuff in your room and meet me in the hotel lobby in twenty minutes," he said when the taxi dropped us off at the hotel. I promised I would, and after getting my key to my room, I headed to the elevators. Twenty minutes later, showered, clothes changed, I was back in the lobby. I quickly spotted Akhi in his navy-blue Team USA sweatsuit standing near the water fountain. I walked over to him.

He looked at me and smiled. "Well, you look much more awake. Are you ready?"

"Ready for what?" I said. "Where are we going?"

"We're going to go check out our surroundings," Akhi said. "This is going to be your home for the next four days, and you need to know how to get around, where to go for food and water, and how to get to the venue. We don't wait to do those things on the day of the competition."

"Makes sense," I said.

"Of course it does, that's why I'm the coach," Akhi said with a knowing grin. "Let's go."

And with that, I followed my coach out of the hotel into the dry heat of Tunis, an ancient city with remnants of its colonial French past evident in the language, Roman rule in its architecture, and distinctive Middle Eastern flavors in its food. We spent the day wandering around the neighborhood, finding restaurants and cafés where we could eat for an affordable price. We caught a cab to the fencing venue, so on game day I would be familiar with the layout. The last stop on our tour was at a small market where Akhi had me buy a package of plain crackers, bottled water, almonds, and two bananas. I showed off a little and used my basic Arabic to thank the storekeeper when we were done. Akhi raised one of his thick, bushy eyebrows in my direction.

"Impressive. I know who to call if I'm in a pinch here," he said.

"I won't be that helpful, because I have the vocabulary of a second-grader in Arabic," I admitted.

Akhi laughed as we headed back to the hotel. He pointed to my bag of provisions. "This will keep you hydrated tomorrow during practice. The last thing I want is for you to collapse because you're malnourished," Akhi said.

I paid close attention to his words of advice.

"You'd be surprised how much traveling takes out of you," Akhi continued. "When you're competing in different time zones and you're asking your body to work harder than it normally does while fending off jet lag, you have to be extra mindful with your nutrition and hydration, and you can't take anything for granted."

I promised I would watch what I ate and drank. As we walked back into the hotel, I thanked Akhi for hanging out with me.

"Hey, I may be new at this as a coach, but after traveling so much as an athlete, I have learned what to do when I land someplace new for a competition," Akhi said. "This is my routine wherever I go. And it should be yours, too."

I nodded. "Okay. Got it."

Even though it was only seven p.m., we both said good night. I had now officially been awake for twenty-seven hours, and I was dying to go to sleep. As I rode up the elevator I realized how nice it had been to stroll around a Muslim country in my hijab and receive nothing more than warm smiles of recognition from the people on the street. Tunisia reminded me so much of Morocco, such that walking around all day with Akhi, I never once felt like I was different. There were no stares or questions. I was just another familiar face blending into the crowd. With a clear mind and a happy heart, now I could fall asleep thinking about one thing—winning.

Like the majority of the other fencers registered in the competition, I began the first day of the Grand Prix warming up for pools. Before I went off for my first bout, Akhi reminded me to be confident and remember the game plan, and that's exactly what I did. Three hours later, Akhi and I were exchanging high fives because I had gone undefeated in the pool round, winning all six bouts, directly advancing on to the second day of competition. I was so pleased with my performance, I already felt like a winner at that point. But now came the tough part—advancing through the bracket of sixty-four. But I decided that whatever happened on day two of the Grand Prix I would simply remember my mantra, "You can do this!"

The following morning, I rose early, even before the sun, to perform my morning prayers in my hotel room. I took an extra moment to thank Allah for allowing me to reach this moment, but also to help me find the strength and courage to win the matches still ahead of me. As I sat on the floor near the hotel window, I thought about my mother, who had agreed to pay for half of my plane ticket and hotel fees. Even though I continued working my two jobs, I still didn't have enough money to fully support my quest for glory. Fencing ate up everything I earned. Having the financial and emotional support of both of my parents made me so thankful because their support allowed me to keep my focus on fencing. I knew it took courage for them to invest money in my pursuits, considering there wasn't an immediate, tangible return on their investment. Plus, Faizah had recently confided in me that some people back home were giving my parents a hard time because of my traveling schedule, so they had to deal with that nonsense as well.

"Mommy said some of the sisters at the masjid were asking about you," Faizah had told me. She whispered even though we were up in my attic bedroom.

"What did they want to know?" I asked, trying to keep my voice neutral, careful not to show my little sister that I actually cared what other people said about me behind my back.

"They told Mommy that they were surprised she let you travel all over the world by yourself. And they said you should be traveling with your father or brother at least. They made it sound like Mommy and Abu were doing something wrong by letting you go to your competitions instead of focusing on a career and marriage prospects." Faizah's face registered her annoyance.

I shook my head. "I don't expect people to understand my journey, and I'm not going to let their opinions cloud my vision."

I didn't want Faizah to think that being a Muslim meant living a restricted life. I was thankful for the peace Islam brought to my life when things proved too painful or chaotic. It was frustrating that I didn't always have the support of the people around me, but I really felt guilty that my mother had to deal with that nonsense, especially at the masjid where she liked to spend much of her free time. My whole family made sacrifices to help me on my fencing journey, and the last thing I wanted to do was cause anyone pain or embarrassment.

"Did Mom say anything back to those women?" I asked my

sister, scrolling through my mental files trying to guess who had been talking about me. It was probably the same women who gave my parents grief for sending us to public school instead of a private Islamic school. It was like they couldn't wrap their heads around the fact that my parents didn't raise their children in the exact same way as other Muslim parents. For some people, seeing my sisters and me actively engaged in sport was a challenge to their beliefs.

Faizah smirked. "You know Mom just did her usual and ignored their questions and changed the subject."

We both laughed. Our mother was our greatest role model and fiercest protector, and I was going to take a lesson from her; ignore the haters and the naysayers and just focus on being my best self.

———

My mother and younger sisters met me at the airport with a bouquet of flowers and a single balloon that read "Sweet 16." I was coming home from Tunis in triumph. For the first time ever, I cracked the top sixteen and came home with a twelfth place finish. Just seeing my name nearing the top of the list at the end of the competition, with Akhi by my side, I'd felt so proud. We'd done this together. And here was my family sharing in my joy.

Now that Faizah was fencing, she could help my parents understand the intricacies of competitions and explain that making the round of sixteen at an international competition was a huge achievement. Initially my father didn't see what everyone was so excited about when I'd made the call from Tunisia to tell them the good news. I'd heard Abu in the background when I called.

"Twelfth place?" he asked, sounding perplexed. I knew my dad didn't intend to be mean, but to him, with very little knowledge about the sport, he understood fencing from the perspective of winning and losing. His reference points for sports were the more common football, basketball, and baseball; fencing was still new for him. But I knew he was proud that I was working hard for something I believed in. And truth be told, I appreciated my father's high expectations that I should shoot for being number one. It motivated me. According to Abu, I could do anything I put my mind and energy to, and I was only too willing to prove him right.

More success was just around the corner for me. Because of my twelfth place win in Tunisia and my earlier gold medal finishes in the domestic tournaments, my national ranking had improved significantly. Some fencers keep close tabs on their rankings; they calculate their standing themselves even before the official rankings are announced. Sometimes they're a little off, but for the most part they know exactly where they rank at all times. I'm a naturally competitive person, but I wasn't so obsessive that I had to know what my ranking was going to be every single second of every single day. That would be an added layer of pressure and stress I didn't need. When the final standings went up, I'd find out with everyone else where I ranked. And that's why, when the news broke that I had qualified for my first United States National Team, I was shocked. I knew I was getting close, but wasn't expecting to make the team so soon. But the numbers don't lie. It was now official; I was one of the top four women's saber fencers in the entire United States, earning me a spot on my first national team. At age twenty-four, after working with Akhi for only a year, I had done what most people would assume was impossible. The seed Coach Mustilli had planted in my mind was sprouting into reality. I was on my way to going all the way.

CHAPTER 11

We are the ones we've been waiting for. We are the change that we seek.

—PRESIDENT BARACK OBAMA

The whispers preceded me into the room. People stopped what they were doing when I walked into the foundation on a Saturday morning after the announcement had been made. Suddenly the space erupted in applause, and people started shouting their congratulations. I laughed and let the tears slide down my cheeks without even bothering to wipe them away. I had made my first national team and would be representing the United States of America at the World Fencing Championships. As an official member of the team, the majority of my competition expenses like airfare, food, and hotel would now be covered. This meant that some of the financial burden of fencing would finally be off my plate, and I could quit teaching and focus the majority of my time on training. As far as I was concerned, I could now say that I had a "career" in fencing.

Technically I wouldn't be earning a salary—instead I received a training stipend from USA Fencing, the official organizing body of fencing in the United States. My stipend was a predetermined amount of money—based on world ranking—to defray the cost of training expenses. Since I lived with my parents, my training stipend—which turned out to be almost the same amount as my teaching salary—would be just enough to subsidize the costs of my personal trainer, gym membership, massage therapist, fencing equipment, and countless other expenses associated with staying in peak physical condition. I decided to keep coaching at Columbia High School because I had developed a close bond with the students there and really grew to love them. And the extra money would also come in handy for unexpected expenses.

Standing there in the doorway of the foundation with my real fencing family surrounding me in applause only made the moment more real. After all my hard work trying to make it, this was the first time since graduating from college that I felt like I had finally achieved something meaningful. I was no longer chasing rainbows; I was looking at my pot of gold and everyone at the foundation had witnessed my fight. They knew how significant it was that another one of us had made it; it was like one more step toward diversifying fencing. Our unwritten foundation motto was, "When one wins, we all win." Peter started the process and opened doors and we, his students, proudly kept marching through. Peter came over and gave me a big hug. He then asked for everyone's attention. There were more than 150 kids on the floor for their Saturday morning lessons and dozens of other adult students and coaches, so it took a moment for the noise level to die down. When it did, Peter started to talk.

"I want everyone here to take a look here at Ibtihaj Muhammad. She has just qualified for the United States women's saber team and will represent our country at the World Championships. She got there with hard work and because she never gave up." Peter paused and looked at me. "Did you ever give up, Ibtihaj?"

I felt awkward with all eyes on me but managed to squeak out, "No."

"That's right," Peter said. "She never gave up, and neither can you if you want to be successful. In fencing and in life. If your coach is telling you that your parry isn't right, don't give up, fix it. If you keep falling short in your attack, don't give up, keep trying until you land that attack with your eyes closed and one hand tied behind your back. And most of all, don't ever give up because someone tries to tell you that you don't belong because you don't look the part. Ibtihaj didn't listen to any of that nonsense, and she stands here in front of you triumphant."

The whole room erupted in applause, and a small group turned to congratulate Akhi, too. I was still in awe of all that he and I had accomplished working together for only one year. My friend Candace still hadn't qualified for a national team, so I truly recognized what an accomplishment I had achieved. I owed much of my newfound self-confidence and knowledge, both on and off the fencing strip, to Akhi. So many people, like Sam, didn't believe in me and doubted my potential. Had I listened to the chorus of male voices at the foundation, I might have given up. I might have bought into their belief that I was too old, not strong enough, or lacked the requisite talent. There were a lot of young women who, over the years, left the foundation because they hadn't felt supported or encouraged to keep going. One of my biggest challenges has always been to see past other people's doubt and negativity so I could define my own path. In the meantime, it didn't make sense to me to hold on to any grudges or focus my energy on the people who hadn't believed in me. I was standing in gratitude, thankful for the ability to see past other people's low expectations for me and fully embrace the future. I smiled at everyone in the room and blushed from all the applause and cheers.

Then everyone started chanting Akhi's name. "Akhi! Akhi" They wanted him to make a small speech. We locked eyes across the room, and he smiled. "I don't have time for speeches," he said with a grin. "Just because I helped Ibtihaj get onto the national team doesn't mean I'm done. Our work has just begun."

And with that pronouncement, Peter sent everyone back to training. I went to the locker room to get changed, and Akhi told me to meet him on the strip.

My spot on Team USA definitely carried with it a new level of respect at the foundation. I was no longer walking around with a giant question mark over my head. Since coming back from Duke, I'd been treated like an afterthought; now all of the coaches saw real potential in me. The upcoming 2012 Olympics were even being mentioned in my presence. But I couldn't let it get to my head. Like Akhi said, making the team was hardly the moment to slack off. Now that I was going to wear red, white, and blue in competitions, I felt even more pressure to elevate my skills and become the best fencer I could.

Like gymnastics, or track and field, fencing is still an individual sport, so even though I had qualified for the United States National Team, I would fence both the individual and team events during competitions. When it was all said and done, I was out on the fencing strip alone, with nothing but my name and country on my uniform. Most international competitions had two distinct parts, the individual event and the team event. So, during the first two days of a competition, it was every woman for herself, and depending on how the bracket was configured, two people from the same team could wind up fencing against each other in the direct elimination rounds. But then on the day of the team event, we competed as a unit—all for one and one for all. That kind of setup made for an interesting team dynamic, because it meant I had to look at my teammates as both my opponents and my lifelines. Luckily, I didn't have to deal with that dynamic on a daily basis.

Qualifying for Team USA didn't mean I stopped training with Akhi. I continued to train at the foundation in Manhattan and lived at home with my parents in New Jersey, but I would compete representing the United States as a member of the national team. There was a national coach for the team, but most team members traveled to competitions with their personal coaches as well. The competition season ran from January through October, with about ten international competitions per season. Theoretically we were supposed to have at least one World Cup in each zone of the world—the Americas, Africa, Europe, and Asia—but due to a lack of resources or sometimes political instability, the competitions were predominantly held in Europe, with a few held in Asia. In between the World Cups, we also had four domestic competitions (NACs) held in different cities around the United States. Those competitions would occur in January, April, October, and December. Every season culminated with World Championships, unless it was an Olympic year. The points accumulated from all of these competitions would make up the US national rankings, and the top four finishers qualified for the national team for the following season.

Since fencing legends Becca Ward and Sada Jacobson retired from the sport in 2008, two women had become staples on the national saber team, and I'd been following their careers since graduating from college. They had consistently been ranked in the top four for years and formed the nexus of the team, leaving the other two spots open for wildcards like me. The anchor of the team was a woman named Mariel Zagunis. Tall, blonde, and the child of Olympic rowers, Mariel was the most decorated American fencer, male or female, and had been fencing since she was ten. She'd won individual gold medals at the 2004 and 2008 Olympics and had been on the national team since 2000. Dagmara Wozniak, a Polish immigrant to the United States, with mousy brown hair and a

sturdy frame, had been fencing since she was nine years old and had
been the alternate on the women's saber team at the 2008 Olympics
and been on Team USA since then. Even though Mariel and Dagmara had been fencing for far longer than I had, we were all around
the same age: Mariel was twenty-four like me and Dagmara was
twenty-one. The third member of the team in 2010 when I joined
was named Daria Schneider. Daria was a strong fencer who had
just missed a chance to compete in the 2008 Olympics but who had
done really well on the college circuit, competing for Columbia University. All told, my new teammates were part of an elite group of
athletes who had been raised to become fencing champions. It was
awe-inspiring to join such a talented team of women. I promised
myself I'd prove myself worthy of my spot on the squad.

Our first competition as a team was World Championships
in October. Akhi and I had been training overtime, and I felt as
ready as I ever had to get on the strip. Because all four team members lived and trained in different parts of the country, we arrived
to the World Championships, held in Paris, France, separately. I
was so excited to be at my first World Championships and representing the United States that I must have seemed like a puppy on
Red Bull; my eagerness showed all over my face. I was so looking forward to bonding with Mariel and Dagmara. Two athletes
I had admired from afar were now my teammates. These were
women who, like me, understood the level of intensity and sacrifice required to reach athletic excellence. Though we lived separate
lives, training in different clubs and in different parts of the country, we were all on the same page trying to find enough time in
the day to eat, sleep, and drink fencing. It was understood that we
were on the same mission.

The national coach for the women's saber team was the highly
respected Polish saber fencer Ed Korfanty. Coach Korfanty had
had an illustrious fencing career in his native Poland before

immigrating to the United States and starting a career in coaching in Portland, Oregon. Not only had he coached Coach Mustilli's elder daughter when she was on the US women's saber team back in 2000, he was also Mariel's personal coach. Ed didn't show much emotion upon my arrival in Paris. He didn't act like he cared very much that I was the newest member of the team. For that matter, none of the other team members greeted me with high levels of enthusiasm, either. It certainly wasn't the welcome I'd been hoping for or expecting, but I tried not to let the lack of warm smiles and encouraging words from my teammates deter me from my mission. Besides, I had brought my own cheering squad with me.

My sister Brandilyn and my mom came with me to Paris because this was my first time competing for Team USA, plus it was Paris! The excitement of being in Paris and competing at this high level was intoxicating. They say everything is better in Paris, the food, the architecture, the romance; I found even fencing belonged on that list. I had traveled to a handful of other countries to fence, but this World Championship felt magical. The entire experience felt like something out of a Disney movie.

The competition took place at the historic Grand Palais, an exhibition hall normally reserved for art and cultural exhibits. The grandeur of the ornate glass structure, built in the Beaux Arts style in the early twentieth century, makes one think it must have at one point been a playground for royalty. I was used to fencing in convention centers or sports arenas, so this was on a whole different level of spectacular.

Mom, Brandilyn, and I toured the Palais the night before the competition. If Akhi had been with us, he would have been leading this mission, but he hadn't been able to make it to Paris.

Stepping foot in the historic glass palace with vaulted ceilings that offered unobstructed views of the dark night sky was a sight to behold. It was so gorgeous, we stood in awe, drinking it all in. Not a single word passed between us. And then I broke the silence.

"I am going to love fencing in here. It will truly feel like a fairy tale."

"You are so corny," Brandilyn joked. "But this place *is* gorgeous."

Mom just shook her head, too overwhelmed to put into words what she was feeling. Finally, she just smiled and said, "This is truly a blessing to be here."

———————

The next morning, I headed over to the venue early while my mom and Brandilyn went off to sightsee. I wore my national team warm-up and headed out the door of our hotel. Right before I reached the Grand Palais, a young Muslim girl in hijab stopped me.

"Excuse me," she said with a thick French accent. "Can I have your autograph?"

I gave her a funny look. "You want my autograph?"

"Because you are the famous American fencer wearing a hijab. We have read about you in the newspaper. I want your autograph because I look up to you. I want to be an athlete like you."

I had no idea that the few small articles that had been written about me back home had made it all the way to France.

I didn't want to tell the girl that I wasn't actually a celebrity, but I signed her paper and wished her good luck. She thanked me profusely and ran off. Before I could process the interaction, another hijabi girl and her mother approached me, and before I could even get to the doors of the Grand Palais, I'd signed three more autographs.

This was a totally new experience for me; I felt kind of weird getting extra attention because people hadn't seen a Muslim woman fence before. After getting over the initial shock of being considered "special" for wearing hijab, I thought it was kind of cool. I'd never thought of wearing hijab as anything extraordinary—it was just something I did. It was other people who defined it as exotic or dangerous. I was happy to be a source of inspiration to young Muslim girls in France, or anywhere else, but I hadn't really thought of myself as a role model for kids except as a fencer. But that day was the first day I saw myself in a new light, with a new mission. If I could provide a vision of hope for these girls, hope that would help them craft their aspirations, manifest their dreams, and demonstrate that wearing hijab didn't mean limited opportunities, then I was fully on board.

When it came time to fence my first bout in the Palais, the faces of all of the young women who had asked for my autograph that morning flashed before me. As I placed my mask over my head, and forced myself to block out the noise of the audience on all four sides of the strip, I decided to fence for young Ibtihaj, and I fenced for the young Muslim girls I'd met that morning. I told myself that I would win for all of us. As I wielded my saber against one opponent after another, I felt the strength in my whole body respond to my demands. I smiled behind my mask as I locked out opponent after opponent. I felt invincible on the strip, and for a long time I was. I kept winning, fighting my way to chance at the final, before losing a close match to 2008 Olympian champion Olena Khomrova by a score of 14–5, and eventually finishing with a fourteenth place finish. I was ecstatic. It was my highest finish ever in a competition of that high quality. And my career was just getting started.

During my first year on the national team, I was a workhorse who showed no mercy on the strip, but I was a lamb among my teammates, with the goal of forging friendships with them. I tried my best to fit in. Even though we all maintained our own individual training schedules, we would often be required to attend training camps together both in Oregon at Ed's club and overseas, so I figured I'd have plenty of opportunities to bond with my new teammates.

One time, at a training camp during the beginning of the season, Ed instructed us to free fence, and I was paired with an up-and-coming fencer named Melanie. She had hopes of making the team the following year.

"Can we stop for a minute?" Melanie huffed, taking her mask off.

I glanced at the clock on the wall and realized we'd been fencing for a while without any specific direction from our coach, and I noticed him in a huddle with Dagmara on the other side of the room. From where I stood, it looked like they were talking tactics.

"Hold on, Melanie," I said. "Let me go see what Ed wants us to do."

I jogged across the gymnasium, and as I got closer to the two of them, I stopped running and hovered at a respectable distance. I didn't want to barge in on their conversation. I stood there for a minute waiting to be acknowledged and realized that Ed wasn't speaking to Dagmara in English. I strained my ears and listened for any familiar-sounding words and when I could hear none, I assumed it was his native Polish. I stood there for a minute longer and finally cleared my throat, even though I figured he must have noticed me by then.

"Excuse me," I said. "Melanie and I were wondering if you wanted us to rotate partners?"

"Ibti," the coach said, struggling to pronounce even my shortened nickname correctly, "please keep working on what I told you. I'll let you know when it's time to stop. You must keep working and not be so quick to give up. Don't be lazy."

I pressed down on my lips, sealing my mouth shut. I didn't want to say something I might regret. But me, lazy? Did this man not understand that all I knew was hard work? That in the dictionary under work ethic there is a picture of me? The insult—especially in front of my teammates—burned inside me. I clenched my teeth and turned to head back over to Melanie. As I walked away the coach said something in Polish, and he and Dagmara shared a laugh.

Getting off to a rocky start with the team didn't sit well with me, but I didn't let it distract me from my purpose of becoming one of the world's best fencers. And I didn't let it deter me from continually trying to break the ice between my teammates and myself. It wasn't easy to always be the one making the overtures of friendship, since I was, after all, the new member on the team. I felt a sense of "othering" was happening—because I was Black and a Muslim—but I wholly rejected the idea that it was my responsibility to make everyone else feel comfortable with me being different. I didn't believe that was my burden to take on, yet at the same time I wanted to show them that if they gave me a chance they'd see we were more alike than different. I'd been in this position so many times before. I knew what I had to do.

I put a lot of effort into being a great teammate. I tried to keep a smile on my face all the time. When we were on the road, I tried to initiate team dinners and arrange group outings when we landed in a new country or city for a competition. I held my tongue in times of dispute. I would compliment my teammates to show them I appreciated their skill and expertise on the strip. I barely recognized myself, as I tried to assimilate into the team. I went above and beyond to show them my best self. But my efforts to extend the olive branch of friendship were rarely if ever reciprocated. My dinner invitations were often turned down, as were my invitations for movie nights in our hotel rooms or sightseeing when we arrived in a new city.

"Is there any plan to go out for a team dinner?" I asked the team manager once after practice. We were at a World Cup competition, and I had heard some talk of going out to a restaurant instead of eating at the hotel.

"No, not this time, Ibtihaj," the manager told me. "You should probably just order in and be ready for the competition tomorrow," she said.

I went back to my room. All of the travel for competitions was beginning to weigh on me. I was lonely and homesick. Akhi hadn't been able to make it to this tournament, so I had no one to talk to and no one cheering in my corner. I consoled myself with the knowledge that with no dinner plans, I'd have more time to sleep and prepare for tomorrow's competition

The next morning when I boarded the bus to the venue, I sat next to Daria. I tried to make small talk as I knew we had a thirty-minute ride ahead of us.

"What did you do for dinner last night?" I asked. "I ordered from the restaurant in the hotel and it was really good."

Daria turned to Mariel before answering. "Oh, we all went to this restaurant near the hotel."

"We tried to call your room but got no answer," Dagmara jumped in.

"That's strange," I said. "My phone never rang, and I don't show any missed calls."

Dagmara shrugged. "I don't know who made the call, but I know someone did. But anyway, you didn't really miss anything. The food wasn't that good."

I turned to our team manager, Cathy, who happened to also be

Mariel's mother. (Yes, our team manager was the parent of our star team member.) "You told me there was no team dinner," I said.

Never taking her eyes from the pages of her magazine, Cathy said with an annoyingly false note of concern, "Ibtihaj, it was nothing official. If it had been, I would have told you."

"Right," I said doubtfully. Inside I was hurt. They clearly hadn't invited me on purpose. I leaned my head against the window and closed my eyes. I tried to sleep, willing the ride to be over as soon as possible.

I spent the rest of my first year on the national team progressing as an athlete as I worked to climb the rankings, but socially, despite my best efforts, my attempts to bond with my teammates were consistently met with resistance deserving only of a pariah. I realized these women had known each other longer, but I couldn't help but wonder if their behavior was intentional. They would routinely watch movies together in one of their hotel rooms but never invite me. When they made plans for dinner, I never got a call to tag along. And because we were only a team of four, being the one person left out when the other three gathered was all the more hurtful. Sometimes I would go to my room and call my mother and just cry from sheer frustration. I felt so foolish crying over the fact that my teammates were being mean to me, but it was just such a letdown to have finally "made it" and yet feel so alone at the top.

My mother would try to console me, telling me, "Ibtihaj, when you have three sisters, you have all of the girlfriends you need. You don't need your teammates to be your friends."

I knew my mom was right. I didn't *need* them to be my friends, but spending so much time on the road, away from my family and friends, was hard enough without the pain of feeling like "the other" all the time. The feelings of dismissal and exclusion were overwhelming and suffocating for me.

In general, it seemed my teammates and the coaching staff had a very superficial idea of who I was as a fencer and a person. They attributed my qualifying for the national team as a stroke of luck instead of the result of hard work and talent, and they attributed my wins on the team to brute strength and blind speed instead of intelligence and planning. Like so many other Black athletes, I was being pigeonholed as strong but not smart. The stereotyping and bias was incredibly exasperating, not to mention disheartening. The seemingly small events like leaving me off a team email chain or forgetting to include my name on the team list while on the road added up to a bigger problem. Despite my success on the strip, I was feeling increasingly unhappy. I wanted so badly to understand what I had done to make my teammates and the coaching staff treat me so coldly. I had never felt more lonely or disconnected in my life.

Because I spent so much time alone during our competitions, I dedicated far too many hours to trying to dissect what was happening with my team. It was too easy to assume that their behavior toward me was based on some sort of racial or religious prejudice. But I wasn't convinced that was it. I would lie in bed and wonder if it was because I was unapologetically competitive on the strip. Even if I had to fence against one of them in competition, I didn't suspend my desire to win. Maybe they saw me as some sort of threat. Maybe I was breaking some sort of long-standing code that the newest member on the team wasn't supposed to win and make her teammates look bad. But Mariel and Dagmara were seasoned competitors and had been on Team USA consistently. They didn't need to fear me. Yet the more success that came my way, the harsher the treatment from my teammates and coaches became. After combing through all of the possibilities, my head would ache and I was back to where I started. In the end I decided that the women's saber team simply wasn't ready for change—an African-American Muslim was too much difference all at once. I think my team viewed me as so different from themselves they didn't know how to relate, and they weren't willing to put in the effort to figure it out. It was a sobering thought, but it was what I'd been given. And I recognized that I couldn't force my teammates and coaches to push past their own limited thinking. That was something they would have to do on their own. I had to focus on fencing. Nothing else.

CHAPTER 12

We realize the importance of our voices only when we are silenced.

—MALALA YOUSAFZAI

Once I realized that the women on my own team were not going to be my friends, I sought companionship elsewhere when I was on the road. Rather than hanging out in my hotel room waiting for an invitation that was never going to arrive, I started to spend time with fencers from other nations and would end up finding any number of people willing and eager to share a meal or go sightseeing. It was often a struggle, still feeling like an outsider on my own team, but I made up my mind that I wasn't going to let my teammates' behavior affect my goals. And my new goal was to make it to the 2012 Olympics in London.

Because I was the newest member of the national team and because no one had ever even mentioned my name in the same breath as the Olympics, I didn't talk about my Olympic dreams. I didn't know the exact qualification path to make an Olympic team, but my plan was simple: work as hard as possible, maintain focus, and the success would come. I knew Mariel and Dagmara were favored to qualify, but I just kept telling myself, why not me too? When I fenced with Mariel and Dagmara they were formidable opponents, but they didn't have anything I didn't have. What I lacked in experience, I made up for with heart and determination. I told myself that the Olympics were a real possibility.

But I had to fail first. And fail I did. It wasn't a spectacular fail. To some it might have just seemed like an off day, but after a season of only podium finishes on the domestic circuit, a tournament where I failed to make it to the top sixteen crushed my spirit. The mental game plays such a pivotal role in fencing, and on that day, my mental game had been off. I had a hard time finding my way on the strip. For some reason my feet wouldn't move fast enough, my arm felt heavy, and I was always one step behind where I wanted to be. For the first time in a long time, when my match was over, I cried. I cried not because I lost, but because my mind felt separate from my body, and I wasn't able to get my head in the game.

Back in my hotel room, I called my sister Faizah. She had graduated from high school and was now attending Rutgers University along with my other sister, Asiya. Faizah had now started competing on the national and international circuits as well and understood how devastating a loss could feel. She also understood the devastation of such a spectacular loss.

"It was awful, Faizah," I said, as I felt the tears forming again. "I haven't lost like that in a long time," I said.

"What was the score?" Faizah asked.

"Fifteen to seven," I murmured.

"That's not so bad," Faizah cooed into the phone. "And this was just one tournament. You've won so many more than you've lost."

"But this whole tournament I felt off, and it didn't help that Ed yelled at me afterwards."

Faizah sighed. "Ignore him. He doesn't care about you or how you do. If he doesn't say anything positive to you when you win, then he doesn't get to say anything to you when you have a bad day. Period."

My little sister was so wise. Not only did she know the

intricacies of the sport and all of its rules, but she knew me and all of my idiosyncrasies as well. She knew I put on a fierce face during competition, but that my inner core was soft. My sister knew me better than anyone else. She was becoming my closest confidante and I depended on her more and more to help me ride through the ups and down of being a member of Team USA. She was the newbie on the circuit, but she was my ride-or-die all the way.

————————

The tournament was going to officially start in one hour. I was going through the motions of my warm-up, but all I was really doing was fighting the urge to go curl up in a corner somewhere and take a nap. The thing was, I had gotten plenty of rest on the flight over from the States and had a good night's sleep the night before. I knew I wasn't sleep deprived, yet the feeling of fatigue was overwhelming me and the desire to go to sleep was so strong. It took every fiber in my being not to give in to it and take a nap right there on the strip.

I went to the bathroom and splashed water on my face. I forced myself into a longer warm-up routine than normal, including some basic calisthenics and my usual stretching routine, but I couldn't shake the fatigue I was feeling. In fact, I had this strange sensation like someone was pouring warm water over me, and I could feel it wash over my body starting from my temples all the way down to the tips of my toes, and I just felt so tired. Almost too tired to fence. I glanced up at the clock and realized I only had thirty more minutes before my first bout, and I was sitting on the ground feeling like a sloth. This was so unlike me, it felt strange. Somehow, I had to push through this feeling and get on the strip. This same thing had been happening to me for the last couple of competitions, and I knew once I started fencing, the fatigue would eventually fade as swiftly as it had come. But once the bout was over, another tidal wave of exhaustion would hit me. Since saber is all about speed and explosive energy, feeling slow and lethargic before every competition was distressing. I didn't know if the problem was physical or mental, so I wasn't sure where to turn for help. And I worried about telling my coach and the other members of the team.

Sometimes the universe conspires to help those in need. This was one of those occasions. While I was in the midst of having another abnormal attack of fatigue, the United States Olympic Committee assigned us an official team psychologist, Jamie Harshaw. It was one of the perks of being on the national team that I never knew about. Jamie met with each team member individually for a basic psychological evaluation and check-up. When it was my turn to meet with her, my issue of battling precompetition fatigue was at the top of my list. After breaking down exactly what I had been feeling, it was she who suggested that perhaps what I was experiencing was anxiety manifesting itself as fatigue. Where other people may hyperventilate or feel faint when having a panic attack, my anxiety essentially caused high levels of tiredness, leaving me feeling incredibly drained. Jamie's assessment made total sense considering my experiences with this were recent and only happened at competitions. Perhaps the anxiety stemmed from a fear of failure or maybe even the perceived catastrophic consequences of not meeting my own expectations. To deepen the weight on my back was the disapproval of my teammates, who were less than forgiving when I lost a point or didn't measure up to their expectations. I realized I had been suffering from performance anxiety in the moments before competing and had to learn how to manage these anxieties and disarm some of the triggers.

Jamie and I met regularly, and she gave me exercises I could walk myself through to deescalate myself out of an anxious state. With Jamie's help, I learned different breathing exercises and ways to use guided imagery to help prevent and mediate my anxiety. I would take fifteen minutes before I began my warm-up to focus on my breathing and my thoughts. I would tell myself, "I'm ready. I'm prepared. I'm strong. I'm a champion." These mantras helped me visualize the future, to see myself winning. Remembering past losses wasn't helpful, and those thoughts creeping into my psyche before competitions were what created the anxieties in the first place. I had to remind myself that I was prepared for battle and I had no reason to doubt my abilities. I learned to use my imagination to shape my reality and harness it to serve my needs. It was truly amazing what the mind could do when directed the right way.

It didn't happen overnight, but by using these techniques I slowly learned how to manage my anxiety so that it wouldn't derail my career. Feeling better and more in control, I returned my focus to the next big thing, and that next big thing was making the 2012 Olympic team.

Despite having to deal with my anxiety issues, in the two years since making the US National Women's Saber Team, I was doing more winning than losing. I had qualified for my first Pan American Games in 2011, held in Guadalajara, Mexico, and captured the gold medal along with my teammates. We'd won two team medals at the Fencing World Championships, both bronze, one in 2011 at Catania, Italy, and the other in 2012 in Kiev, Ukraine. And I had won a few individual medals at World Cups throughout the season, helping both my domestic and world rankings. In early 2012, I was ranked number two in the United States and thirteenth in the world. With those stats, qualifying for an Olympic team was now a real possibility.

Akhi thought I could qualify. My family believed I would qualify, and even the media was speculating that I would be going to the games in London. The New Jersey *Star-Ledger*, the state newspaper, wrote a long feature story on me, as an Olympic hopeful.

The headline read, "Maplewood Woman Could Be First American Muslim to Wear Hijab While Competing at Olympics." The journalist interviewed my parents and came to watch me practice in New York at the foundation. Although the headline made mention of my religion, the article mostly focused on me as an athlete, which I appreciated.

It used to make me feel a little awkward to have people single me out because I was a Muslim. I knew I was unique for being the first potential Olympic athlete to represent the United States wearing a hijab, but I didn't know if it warranted the level of attention it brought me. I was also the first woman of color on the women's saber team, but no one ever wrote about that. On the other hand, I was extremely proud to represent Muslim women in sport and show us in a different light than how we had traditionally been portrayed in the media. The acknowledgment of "firsts," especially in sports, was important to show not only how far we've come as people of color, as women, and as a religious minority, but also how far we still have to go to make our world more inclusive. Making the Olympic team would have been an amazing triumph for that reason alone. Every time I spoke to a Muslim audience, someone would always tell me how grateful they were to see a woman of faith succeed at such a high level of sport. It made me proud to know that I was actively changing the narrative for other Muslim women, and it motivated me to continue reaching for the highest levels of sport, like qualifying for the Olympics.

But I didn't qualify.

Part of the reason I didn't qualify was beyond my control. In 2012, there was no women's saber team event in the Olympics, only the individual event. As a rule, fencing is only allocated ten medals during the Olympic Games, even though there are technically twelve events. So, every Olympics, they drop two team events. In 2012, they dropped the women's saber and the men's épée team events. That only left two possible slots for Americans in the individual competitions instead of the usual four. So, when the qualification year came to a close, I wasn't one of the top two women saber fencers. Mariel and Dagmara ranked one and two and went to London to represent the United States. For the record, they finished fourth and eighth respectively.

On the day the team was named, it felt like everyone in my corner wilted in defeat. My family was heartbroken. I was disappointed but not entirely surprised. I didn't have a real strategy to qualify for the games. There was no plan in place, other than to continue to train hard. But that isn't enough. People had hinted that I could qualify for the Olympic team, but no one, not even my coaches at the foundation, actually helped lay out a specific plan to help get me there. It wasn't until after I failed to qualify for the Olympics that I really started to consider what making an Olympic team would mean, not just for me as an athlete but for the communities whom I represented, particularly the Muslim community here in the United States.

There are about 6.5 million American Muslims in this country, making them one of the largest religious groups in the United States. American Muslims are a diverse and growing population with a thriving social and cultural scene catering to their unique needs. Throughout the year, thousands of Muslims attend regional and national conventions throughout North America. There are Muslim schools, stores, restaurants, and of course mosques. There are Muslim newspapers, magazines, radio stations, publishers, websites, apps, and YouTube channels. At almost every college and university in the country there are Muslim student groups. There's even an annual Muslim Day at Six Flags amusement parks around the county. And it is within this Muslim community that I gained my first level of "celebrity" status as an athlete. This made sense to me because, while expansive, the Muslim community in the United States is still relatively small. When it came to professional female athletes who wore hijab, I was one in a group of one. So I quickly became a public figure within this Muslim world, regularly traveling to speak about my experiences as a minority member of Team USA. From campus visits to conference keynotes, I was getting invitations from all across the United States. My name and unique story as a hijabi fencer had spread quickly throughout the community.

———

The only problem was, people in the Muslim community often referred to me as "the Olympic fencer" because I was building a reputation as a professional athlete who competed on a United States national team. I knew it was an honest mistake for people to equate my career as a member of Team USA with Olympic stature. Add to that a handful of media articles referring to me as an Olympic hopeful in the run-up to the 2012 Olympics, and it's understandable why I was being mistaken for an Olympian. While I didn't fault anyone for the confusion, as someone who had failed to qualify, it was a painful reminder every time I had to correct someone to say, "Sorry, I'm not an Olympian."

———

One day soon after the 2012 London Summer Games had actually transpired, I was out shopping with my friend Habiba in a department store at the shopping mall. Habiba and I have known each other since our summers playing at the mosque together when we were in elementary school. She was always busy buried in paperwork at her corporate job, and I was constantly traveling for competition, so we often went months without seeing each other, but we did our best to keep in touch. The store had a dazzling array of formal dresses perfect for some of the special events I had coming up. I had an important keynote scheduled at an Islamic conference in Chicago, so I was happy to find some modest options tucked in the racks of elegant dresses. As a professional athlete who spent the majority of her time in sweatpants and sneakers, I jumped at any opportunity to dress up. That was another stereotype I was trying to break—that fashion and sports were mutually exclusive. I was an athlete *and* I loved fashion. I wore eyeliner most days, even when I fenced, and wasn't interested in how anyone felt about it. My eyeliner was like war paint; I never went anywhere without it

"Habiba, everything in here looks like it was made for older women," I said to my friend, making moves to leave the store.

"Don't give up so quickly," Habiba said, pulling me back to the rack of dresses. "We should be able to find something." She pulled out two long, dark-blue dresses with intricate beadwork around the sleeves. "What about these?" she said.

I eyed the two dresses and thought they looked more mother of the bride than something I as a twenty-six-year-old was interested in wearing. Before I could voice my disapproval, we were interrupted.

"Excuse me, are you Ibtihaj Muhammad? The Olympic fencer?"

A young girl stood in front of me, a scrap of paper and a pencil in her hand. She was wearing blue jeans, a pink-checkered button-down shirt, and a blue hijab. A shy grin decorated her face. I guessed she was probably eleven or twelve years old. I started to respond, but Habiba jumped in to answer for me.

"Actually, she's not an Olympian."

I turned my head and shot Habiba a glare.

"Can I still have your autograph?" the little girl asked.

"Oh, of course," I said, taking the paper from her hand and scribbling my name and some kind words.

"Thank you," she said and rewarded me with another huge

smile. "I want to be just like you when I grow up. Except I don't want to fence. I'm going to the Olympics to run track."

I smiled at the little girl, wishing her the best of luck, and told her to never give up on her dreams. It was such an endearing moment, but I was annoyed at Habiba for butting in. Was I mad at her for embarrassing me? She had only told the truth. I *wasn't* an Olympian, and the reality was it hurt to even think about it.

"Let's go, Habiba," I said as I headed for the department store exit. "I'm going to order a dress online," I said, making an excuse to cut our afternoon shopping spree short. Luckily, Habiba didn't try to change my mind. She probably sensed I was irritated. We said our goodbyes in the parking lot, and I hopped in my car and headed back home to Maplewood.

While I was driving, I replayed the events that had just transpired in the store and the visceral reaction I'd had in my gut. When Habiba announced that I wasn't an Olympian, it reminded me of all the naysayers and people who hadn't believed in me or my fencing potential. From the coaches to the competitors in my life who doubted my abilities—because I was Black, because I was a woman, because I was Muslim—they all ran through my mind. All of the times I'd been told no crowded into my memory until I wanted to scream. I gripped the steering wheel tighter and forced myself to breathe calmly, but I couldn't tamp down the emotions brewing inside of me. That little girl from the department store deserved a role model. She deserved to see someone who looked like her in sports. Representation and inclusion matter. When I started on this journey I always told myself that I wanted to see how far fencing could take me, and now I realized that the journey was bigger than me. My success would mean so much to so many people. Watching Dominique Dawes flip her way to Olympic gold in the 1996 Atlanta Olympic Games was the reason my sister Asiya had started gymnastics. And if it weren't for Venus and

Serena Williams, I know I would have never picked up a tennis racket that summer back in middle school. It was in that moment in my car, heading south on the turnpike, that I decided that I was going to make an Olympic team. I didn't care that it would be four years of grind. I didn't care how old I would be. I was going to be on the United States Olympic Team in the 2016 summer games. There was no other option.

CHAPTER 13

To be a champ you have to believe in yourself when no one else will.

—SUGAR RAY ROBINSON

To do the same thing and expect a different result is the definition of crazy, so I knew everything in my training regimen had to be fine-tuned, altered, and adjusted to get me where I wanted to be. I knew I needed to find people who could help me make the Olympic team, so I started building a cadre of trainers who could help me formulate a plan, a training schedule, and a mind-set that would take me to the top. The individuals I was looking for had to be smart and trustworthy. I was looking for people with positive energy and a track record of excellence.

It had become painfully obvious that Akhi was no longer able to maintain our same level of training. It felt like once he had proven himself capable of helping me qualify for the national team, his priorities shifted. Officially, he was still my personal coach at the foundation, but his work ethic and interest in pushing our training to the next level had slowly dissipated. Now he was frequently absent from the foundation and my competitions. Too often he was late or simply didn't show up for our lessons. During this time, Akhi became a father, so fatherhood was likely pulling his attention away from fencing. I understood that Akhi had different goals as a coach than I did as a competitor and that I wasn't his only student, but selfishly I wanted him to stick with me. I wanted a committed coach who had made an Olympic team, who knew exactly what it took to get me to the promised land. I wanted a coach who had a shared interest in helping me grow technically and tactically and whom I could count on 24/7. But after all of these years, I had finally come to realize that depending on anyone other than myself was a recipe for failure. Ultimately, I was the one responsible for my own success, and if that meant I had to seek out help to push forward, then that was exactly what I was going to do.

Keeth Smart was the first person I sought to be my mentor. He wasn't a coach, but I still wanted him to be on my personal team of advisors. Keeth had led the US men's saber team to a silver medal in the 2008 Olympic Games in Beijing and was arguably the best US male saber fencer of all time. He had since retired from competition, but he liked to come back to the Peter Westbrook Foundation—where he had gotten his start—to mentor and teach the younger kids on Saturday mornings. He said it was his way of giving back after fencing gave him so much. After watching the way Keeth worked with the kids, it was easy to see he had a vast knowledge of fencing and he would be able to help me master tactical avenues of the sport I was missing. I started to pick Keeth's brain about his training prior to qualifying for the games, what kind of things he focused on with his trainers, which drills I could incorporate into my training to help with my speed, and any other tips he might have for me. Keeth had a demanding, full-time job and wasn't even at the foundation that much, but he was kind enough to give me his cell number and make time despite his busy schedule. Keeth's love for the sport was genuine, and he saw how invested I was in progressing. I was lucky and grateful to have him in my corner.

One of the most useful things Keeth did for me was to give me a list of simple exercises to do every day to make me a better fencer. He told me if I focused on these seven simple things before practice for thirty minutes, if I got to the foundation thirty minutes earlier than everyone else and plowed through these exercises, they would add up to make a difference. When I looked at the list, I was skeptical. How could doing what seemed like nothing more than warm-ups make any real difference? These were plyometric exercises, like jumps and lateral lunges that Keeth said, with repetition, would help increase my explosiveness and foot speed. He said if I did these exercises for thirty minutes at least four times a week, that would be two hours of extra practice that I was getting, not just more than my teammates at the foundation and more than my US teammates, but also more than my competitors on the world circuit.

"Don't cheat on these," Keeth said to me, noting the look of doubt on my face. "If you can commit to doing these drills, you will be building your craft exponentially and getting ahead of the competition," he said. "Trust me. It will work."

I took the list and promised I would start doing the exercises.

Keeth wasn't just a great fencer, he really was a smart guy. He was committed to having an equally stellar career outside of sports. Keeth had parlayed his skills and work ethic from fencing into an MBA from Columbia University and a job in the financial sector.

When I first sought Keeth's advice, he asked me how much studying I did of my competition. I told him about that first World Cup in London where Candace and I had sat with our notebooks watching the competition. I ran to my locker to grab my fencing journal—a simple black moleskin notebook with lined pages and furious handwritten notes—and then showed it to Keeth. He flipped through the pages and saw the detailed descriptions I had of almost every woman I'd ever competed against over the years. I wrote things like, Fencer X "will take parry but often misses repost. Use long attack and finish under." I recorded everyone's techniques, and I strategized how best to beat them.

Keeth was impressed. "This is really good. You can be the fastest woman on the strip, but it's important to fence every match smart. At the start of every competition, know who you're up against so you can strategize. You've put in too much time and energy to wing it. You can win sometimes with speed and strength, but if you want to be consistent and if you want to be the best, you have to be smart."

"Well, I guess since your name is Keeth Smart, you're in a good position to know." I couldn't resist making the joke.

Thankfully, Keeth laughed, too. "Who knew you have a funny side under all that bravado."

"I can be funny," I said, pretending hurt. "Ask anyone in my family."

Keeth laughed again. But I didn't want to get off track.

"How do you draw the attack out of your opponent?" I said, turning the conversation back to fencing. "When I watch you fence, you're so good at making people fall short in their attack. How do you do it?" I said.

Sometimes Keeth would give me scenarios to try in practice that he thought would work against certain fencers based on their style of fencing. I would write those down in my journal and refer to them often when I was on the road. My journal became my guide. It was what I relied on, being that I often didn't have a personal coach by my side, given Akhi's increasingly spotty attendance. More often than not, I would be the only fencer at a major international competition without a personal coach by her side. It makes fencing on the world circuit really tough, given that our personal coaches act as our advocates and voices on the strip. Whenever the calls are left to the referees, it is our personal coach who steps in to persuade the refs to call a point one way or the other. With Akhi missing, there was no one to speak up for me. And his absence was not only felt on the strip. During competitions our personal coaches gave us lessons to keep us in the best shape while competing, so with no Akhi, I was left to my own devices. Here I was doing everything I could to qualify for the Olympics, but I was missing a large part of my training that each of my competitors had ample access to. Sometimes that thought would bring back those feelings of panic, and I feared I'd never get to see my dream realized. Once again, I felt like I was putting in all of the work required of me, but I lacked a coach willing to show me the way. It seemed a particularly cruel place to be.

For years, I had been working out at an all-women's gym in New Jersey—the same all-women's gym my mother belonged to—but I could tell I wasn't getting anything out of the facilities anymore. I knew that I needed a facility that catered to athletes, not just women trying to make good on their New Year's resolutions. I found a gym a few towns over in Springfield. Once I started, it took me a while to find the right trainer. Because of my faith, I debated whether or not I wanted to work with a male or female, but ultimately, I decided I wouldn't limit my choices by gender, I would simply find the best person for the job. So when I met Jake, I knew he was the one. Initially, I didn't tell Jake I was on a national team, but I told him I was a fencer and that I wanted to work on speed, strength, and agility. Jake was the type of trainer that no matter what mood I was in or how much I might complain, he wouldn't accept anything less than 100 percent in every workout. I loved his tough love, humor, and that we were the same age. He was easy to get along with. The thing I enjoyed most about Jake, though, was that he was totally dependable. If I needed or wanted to work out at six o'clock in the morning or ten at night, Jake would be there, no questions asked and ready to work.

After working with Jake, I realized that circuit training was the piece of the puzzle that I had been missing prior to 2012. It was high-intensity metabolic strength training that I needed to make me more dominant on the strip. I could lunge farther and faster. I was stronger, and my speed picked up with this new level of training. Suddenly, with this small change in my workout regimen, I was a better balanced athlete. I diversified my training, too, by incorporating Pilates reformer, kickboxing, interval running, everything and anything to increase my stamina and strength. My performance on the strip started showing that I was headed in the right direction. I qualified for every national team for seven years straight, and that wasn't an easy thing to do. There were always women cycling on and off the team, as no one's ranking was guaranteed. I had to battle for my place at the top every single season, but I made it because I was stronger and fencing smarter. And as a team we had some impressive showings as well. In 2013 we won the bronze medal at World Cups in Italy, Turkey, and Belgium. At the end of the season, we captured the bronze medal at the World Championships in Budapest, Hungary. My individual results continued to climb as well, improving both my national and international rankings, being recognized both on and off the strip for my efforts. Despite our success as a team, however, I was still wading through the minefield of micro-aggressions and psychological warfare from my teammates and the coaching staff. My contributions to our winning record did nothing to stem the abuse.

It was March 2013, and we were in Moscow for a Grand Prix. At that point, the national team still consisted of Mariel, Dagmara, Daria, and me. Although she wasn't officially on the team, a younger fencer named Eliza Stone was also traveling with us for the competition. Many people believed she would make the team at the end of the season because she had been having a breakout year so far. Both Eliza and I had fenced well on the first day of competition in Moscow. I advanced through my bracket, eliminating some heavy hitters on the world circuit, including my teammate Dagmara, by a wide margin. Eliza and I tied for third place and were both really happy with our results and wanted to celebrate. We were rather limited in dinner options, as we were instructed not to venture far from the hotel for safety reasons. There was a decent Uzbek restaurant most teams frequented whenever we traveled to Moscow. Because it was late and adjacent to the hotel, Eliza and I decided to go there.

It wasn't surprising to me that during our matches the rest of the US fencers hadn't bothered to cheer for me, especially since I beat Dagmara to get to the semifinals. Daria and Mariel hadn't had their best day, either. But Eliza was disappointed that the team she hoped to join one day wasn't in her corner. The team members hadn't cheered for her as she made her run to the semifinals. I didn't want to dash her hopes by telling her all I'd witnessed on the team, so I downplayed my teammates' behavior.

"Don't worry about it," I said to Eliza, trying to boost her confidence as we walked into the restaurant. "You fenced well today."

Eliza smiled. "I still can't believe how well we did."

As we stepped into the dimly lit restaurant with a handful of mostly empty tables we both stopped in our tracks. There in the far corner of the restaurant sat the rest of the team—Mariel, Dagmara, and Daria—in the middle of dinner.

We waited to see if our teammates would invite us to join them. They didn't. They didn't even pause to wave or say hello.

A hostess appeared and greeted us in English.

She smiled at us and led us to a table next to our teammates. She probably assumed we'd want to sit close by. No sooner had we sat down than Mariel, Dagmara, and Daria abruptly stood up and left the restaurant. They left their half-eaten dinners on the table without saying a single word to us. I think Eliza was shocked. I know I was. Even after all of these years with the three of them and their cold behavior toward me, I could not understand why they acted like that toward me and now Eliza.

"What was that about?" Eliza asked as we watched their retreating forms.

I shrugged my shoulders. "I honestly do not know," I said. "I could make something up or say it's because they are upset about their performance, but anything I say would be a guess. And to be honest, their behavior is so bizarre to me, I can't even begin to imagine why anyone would act that way to other human beings."

Eliza didn't look like my answer satisfied her. She clearly wanted to know more, but we agreed not to talk about them for the rest of the evening. We could have spent the whole evening and the rest of the night dissecting Mariel's, Dagmara's, and Daria's behavior, but I wouldn't let them ruin my evening. And I didn't want to color Eliza's opinions about her future teammates. She could form her own thoughts.

So we ate and celebrated our success on the strip.

Despite her discouraging introduction to the team dynamic, Eliza continued her quest to make the national team, and she displaced Daria as our newest team member. I was excited to have Eliza on the team, hoping for a friend in what had widely been a lonely experience. Unfortunately for me and Eliza, her befriending me meant being iced out by Mariel and Dagmara, so her entrance onto the team did nothing to quell my discomfort. The national coach was primarily interested in Mariel's success, and Mariel's mother was still our team manager. My hopes for a change in the team dynamic quickly disappeared as things pretty much stayed the same. I was the odd woman out, and no one cared to bring me into the fold.

One year we were at a training camp in Poland before the World Championships, and the training camp happened to fall during Ramadan, the religious month when Muslims abstain from food and drink from sunrise to sunset for thirty days. Because it was summer and the days were quite long, I was fasting for sixteen hours a day. I would go to the cafeteria during dinner, pack my food into a container, and then eat in my room once the sun set around eleven p.m. And then at three or four in the morning, when the sun was poised to rise again, I would start the fast all over again. In that short window between eleven p.m. and four a.m., instead of getting good rest, I would spend my time drinking copious amounts of water to make sure I didn't become dehydrated during practice. The coaching staff and my teammates didn't understand why I was fasting or make any attempts to understand the reasons it was important to me. As for most Muslims, Ramadan was a special time for me; fasting allowed for spiritual reflection and a remembrance of God and His mercy. I had been fasting since I was a little kid when we'd wake up with my parents early in the morning to eat and pray together. It never occurred to me not to fast, just like it never occurred me to stop training during Ramadan. I was more than ready to make sacrifices so I could do both things. But the coach and my teammates had no sympathy for my situation.

Instead, Ed continued to push me without pause. If I took a break or had a hard time catching my breath, I was told I was being lazy. That made me so angry because I had always been one of those people who worked harder than the next person no matter what. And not just in fencing, but in every aspect of my life. So when the coach would suggest that I was slacking off, I wouldn't say much, I'd just get back on the strip and do my best. I didn't feel comfortable defending myself because I didn't want to perpetuate the stereotype of being an angry Black woman. I was always conscious about how I would come across to my white teammates and my white coach in this mostly white sport. I didn't dare give them the ammunition they craved to justify their cold behavior toward me.

I had been on the team for almost three years at this point, and Ed had shown zero interest in understanding what Ramadan was or why I was fasting. He had no desire to know me as a person. I wasn't looking to force my religion on anyone, but a tiny bit of understanding on his part could have gone a long way. It's what a good leader should have done. But his attitude toward me and fasting felt like, "I don't understand why you would choose to starve yourself." I found his behavior completely baffling and totally disrespectful. I wondered why he couldn't approach me with just a hint of empathy, knowing how hard I worked every day. But the words, "Are you okay, Ibti? Do you need to rest for a minute, Ibti?" never came out of his mouth.

By this point, my fencing career on Team USA had become a mental game. I had to find ways to block out all of the distractions in order to fully focus on the goal ahead of me. There was an art to it, and it was something that, by the grace of Allah, I was able to eventually figure out. But not before I spent dozens of hours crying and unhappy, surrounded by people who made me feel inferior and devalued.

"Ibtihaj!" my mother shouted one day. "Are you even listening to me?"

"Sorry, Mommy, what did you say?" I said, looking around the crowded café. We were sitting in one of our favorite girls' getaway spots in Maplewood on a rare Sunday afternoon that I wasn't traveling for a competition.

"What I said," my mother repeated in a more soothing tone, "is that I'm worried about you. You're killing yourself at the gym and at the foundation and I understand that, but then you come home from these competitions so upset. Is it worth it, baby? Because you know your father and I don't think you need to prove anything to anyone. Your health is more important."

I could feel a wall of tears gather behind my eyelids. I wanted so much to let them fall, but then it felt like I would fall, too, into a million little pieces. My mother's concern was almost too much to bear because it meant I wasn't hiding my anguish very well. I was miserable much of the time. I was in physical pain after almost every workout. Sometimes I couldn't sleep because I was so worried that I hadn't trained hard enough. All of that coupled with my teammates and coaching staff who made no effort to mask their disdain for me. To confront that kind of energy day in and day out was mentally and emotionally exhausting, and now my mother could see it on my face. She was giving me permission to quit. I knew she'd never say the words aloud, but I could see the concern etched in her eyes.

I pulled in a deep breath of air and released it slowly. I forced a smile on my face and prayed my mother believed me when I said, "I'm okay, Mommy."

"No, you're not," my mother said, taking a big gulp of her coffee. 'I'm your mother and I think I know when my child is not okay."

I placed my hand over my mother's hand and gave it a squeeze. "I said I was going to do this, and I am not going to quit now because things are hard."

Now my mother looked like she was going to cry. Now it was her turn to breathe deeply.

"Ibtihaj," she started, "you have always known what you wanted to do and no one could stop you once you made your mind up, so I'm not going to try to stop you now, but I want you to understand that no one will think any of less of you if you decide to move on."

"I know," I said to my mom, but inside I was thinking of the one person who would think less of me if I quit. Me! I couldn't let myself down. I had made a promise to myself to make the Olympic team. I had promised myself and all of the little girls who looked like me that I was going to go all the way. If I gave up now, how would I face them? How would I face myself? But to my mother, I just said, "I promise you, Mom, that if it ever gets to be too much, I'll stop. But I'm not there yet."

My mom stared at me. "If you say so."

"If you just keep cheering me on and taking my late-night phone calls then I'll be okay, Mommy. I promise," I said.

"Okay," my mother said, eyeing me carefully. "Okay."

I wasn't just trying to make my mother feel good. It was true that I couldn't have survived my journey to the Olympics without her. She was the nexus of my support team. She started coming to more of my international competitions and always had her phone available to take my calls when I needed a loving voice to remind me that I could triumph on the strip. The same criteria I used to assemble my training team, I used with my emotional well-being team. I kept a small group of people around me, as anchors in my storm, but more importantly a smile and some sunshine during the darkness. Paola Pliego was a star fencer on Mexico's women's saber team. She was almost ten years younger than me, but our paths always crossed during World Cups, and soon we became best friends. I loved her positive outlook on life; she always had a smile on her face. Like me, she was relentless on the strip, but she was always able to leave fencing behind once she took off her mask and carry on with life in a loving way. I loved that about her, and as our friendship blossomed on and off the strip, she helped me not to feel so alone when the team traveled abroad. Whenever we could, we'd coordinate our schedules, meet for meals, and go sightseeing in whatever city we were competing or training in.

I also began to depend on my sister Faizah in more ways than one. Now that Faizah was fencing more regularly, we often traveled together to the same competitions. Sometimes Faizah and I even fenced each other at tournaments: that's how good she was. My sister's national and international ranking was climbing steadily, even though she was balancing competing with a heavy courseload at college. She wasn't able to make it to every tournament, but things were so much better with her around. She witnessed firsthand some of the outlandish treatment I received at the hands of my teammates. Just having someone else see what I was going through helped in the sense that I knew I wasn't crazy.

"I can't believe they 'forgot' to tell you about team practice," Faizah said to me one night after a day spent training before a tournament.

Somehow no one figured it important to tell me the time of a mandatory team practice Ed had scheduled. Then I was chastised when I arrived one hour late. This type of "accident" had become so common to me—sometimes the team manager would forget to include me on team emails—that I hardly blinked. My sister, on the other hand, was bewildered as to why I was willing to put up with it. I had gotten so used to being treated like a second-class citizen that these slights didn't even faze me anymore. But Faizah was incensed.

"I think they're just jealous because you're doing so well," she surmised.

"Maybe. I hope it's jealousy and not something worse. I don't even know, Faizah," I said, throwing my hands up in mock surrender. "All I do know is that I can't give them any more of my energy by worrying about their issues."

"It's so not fair," Faizah said. "You work so hard. You don't deserve to be treated like this."

After three years on the team I had finally gotten to the point where I refused to give it any more attention.

"Hey, don't worry about it," I said to Faizah. "Just having you here with me is enough. I want you to maintain your focus on winning as well. Don't let these people distract you from winning."

"Is that how you handle all of this?" Faizah asked, a look of concern still marking her face.

"Yeah," I said, keeping my voice neutral to protect her. I needed to give her the strength that no one had given me. "I try to put this stuff aside so I can focus on the sport."

Faizah and I didn't spend a whole lot of time discussing my teammates, but even though nothing was ever said aloud, I got the distinct impression that my little sister appointed herself my protector on the fencing circuit. She was always there when I needed her. Sometimes it was just a look she shot me across the room, or there were times when she'd give me a high-five to congratulate me on a bout well fought. Sometimes it felt like she was the older sister, given how much I grew to depend on not just her skills and advice as a training partner but also on her comforting presence in what too often felt like enemy territory.

I still often found myself without a personal coach in my corner at competitions, but I almost always had some combination of my mother, Faizah, and Paola as part of my cheering squad.

Though they didn't carry the same weight as a coach in the coach's box, they soothed my soul and buoyed my spirits to no end. I thanked Allah I had them in my life.

———————

In 2013 toward the end of the season, we were at a World Cup in Bologna, Italy. I remember looking at my bracket after qualifying for the second day of competition and realizing it was one of the toughest brackets ever. I would be competing against some of the best fencers in the world, women I'd yet to face off against on the strip. These were the women that I'd been admiring since I started fencing, women whose bouts I studied on video replay as part of my training, women like the Russian fencer Sofiya Velikaya, who had several World Championship titles and an Olympic medal to her name. To me Sofiya, or Sonia, as I called her, was like the Serena Williams of women's saber. And I had her in my bracket.

Sonia was so smooth and dominant on the strip that as I put on my mask, my last thought before turning on fight mode was to try to fence like her. I wanted to be strong and confident in my actions, and that was exactly what I did. I beat the great Sofiya Velikaya, arguably one of the best fencers in the world, by a score of 15–10. My confidence was sky-high after that win. From there, it was almost like this mental courage built up inside of me because I had toppled one of the greatest. I felt invincible all day. I made it all the way to the semifinals, which meant I was going home with a medal.

The semifinal match did not start out well. I was losing miserably, 13–4, but then something clicked inside of me. I found this awareness that if I could beat Sonia, then I could beat anyone. My body caught up with my mind, and I rallied back on the strip to win the match against Ilaria Bianco from Italy 15–14. I ended up taking second place that day in Bologna, earning my first individual medal at a World Cup. I was ecstatic. When I stood on that medal stand I was so proud of myself. Nothing could contain my happiness.

From the medal stand I could see my teammates were watching me. But not one of them was cheering. And that's the moment I realized I really was out here all on my own. It was a cold jolt of reality. Fencing is not the Girl Scouts. We're not going to do a kumbaya as a team and rejoice in our joint success. Fencing doesn't work like that. We are individuals first, a team second, and I would be smart to always remember that.

CHAPTER 14

Success isn't handed to us; we earn it.

—MISTY COPELAND

The phone rang. Someone from the United States Department of State was calling and wanted to speak with me. It was a spokeswoman from Secretary of State Hillary Clinton's office, and she was calling to ask me if I was interested in serving on the United States Department of State's Council to Empower Women and Girls through Sports. This new initiative would be composed of American trailblazers in women's sports who embody and support the secretary and department's efforts to empower women and girls globally through sport. As a council member, I would travel to different parts of the world to share my story and encourage women and girls from around the world to pursue their potential through sports. By accepting the invitation, I would be joining an elite group of athletes, coaches, and sports journalists—like legends Mia Hamm and Billie Jean King—who were standouts in their field.

I didn't know what to say. This was so humbling. I was honored to be acknowledged for breaking barriers in sport, as the first Muslim woman to represent the United States in international competition, but I hadn't even qualified for the Olympics. My mind immediately went to that little girl who wanted my autograph in the clothing store. Was I accomplished enough as an athlete to be sent out into the world as an ambassador? Did I have a good enough story to share?

The State Department representative informed me that I didn't have to give her an answer right away and could get back to them in a couple of days. I was grateful for the time to consider the offer. I used the time to talk to the people in my life I trusted most, beginning with my parents. I also talked to Peter Westbrook and Keeth Smart to gauge their thoughts on the opportunity. My parents told me I should be honored to show the world that a Muslim woman could excel in sports on an international level. Peter and Keeth both told me to seize every single opportunity that came my way. When I stopped to consider what this position really was about, I realized it fit perfectly with my aspirations since college. Being a part of this global initiative would be an amazing opportunity to merge my interests in diplomacy with my love for sports.

When Secretary Clinton's office reached out again, I was happy to accept the position.

One of the first assignments I had as a council member was a series of speaking engagements at local schools in London about my journey as a minority member of Team USA. I had a World Cup in London at the end of the week, so I flew in a few days before to meet with cultural attachés and representatives from the United States embassy.

While on the airplane, I went over my speech a dozen times. I was still getting the hang of speaking in front of large audiences, but this would be one of the biggest assignments yet. I wanted to make sure I was prepared, because there was so much I wanted to say. I had to motivate these kids to follow their dreams no matter their gender, race, religion. I wanted to make sure my words reached them, and most of all I wanted them to know that I believed in them even if they didn't yet believe in themselves.

As it turned out, the first school I visited, the Sarah Bonnell School for girls, had a large contingent of Muslim students. London is such a diverse city, with a large Southeast Asian Muslim community. As the students filled the auditorium, many of the girls wearing sky-blue hijabs smiled when they saw me, and I returned the favor. I shared my experiences growing up in a town with few Muslims, and I spoke about how hard it was to be the only person with brown skin or the only person wearing hijab in the sport of fencing. I also shared with them that my secret to success was to never let other people's opinions about me stop me from pursuing my passions.

"When other people told me 'no, you can't,' that's when I told myself, 'yes, I can,'" I said. Looking out into a crowd of eager faces, I felt fulfilled. The rush of making a room full of young girls feel good about themselves was amazing.

Before the students had to file off to their next class, I did a demonstration introducing some fencing basics followed by a short question-and-answer session. They asked if it was hard to train when no one else on my team looked like me. They wanted to know how heavy my saber was and if I could really kill someone with it. My favorite comment came from a little girl in one of the front rows who said that she had never seen a fencer who looked like me and now that she had, she realized she too could be the first at something, like the first Muslim woman astronaut from the UK. A bunch of other students added their own dreams of what first they wanted to achieve. It filled my heart to know that my story provided hope, and it confirmed my belief that there weren't enough people like me in the public view for younger generations to find inspiration in. Black and brown young people, old people, Muslims and non-Muslims alike need role models to show that their dreams are possible.

And from that moment on, I made it a point to share my story as often as possible—not only through Secretary Clinton's initiative, but whenever the opportunity presented itself. I realized I was in a unique position to transform the way society sees Muslim women and Black women in predominantly white sports, and the way we as ethnic and religious minorities see ourselves. I asked myself, *If not me, then who?* Looking back, I wondered how my own journey might have been different, easier maybe, if there had been someone who looked like me for me to look up to when I felt alone and defeated simply because I was deemed different.

Once I made the mental commitment to share my story, more and more speaking opportunities came my way. I was regularly speaking at universities, Muslim conferences, and different cultural organizations, in the United States and some internationally as well. Again, the Muslim community was particularly receptive to hearing about my experiences and cheered me on in my pursuits. In 2011, I received the Inspiration Award from the New Jersey chapter of the Council on American Islamic Relations (CAIR). In 2012, I was named Sportswoman of the Year by the Muslim Women's Sports Foundation, an organization based in the United Kingdom.

Because there were so few Muslim women on the professional sports circuit, I was an inspiration for a lot of people, especially as the first professional athlete from the United States who also wears hijab. There were misconceptions about Muslim women that existed both inside and outside of the Muslim community. While Islam doesn't restrict women from exercising—in fact all Muslims are required to care for their bodies through exercise and healthy eating habits—women face a unique set of challenges with sports. A lot of Muslim women find it difficult to lead an active lifestyle while adhering to their religious principles around modesty, with most gyms being coed and workout wear being formfitting. These minor obstacles leave room for excuses not to make exercise a priority. It became common for certain groups within the Muslim community to encourage their boys to be involved in sports, while leaving their girls to sit on the sidelines. As a woman who pursued sport professionally in hijab, I proved that being a modest Muslim woman and being active were not mutually exclusive.

Another reason the Muslim community at large was embracing me was because they were simply starved for positive representation in the media. Media depictions of Muslims as terrorists and foreigners had inundated our televisions and movie screens, and these harsh misrepresentations fueled anti-Muslim bigotry and policies in America. My journey as a Muslim woman on Team USA flipped the Muslim narrative onto its head and became a source of pride for Muslims of all backgrounds. I bucked every single stereotype of the media depictions of Muslims. I was an American. I wore hijab by choice, and I proudly represented my country both on and off the fencing strip, both in victory and defeat. My journey was bigger than me. I was a vision that publicly counterbalanced the negativity surrounding Muslim identity in the United States.

———————

Of course, there would always be people, even within the Muslim community, who didn't want to see me succeed. They had complaints and critiques they couldn't keep to themselves. Some questioned my traveling alone without a family escort, others opined that my fencing uniform was too tight. But these were exceptions to the overwhelmingly positive responses I received from my faith community. I was blessed to always have my parents around to remind me that what I was doing as an athlete, as a woman, and as a Muslim was brave and exceptional, and I should never let anyone make me feel guilty about the path I had chosen.

Everything seemed to be headed in the right direction. In addition to my speaking engagements at universities, with the State Department, and in the Muslim community, there was now a growing interest in my career by mainstream media outlets who found my story as an African-American, hijab-wearing Muslim in a traditionally white and elitist sport to be fascinating. It was kind of ironic that as anti-Muslim sentiment in the United States and the rest of the Western world increased, the media's interest in my story grew in tandem. Because so few Americans personally knew a Muslim, and media misrepresentation of Muslims was at an all-time high, I was mindful that as one of the few Muslims receiving positive attention, I was in a unique and potentially precarious position. I wanted to continue to be a beacon of light for the Muslim community, challenging the negative stereotypes being perpetuated in the media. But I also wanted to be a voice who spoke up in defense of our religious rights.

This newfound weight on my shoulders changed and reshaped my conversations with God. Instead of praying for a win or praying during times of difficulties, I started to ask Allah to allow me to represent my community and my family well. I asked Allah to protect me from those who didn't want good for me and surround me instead with those who would encourage and uplift me. I asked Allah to help me show patience even when the world was testing me.

And, oh, boy, was I tested.

I had been traveling overseas for a series of training camps and competitions. My mom had been with me in Belgium for my last competition, and now we were heading home. As we were passing through a security checkpoint at the airport in Brussels, we were pulled out of line.

"You must take this off," the security officer barked at me in halting English, pointing at my hijab.

I turned to my mother, who was standing behind me in the line. She must have seen the fear in my eyes.

"What's the matter?" she said.

"I think he's saying I have to take off my hijab."

Sensing the agent's belligerent energy, my mom stood next to me and tried to deescalate the situation by calmly asking the security officer what the problem was. He repeated his words verbatim, indicating with hand gestures that we would have to remove our scarves. The officer had thinning brown hair and pale skin and looked to be in his late fifties. Maybe he was having a bad day or didn't care much for his job, but either way he did not look happy with my mom and me.

"I'm sorry, we're wearing this for religious reasons. We're not taking them off," I said firmly.

With the color in the officer's cheeks rising, he looked like I had insulted him personally.

"Off or no flight," he said. "You will not board the airplane if you do not take it off for the security check."

This had never happened to me before. My passport was now filled with stamps from dozens of different countries, and I had never been asked to remove my hijab at an airport for security.

"We're from the United States, and we've never had to remove our hijabs for security," I said. My tone was defiant, but I was offended by the insensitivity of the officer and suspected this wasn't a required safety precaution. This was profiling.

"Take it off," the officer shouted, "or you will not fly on any airplane leaving this airport."

I looked around to see if anyone else had noticed our mistreatment by the security officer. I was now starting to panic and wondered if anyone would step in to help us. Removing my hijab would feel like a severe violation of my privacy. It would be like asking someone to remove their underwear in the middle of the airport. I tried to be cordial and plead our case, but the officer seemed firm in his words. As desperation started to kick in, I tried to think of alternate routes my mom and I could take to get out of Belgium. Luckily, my mother kept a cooler head and intervened. "Sir, how about you pat our heads down like this to check. That's how they do it in the United States," my mother said, pantomiming with her hands.

"What is the problem here?" A female officer finally came over. The two officers spoke in hushed but heated tones in French, and then the female officer indicated that we were to follow her. Mindful of the time, Mom and I exchanged looks and then followed the woman into a room not far from the security hall. It was an unadorned gray room with a small table with two metal folding chairs. I imagined it was an interrogation room, and I feared what was going to happen to us. I reached for my mother's hand for comfort.

"Okay, ladies," the officer said. "Who is first?"

"For what?" I said.

"For the head check. I will pat you down over the scarf," the woman answered.

Before I could answer, my mother stepped forward. The whole procedure for both my mom and me took five minutes. The female security officer was brisk and efficient. When she was done, we were free to go. We thanked the woman and hightailed it out of there, eager to make our flight back to the United States.

I didn't want to think what would have happened if my mother hadn't kept her cool. I was not going to remove my hijab—it was a violation of my religious rights to be forced to do so. But as I sat there I realized how close I'd come to a potentially hostile situation. I knew it was important to stand up and fight against discrimination, but I also knew that the next Muslim woman wearing hijab would feel the repercussions of my actions either in a positive or negative way. I prayed no other woman would have to choose between her hijab and getting home.

Sometimes I had to pinch myself when I stopped to think about all the blessings, self-awareness, and lessons I learned because of my commitment to the sport of fencing. I thought back to my darker days after college when I battled depression and uncertainty, unable to find a job in the corporate world like my friends. It reminded me to be thankful for every moment in my journey, including the obstacles, that had led me to this place where I could find happiness and purpose. If only I had known then what I know now, that my life would lead me to a place where I would have a greater impact on the world than I likely ever would have had sitting behind a desk in an office in Manhattan. The blessings now seemed endless, and there was always something new to experience.

But all of those blessings came at a cost. I was training, competing, and showing up for speaking engagements. I was spending so much time on the road that exhaustion felt like my permanent state of being. Sometimes I wondered if I would be able to make it through a single day. I didn't complain about any of these bonus activities, though, because they were a rewarding and uplifting way to balance out the rigorous training I continued to do. But when I wasn't on the road and had the opportunity to be home, my favorite place to be was curled up in my bed or spending time with my family. I didn't have much time for a social life. I would see friends every now and then, but similarly to my time at Duke, I chose to focus on fencing and training. I didn't always answer the phone and took hours to reply to text messages from friends, but they understood my schedule was hectic and overwhelming. That's why most of my friends thought I had lost my mind when in 2014—one year away from Olympic trials—I decided to start a business.

Any good business begins with a problem that needs solving. I was having trouble finding modest clothing options to wear to the speaking engagements now filling my calendar. When I stood in front of these large audiences, I wanted to be modest in my clothing options, but did not want to sacrifice my sense of fashion. I had decided that finding an on-trend, long-sleeved maxi dress in the United States market was like finding a unicorn in the desert. And even when I was lucky enough to find one online, it was often from overseas and expensive. I would end up paying too much for a dress I didn't even like that much.

I would never complain in public about my fashion dilemmas, but I felt perfectly okay pouring out my frustrations to my brother on one of our regular weekly phone calls. Qareeb was happily living in Los Angeles with his wife and toddler son. We didn't see each other that much, but we talked on the phone often.

"Why don't you make your own dresses?" Qareeb said.

"I don't know how to sew," I said. I'd been scrolling around online for an hour looking for a dress for an event I had in a few weeks, and absolutely nothing looked right.

"No, silly," Qareeb said. "You should hire someone to make your dresses for you so you don't have to do this every time you're looking for something appropriate to wear."

I laughed. "Qareeb, I don't know what you think my life is like, but I'm not trying to hire my own private seamstress."

"That's not what I mean, Ibti," Qareeb clarified. "You should start your own business making the types of dresses you're talking about. I'm sure there are plenty of Muslim women like you in the same boat. I know a manufacturer out here if you wanted to have some dresses made."

My first thought was that my brother sounded crazy. How was I going to start my own clothing line while in the midst of trying to qualify for an Olympic team? I could barely find the time to sleep, but still, I heard myself open my mouth and ask my brother, "So, how would it work?"

I could hear my brother's smile through the phone. "You, Asiya, and Faizah come up with some designs, and the next time you come out here I'll take you shopping for fabric. We can bring the sketches and fabrics to this manufacturer I know out here in the garment district. She can make you some samples and see how you like them. Once you okay the samples, we can have them produced and upload them to a website. You could do everything online. And just like that, you'd be in business."

Despite the fact that I was so tired that I often fantasized about taking naps, I actually started to think it was possible to start a fashion company. My brother made it sound so easy. "Okay, Qareeb, let me think about it," I said.

"All right," Qareeb said. "And I don't think I need to remind you that you can't fence forever. You gotta have a backup plan."

Once I hung up the phone, I stared at the clothes on my laptop screen. I was lying on my bed with my computer balanced on my pillow. There were so many dress options online, yet the few that fit the definition of modest were painfully dull and matronly. Why was it so hard for designers to understand that being fashionable was not antithetical to being modest? I was growing tired of spending time and money trying to cobble together a wardrobe that satisfied my aesthetic and my religious beliefs. There had to be a solution to Muslim women having to layer their clothes to achieve their modest look. I knew there was an opportunity to fill a void in the United States' market, and if no one else was going to do it, I would have to do it myself. That had always been my motto.

A few years earlier, my mother had said she was tired of the tile backsplash behind the stove in the kitchen. When she told me the ridiculous price the contractor had quoted her for replacing it, I went online to find a tutorial on how to lay tile. Then I went to the hardware store and bought the materials I needed, busted out the old tiles, and replaced them with beautiful new ones. It took me two full days to complete the project, but I did it all by myself, and everyone loved it. If I saw a problem that needed fixing, I generally just handled it. And that's why I ultimately decided to take my brother's advice and start a business that would satisfy not only my desire for affordable modest fashion, but thousands of other women's desires as well.

Soon after that conversation with Qareeb, my sisters and I brainstormed ideas for the types of clothes we wanted to make. Full-length long-sleeved dresses. Long-sleeved jumpsuits. Pants sets and tunic tops. All the components a woman needed and wanted to put together a stylish and versatile wardrobe. And we wanted all of our pieces to be affordable so that being fashionable was accessible to all, not just the wealthy. Asiya and Faizah were just as excited as I was to launch this company because they struggled with the same issues of finding modest clothing options as I did. But unlike me, who wore sweatpants to work, they needed these clothes for daily wear to work and school. This crazy idea Qareeb and I had cooked up was truly becoming a full-on Muhammad family project. Even my mother got involved.

With Qareeb doing most of the legwork in Los Angeles to figure out the production side of the business, my sisters and I focused on researching fashion trends for design inspiration and finding the perfect designer to create our website where we would sell everything. We wanted our store to be fully e-commerce-based so it would be accessible to everyone. Thanks to Qareeb's hard work finding a manufacturer, there was a quick turnaround for our dress samples. Once we were able to hold the clothing samples in our hands, samples that had started off as sketches on a notepad, things felt real. "This is really happening, you guys," I exclaimed to my sisters as we sat around our dining room table and passed the dresses and tunics around between us.

Before we could truly embark on this journey as small business owners, we needed investment capital to help launch the business. We decided my mom's sister, Aunt Diana, or Auntie, as we liked to call her, would be the perfect person to pitch our business proposal to. Auntie and my uncle Bernard had always been more like grandparents to us kids; over the years they had helped alleviate some of the financial burdens on my parents by helping out wherever they could, like paying for extracurricular activities. Because Auntie and Uncle Bernard didn't have children of their own, they always said that helping us succeed made them feel like their money was being put to good use. But like my parents, Auntie's money only went where she saw potential and passion. After she heard my pitch for our company—I had her sit through an entire PowerPoint presentation so she knew how serious we were—she too was all in.

"What are you going to call the company?" she asked me when I finished pitching the idea and was seated next to her on the couch in her living room.

"We were thinking about calling it Louella by Ibtihaj Muhammad," I said. "Louellashop.com for the website," I clarified.

"You mean after your dad's mother?" she asked.

"Yeah," I said. "It's such a beautiful name, and I thought it would be a great way to remember her. She was such a source of inspiration and strength for me, and I wanted to have her memory live on this way." I thought about our last days together in Newark and how much she wanted to see me succeed. I was so sad she hadn't lived long enough to see me make Team USA. This felt like a way to keep her memory alive.

"That's really sweet," my aunt said with a smile. "You know family was the most important thing in the world to her."

"I know," I said, thinking back to all of the family gatherings we used to have at her house over the years.

Without hesitation, Auntie Diana said she would have a check ready for me the next day.

Louellashop.com was a certifiable success. Within the first year, we quickly expanded our offerings from our initial ten items to more than fifty, and were already making a profit. I wasn't surprised at how well received Louella was by the community. All of my research on Muslim purchasing power indicated that if we created a product that appealed to and satisfied the needs of Muslim consumers, the company would be successful. Louella was new and bringing something different to the fashion industry that specifically focused on the needs of Muslim women. Our customers loved that our dresses were full-length and came in variety of vibrant colors. We also took pride in the fact that most of our items were $100 or less, and that all of our clothing was made in the United States. Even though I was still busy fencing, it was so much fun bringing Louella to life because I knew there was such a strong need for it within the Muslim community. People were so grateful that we were making clothing that was simultaneously modest, fashionable, and affordable. A pleasant surprise was discovering that our clothing appealed to non-Muslim women as well. Our customers came from different backgrounds and even different countries, but all had one thing in common: appreciation for modest fashion.

As someone who had matched her hijab with her sneakers since she was in middle school, I was thrilled to have this creative business venture that was also helping other women look and feel good. Running a small business was a heavy load to take on, but I loved working on Louellashop.com so much, it didn't feel like work. This was truly a passion project for me. But in order to fit it all in, I knew I had to squeeze every minute out of a twenty-four-hour day, and my family was working just as hard as I was to keep things running smoothly. After training all day, I would come home and review sales for the day and respond to customer emails. My sisters and my mother were busy managing orders and researching new design options for the next season. There was never a spare moment. I used my time commuting to and from New York City to upload content to Louella's social media accounts, like Instagram or Twitter, urging people to shop Louella. Everything about running an online clothing company was new to me, but I loved the challenge and the added perk of never being at a loss for what to wear. But perhaps the best part of starting Louella was that it gave me balance, something outside of fencing I could focus on. I was now looking at my thirtieth birthday looming on the horizon, and I often thought about life after sport. I always knew I wanted to have something in place that I could easily transition to once my fencing career ended. Qareeb and I often spoke about building something for our family together. For me, Louellashop.com was that something, and I looked forward to seeing her thrive well into the future.

CHAPTER 15

*Be careful what you set your heart upon—for it will surely
be yours.*

—JAMES BALDWIN

By the beginning of 2015, I knew the time was approaching,
time for me focus 100 percent of my energy on Olympic qualification. No sooner had Louella proven itself a success than I had
to abandon the day-to-day operations of the company and let my
family handle the business full-time. I didn't fully let my baby go,
but I did have to loosen my grip significantly. I cut out all distractions from my life so I could focus only on fencing, and yet alarm-
ing current events continued to dominate the headlines, making it
very hard to stay focused.

On February 10, three young Muslims, Deah Barakat, twenty-
three; his wife, Yusor Abu-Salha, twenty-one; and her sister,
Razan, nineteen, were shot execution style in their home in Chapel
Hill, North Carolina. The assailant was a neighbor who claimed
the killings were motivated by a parking dispute he had had
with the students. But every Muslim and plenty of non-Muslims
saw the murders for what they were, a vicious hate crime, pure
and simple.

Islamophobia was on the rise in the United States, perpetuated by violent stereotypes and religious extremism portrayed in

the media. And as a result, Muslims were being marginalized and discriminated against in record numbers. The senseless murder of these three young Muslims hit me hard. They were killed in their own home by a neighbor. *Is anyone safe in this country?* I wondered. My travels on the speaking circuit took me to different corners of the United States. Would a crazy, gun-toting nutcase like the murderer in North Carolina put me on a list? These thoughts ambushed my mind, and I couldn't fight the cloud of sadness that descended over me. But as I watched the coverage of the story unfold, I was angered to hear that the Chapel Hill police weren't considering the murders a hate crime. In response, a community of activists spoke out against the Chapel Hill police department's decision on mainstream media outlets, citing the constant fear Muslims in the United States were living in with incidents like this happening far too often. With so few Americans having a favorable opinion of Muslims, Islam had grown to be one of the most stigmatized religions in the country. Like the activists who were taking their messages to the media, I, too, wanted to do more to help change the perception of my faith. With my growing platform, I could be a voice for those who lived in fear. I could stand up and demand fair and just treatment by law enforcement and our elected officials. But first I had to shrug off my own fears and push the sadness aside. I knew that making the Olympic team was the best way I, as a Muslim American athlete, could help dismantle stereotypes and provide a vision of hope and inspiration. So, I dug deep for courage, sat firmly in my faith, and promised to work as hard as I could to make the 2016 Olympic team.

The Olympic qualification period culled points from competitions held between April 1, 2015, and March 31, 2016. As I had in the past, I completely compartmentalized my life and prioritized fencing above all else. I'd learned that mental training was just as important as physical training, because despite our team's upward trajectory in competitions, my teammates and coaching staff were intent on standing in my way. This had become abundantly clear ever since a competition in Seoul, Korea, earlier in the year when for the first time ever, I beat Mariel at a competition.

The Seoul Grand Prix was the last competition before the Olympic qualifiers began. I had a tough bracket, but had successfully knocked out some of the world's top fencers, including Ekaterina Dyachenko of Russia and Azza Besbes of Tunisia. I advanced through to the finals and found myself facing off against Mariel in a semifinal round to determine who would fence for gold against the Ukraine's Olga Kharlan. It was always a bit awkward to fence against one's own teammate, but it was a casualty of war. Once I put my mask on, my mind switched over to one thing, and that was winning. We were competing in a large venue in central Seoul, where Peter Westbrook had captured Olympic bronze nearly twenty-seven years earlier. There were more spectators than normal as they held the men's and women's finals at the same time. I fed off the crowd's energy and focused my concentration fully on taking Mariel down. I knew it would be tough, but after being teammates with someone for so long, you learn their strengths and weaknesses. Mariel and I had fenced countless times before. In a lot of ways, I was more prepared to fence Mariel than any other fencer I'd seen that day. Still, Mariel was the most decorated fencer in United States history for a reason, so I knew she wouldn't go down without a fight.

I said a prayer and stepped into it.

For the first quarter of our bout, Mariel was winning decisively. After I scored the first point of the match, I think she was out for blood. She managed to stay ahead of me by one or two points for a while. But I could tell I was getting under her skin. I could tell she felt threatened with how close I was keeping the match. She had to stop to check the laces on her shoes. She repeatedly asked the referee to verify if the score posted on the machine was correct. It was apparent Mariel didn't believe I was able to keep up with her. Maybe it was gamesmanship to try to throw me off, but it wasn't working. I was closing the gap between her score and mine. At the half, I was ahead by a score of 8–7. At that point, I think she started to get nervous. The lead kept going back and forth between us. I'd score a point, and then she would. I heard her hiss "Lucky" once after I scored. She didn't believe in my ability to beat her. But I believed in myself. We were tied at 12–12 and then 13–13. I wanted that win more than anything. I wanted to show her that underestimating me was a mistake.

With Mariel leading with a score of 14–13, I parried her next attack and scored a point of my own. The score was now 14–14. Whoever scored the next point would win.

At the start of the last point, I came out of the blocks fast. Mariel used a false advance to get me to fall short in my lunge. Most fencers would have felt their backs against the wall on defense, but this was actually where I felt most comfortable. Mariel staged her attack, pushing me down the strip, and as she accelerated with her arm a little behind in speed, I was able to hit her in preparation of her attack.

Point for me! 15–14. I won!

I was so happy I ripped off my mask and jumped in the air. Mariel threw her mask, too, but she looked pissed. The grimace on her face when she put her hand out for the customary end of the match handshake said exactly what she couldn't say out loud.

I had advanced to the final and was guaranteed that I was going home with either a gold or silver medal, my best finish yet at a Grand Prix. People in the audience clapped and cheered; even the referee applauded my efforts. As I passed by Ed I was sure he would acknowledge how well I had just fenced, but I didn't even get so much as a pat on the back from him. It was like I had done something wrong by beating Mariel.

Instead of congratulating me, Ed ripped into Mariel.

"What were you doing out there?" he demanded of her. "How could you let her beat you?"

Mariel looked hurt. I almost felt sorry for her.

"She got lucky," she said. "They were all lucky touches," she protested, still unwilling to admit that I was a damn good fencer.

I walked away. I wasn't going to let them steal this monumental moment from me. I didn't want to listen to them belittle my hard work and talent yet again

The line in the sand had been drawn. We were not the team I desperately wanted us to be.

After that moment, I was clearly seen as a threat to Mariel's chances of making the Olympic team. Now I became an obstacle, not a teammate, and the treatment I received from my coach and the rest of the team grew increasingly harsh and cruel.

If having to endure mistreatment from my teammates on the road wasn't enough, dealing with Akhi's lack of commitment to my training was also causing a lot of stress.

Akhi had become so unreliable that I wasn't able to depend on him at all. I never knew if he was going to be there for me at practice or at competition. But I didn't have the time or the energy to look for a new coach in the midst of the greatest moment of my athletic career. Instead, I started to take lessons here and there with one of the other foundation saber coaches, a new Georgian coach named Luke Nakani. Whenever I showed up to practice and Luke noticed Akhi's absence, he'd immediately make time in his busy schedule, even if he had a previous lesson or class scheduled.

We never talked about Akhi; it was this unspoken understanding we had between us. He knew that I wanted to make the Olympic team, and he saw how hard I was working, so he did what he could in Akhi's absence. I think he felt sorry for me. Luke was pivotal in helping me maintain my precision and hand speed whenever Akhi fell off the map. At this point, I still attributed much of my progression and success to my years working with Akhi, but I was disappointed by how disconnected we had become.

I often spoke with Peter, knowing he would always impart words of wisdom in our lengthy heartfelt talks. I wanted to be in the right headspace as I approached the Olympic qualifying season, and without a dependable coach in my corner and with the burden of unsupportive teammates to deal with, I needed some guidance from someone who'd been in the same place. If anyone understood having to forge one's own path, navigating everything from his mixed-race identity to dominating a sport where African Americans had never been welcomed, it was Peter. I thought of him like a wise grandfather, who was still in impeccably great shape and good enough to take on any opponent on the strip if need be.

I knocked on the door. Peter was sitting in the coach's room, reading glasses at the tip of his nose, and his eyes buried in whatever he was reading.

"Hi, Peter," I said. I'm sure my voice gave away my internal state of anxiety, because he immediately put aside the papers he was looking at and told me to grab a seat.

I could feel my stomach in knots and pulsing in my head. There was a sense of doom hanging over me, and I knew it was going to ruin any chance I had of qualifying if I couldn't get my head in the right space.

"What's going on?" Peter asked gently, his usual bravado toned down about 90 percent.

"Peter," I started, trying to sound calm and at ease, but then the words just came tumbling out like water let loose from a dam. "I know if I'm not top three in the nation at the end of the qualifying season, there's no chance I'm going to the Olympics. Every time the coach talks about who is going to be on the Olympic team my name is never mentioned, and you know how they feel about me in general."

"Ibtihaj," Peter interrupted me. "You're a God-fearing person, right? The Olympic team isn't in their hands. Whether you make the Olympic team or not has already been written by God. They have no power in who qualifies or not. The second you believe they do, you've defeated yourself," he said. Peter was a deacon at his church, so I knew to be ready for a sermon. "Your success comes from God, not them."

"I know," I said, and I believed it wholeheartedly, but I needed the reminder.

"If you don't stop this negative thinking and if you let those people get in your head, then no, you're not going to make the team, you understand me?"

I shook my head in agreement. "Yes," I said aloud.

"Fencing is an individual sport, Ibti," Peter continued. "And you are the only one holding that saber on the strip. So, don't look to anyone other than yourself for the success you want. You talk to God. You talk to me. And don't look to them for acknowledgment or empathy. That's what you do."

"That's it?" I said, wanting desperately to have faith in Peter's words.

"Yep, that's it. If God wants this for you, then you will get it. Believe that and accept that."

I let Peter's words seep in, and I forced myself to acknowledge their truth. My faith taught me to have faith in God. There is a saying in Islam: "What is meant for you will reach you even if it is beneath two mountains. What isn't meant for you won't reach you even if it is between your two lips." If God wanted me to succeed, no one, not the national coach nor my teammates, could change what was written.

I left Peter with the faith and confidence I needed. I told myself that whatever was meant for me would never miss me, and all I had to do was keep my head down and continue to grind. If it was meant for me to make the team, then God would give it to me. If not, that was God's will and I would accept it as such. I let go of my anxiety and put my total faith in Allah. From that moment on I was able to approach each competition from a place of faith. And believe it or not, I had the most successful year of my life. I had more World Cup podium finishes and reached more finals than I ever had, and I genuinely believe it was because I chose faith over fear. Of course, there were still obstacles thrown in my way that were a test, but I never allowed the obstacles to diminish my faith.

———————

It was November and we were about halfway through the Olympic qualifications. We were in Paris training at INSEP, the national French sports training center, prior to our World Cup. I was training with one of France's top competitors, and we were in the middle of an intense match, when I took a hard fall. I screamed out in agony, the pain shooting up my leg was so excruciating. I thought my foot was broken. I lay on the floor scared to open my eyes, as I feared I would see my Olympic dreams vanish in front of me. The team doctor hurried over to my side, helping me from the ground and over to the trainer's room. It turned out I had severely sprained my ankle. Luckily Faizah had traveled with the team for this competition, and she stayed by my side as the trainer assessed my injury. Members from the French team came to see me to offer their support, as they knew how important staying healthy was during the Olympic qualifying year. Meanwhile, not a single person from Team USA, fencers or coaching staff, inquired about me, despite my screams of pain. Their behavior was hurtful, but not surprising.

The next morning, I didn't go to practice because my ankle had swelled to the size of a softball. The team doctor instructed me to keep it elevated, compressed, and to ice it every few hours. I could barely walk, but that afternoon we had to leave Paris to go to the World Cup competition, which was being held in the city of Orléans, about an hour southwest of Paris. I could barely maneuver with a crutch, but I had to keep up with the team climbing up and down the Métro steps and through the cobblestone streets of Paris as we headed to the train station. I don't know what I would have done if Faizah hadn't been there to help with my fencing bag and other luggage.

We finally made it to Gare d'Austerlitz, where we'd have to wait a few hours for our train to Orléans. I gratefully collapsed onto a bench while we waited. Faizah sat next to me and tried to get me to prop my ankle up on one of my bags to help with the swelling.

"I don't want you trying to be superwoman. If it hurts and you need to slow down, ask for help," Faizah warned me.

I knew my sister was right, but I didn't want to be seen as weak. There were twelve fencers traveling all together—the four from the national team and about eight others who would also vie for a chance to fence at the Olympic Games, including my sister— as well as the coaching staff and the team doctor. One of the fencers came over and announced that Ed was having an impromptu team meeting. I looked at Faizah, and without saying a word she helped me to stand. Together we walked a few dozen feet to a small café where everyone was sitting around a few small bistro tables. Faizah had me rest my injured ankle on an empty chair.

As per his custom, the coach didn't sugarcoat his words, perhaps because English was his second language. Without any warning or prompting Ed looked straight at me and said, "Ibtihaj, I don't understand why you weren't at practice this morning. Do you have an excuse for skipping practice?"

It took me a minute to register what he had just said.

In front of all of these people, he'd just accused me of skipping practice? The coach knew about the injury to my ankle, so why was he calling me out as if I had done something wrong? As if I had a habit of skipping practices?

"Coach, I sprained my ankle. Remember, I couldn't even walk yesterday?" I said, trying, against my better judgment, to give him the benefit of the doubt. Was it possible he forgot about my ankle, even though I was sitting there with my leg propped up on a chair and a crutch by my side?

Ed didn't say anything at first. Instead he stood there looking like he was trying to decide if he should believe me or not.

I turned to the team doctor, waiting for him to chime in.

"Coach, she sprained her ankle," the doctor confirmed. "I taped it up yesterday, but it was pretty bad."

For the first time, the coach looked down at my ankle, like he still needed some kind of verification.

"Well, you can walk now, so I don't believe that you are injured that badly. You should have been at practice. Are you going to be able to compete tomorrow?" he asked.

Something about the tone of his voice pushed me to stand up in defiance even though my ankle was throbbing. "You've got to be kidding me!" I said, my voice raised to levels that caused others to turn and see what was going on. But I didn't care; the coach had gone too far. "I don't need you to believe that I'm injured! Every one of you saw me fall yesterday. I can barely walk. I've never missed a practice. I've never led you to question my work ethic. You all don't even have the human decency to ask me if I'm okay!" By now angry tears were streaming down my face. I didn't get it. Did my coaches and teammates see me as so different from them, that somehow I didn't feel pain? Did they not see me as human, too?

Faizah wrapped her arms around me and pulled me back down to sit. I don't know what the other girls were doing, but I didn't care. I realized in that moment it wasn't about my injuries or missed practices. My place on the US Women's Saber Team was an affront to their sensibilities. They didn't want me there, and the micro- and macro-aggressions were a form of harassment, a psychological game meant to break me down.

No matter what had happened the day prior, I had to be ready for competition. The team doctor taped my ankle as best he could and I left the rest to Allah. I fenced completely on pure adrenaline and faith. I asked God to help me get through it, and my prayers were answered. I don't even remember how I did it, but I won match after match and captured my first medal of the season that day. If the coach and my teammates counted me out of the Olympic running because of an injury, they were wrong.

I knew my coach and fellow teammates were desperate not to see me on the 2016 Olympic team. While I was trying my hardest to fence my best at every competition, they were plotting to get other fencers on the team instead of me. If they could find someone who could challenge me for second or third place, then that was another way they could get rid of me. In other words, they were working on multiple fronts not to have me around. When they weren't busy ignoring me at practice, they put a lot of effort into scouting for other talented fencers with the hope that they would surpass me in the rankings. Their great hope was Eliza Stone, who had now been on the team since the 2013–2014 season. She was a strong fencer and had been ranked as high as number seven in the world and number four in the United States. It was clear she had a really great shot at making the team, and it seemed that the coach and my fellow teammates wanted her on the team and not me. I think there was a lot of pressure put on her as well, and it didn't come off in a positive way. Instead of positive encouragement for Eliza, it seemed more like relentless pressure was placed upon her. I think my teammates and coach were so desperate for her to do well enough to move past me in the rankings, they pushed her too far.

Eventually the issue came to a head, and the team psychologist was sent for to discuss our team dynamics. The sad thing was, this wasn't the first time the sports psychologist had been summoned to help the women's saber team work out their personnel problems. The dysfunction was so rampant, we regularly had to have meetings to address the issues that plagued our team.

At this point the psychologist was called in to talk about how we could find a better way to support one another, particularly Eliza. I was hopeful that since for once I wasn't the focus of the dysfunction, perhaps we could address some of the real issues going on. I spoke up on Eliza's behalf to corroborate her feelings of isolation and the examples of unsupportive behavior from Mariel and Dagmara. But Eliza didn't return the favor by acknowledging that she too had witnessed my teammates' unsportsmanlike behavior. Instead, Eliza negated everything I said and suggested I might actually be the problem on the team! I want to say I was shocked that she threw me under the bus, but it made sense. I think her desire to fit in with the team was so strong, she decided that having the black sheep of Team USA defending her was not the way to gain the support of Mariel and Dagmara. It still hurt, considering we had been friendly with each other up until that point. But I had to shrug it off. My success and my purpose did not come from the acceptance of anyone on Team USA. I had learned that lesson a long, long time ago. This was just another day in my strange fencing reality.

As it turned out, Eliza had a bizarre accident in which she sliced open her hand at the laboratory where she worked and had to have surgery to repair the extensive damage. It was her fencing hand, so although she came back after the surgery, she wasn't quite the same fencer, and any hope of her making the team instead of me was quietly put to rest.

Team drama aside, after my ankle healed, I continued to do well throughout the season. Competition after competition, I continued to chip away at my Olympic dream, fencing hard in the hope of a strong result. My ranking hovered between the number two and three spot on the national rankings, and the Olympic team now felt more like a possibility and less like a dream. I stayed true to my habit of not obsessively checking my ranking or trying to plan my results. Still, by early 2016, I knew I had a chance before March—the end of qualifying season—to make the team.

In February of 2016, we were competing in Athens, Greece. This was the second of two back-to-back competitions, and we had had a training camp in between tournaments. I was traveling from Warsaw, Poland, following a weeklong training camp, and my mother and Faizah were flying directly from the United States to meet me in Greece. Mom was flying in for emotional support and to cheer us on as we neared the end of the qualifying circuit. Faizah was in a good position to qualify for the Olympic team as well because her national ranking was around fifth or sixth place. It would be a dream come true to go to the Olympics with my sister. Dreams aside, I was really thankful my mom and Faizah would be in Athens. I could feel the tension in the air everywhere I went. When I saw my mom and sister in the hotel lobby, I was so happy to see them, I breathed a sigh of relief.

Little did I know how soon that relief would be gone.

It was past midnight on the night before competitions were slated to begin. Something woke me up from a deep sleep. There it was. A sharp, grinding pain in my gut. Instinctively, I jumped out of bed and raced to the bathroom. I barely made it to the toilet with explosive diarrhea before my stomach heaved and I found myself vomiting into the bathtub. The pains continued, as did the need to empty the contents of my stomach, and a vicious cycle ensued. The force of the waves of pain was so violent, I couldn't even form a coherent thought as I continued to vomit. I sat curled in fetal position, hovered in the tiny space between the bathtub and toilet, exhausted from the intensity of the sickness.

"Mom," I cried out weakly before I heaved again.

My mom pushed open the door to the bathroom. When she saw me splayed out on the floor and the mess in the tub, she ran for the phone and called the team doctor.

The team doctor came quickly to check on me and decided that I had food poisoning. Apparently, some other women on the fencing team were suffering from the same symptoms, so I was not alone in my misery. The doctor said I was the fourth person she'd seen that night. Rather than prescribe anything to combat the illness that was now wreaking havoc on my system, the doctor told me my body was doing its job and would rid itself of everything on its own. She told me to try to drink fluids and eat crackers once the vomiting subsided. As I lay there on the bathroom floor, my face pressed against the cold blue-and-white floor tiles, I prayed to Allah that I would survive the night. The pain roiling through my body was so excruciating and unlike anything I had ever experienced before, I felt like someone was using a rolling pin to smash shards of glass into my intestines and stomach. After each violent attack, I started to fear that maybe it wasn't food poisoning, but rather that something far more insidious was responsible for the gut-wrenching torture taking place in my body. I considered going to the local hospital. But as it turned out, everyone who had eaten the smoked salmon in the first-class airport lounge during our layover in Poland—like I had—was now suffering these unfortunate consequences.

The team doctor had said my body would take care of the problem, and she was right, but it took *all. Night. Long.* I felt so badly for Faizah, because she had to compete in the morning and I know I kept her awake with my moans of pain and the grotesque sounds of my body ridding itself of the smoked salmon.

The next morning while Faizah competed, I stayed back at the hotel. I still couldn't keep any food or liquids down without vomiting. My head was pounding, my muscles ached like I'd been run over by a bus, and whenever I tried to stand up, I was overcome with dizziness. My back hurt from the violent way I had been throwing up, and my entire body felt fatigued. I couldn't imagine trying to compete in this state. Luckily for me, because I was in the top sixteen in the world, I didn't have to fence until the second day of competition. Some of the other women with food poisoning weren't so lucky and somehow had to find the energy to compete anyway. They didn't fare too well. Unfortunately, neither did Faizah. I felt awful because I wasn't able to be by her side to support and coach her during this really important tournament. I loved watching Faizah fence because she was so talented, and I wanted to be that source of support that she always provided for me. I felt guilty for being sick, and I was thinking my being so sick had interrupted her sleep and thrown her off her game. Now she had failed to make it to the second day of competition. This meant her chances of making the 2016 team, even as the alternate, were pretty much dashed.

But Faizah had other things to look forward to in 2016. My baby sister was getting married! She had met a kind

Egyptian-American man, and the two of them had followed traditional Islamic marriage laws and were going to have their wedding celebration in March. I was so happy that Faizah had found love, and watching her navigate international fencing competitions, college, and now marriage filled me with pride and hope. Hope that one day I too would be able to find that life balance, and pride that my little sister was charting her own successful life path. Faizah truly inspired me.

The next day, the team doctor gave me some medication that would allow me to at least keep water down and stop my head from pounding. I knew only a miracle would get me through a full day of competition. Less than twenty-four hours before, I had been sleeping on the bathroom floor, so I didn't have the highest of expectations, but it was moments like these that I had trained for. I had to be ready.

When I walked into the arena in Athens, the sense of anticipation was palpable. Everyone there had their hopes set on fencing well enough to secure their spot at the Olympics for their respective countries. I was happy that in addition to my mom and sister, Akhi had also made it to this competition and was able to provide me with the support I needed on the strip. I knew I needed to warm up, but my body was too fatigued to make it through my normal routine. I didn't know how I would fare that day, but I prayed my body could function on autopilot. It was possible considering I had competed in dozens of World Cups. Despite my weakened state, I was prepared for battle, repeating my mantra: *You are strong. You are ready. You are a champion.* Because even though I was sick, I still wanted to win.

I had high energy in my first match, like I knew I had to get a jump on my opponent in order to stay in contention to win. I didn't have the easiest bracket, but I made it work. I beat some tough fencers, including 2008 Olympic gold medalist Olga Zhovnir from Ukraine and Yaqi Shao from China. I hadn't seen Shao at too many competitions before, but she had beaten some strong people before me, including 2012 Olympic Gold medalist Ji-Yeon Kim from Korea. Next in my bracket I had four-time Olympic medalist Olga Kharlan from Ukraine. I felt the nervousness begin to creep into my system; not only was Olga a formidable opponent but because when you're fencing the world number one, you almost have to score two points to get one. It was the name of the game in saber, where the sport was subjective and points determined by the referee. Before the match started, I took a moment for myself. I sat in the stands with headphones over my hijab and my eyes closed, focused on my mantras and my breathing. When it was time to fence, I didn't have any extra energy to be nervous. I channeled all of my energy into devising a game plan to fence Kharlan. It's amazing how during a bout of severe fatigue, your body remembers the countless hours of training and is able to push through. I beat Kharlan that day decisively by a score of 15–12. I hugged Akhi, almost collapsing into his arms, happy to have won and happy to see my mom's and sister's faces in the crowd cheering.

My next match was in the semifinal round against Mariel. This time, Mariel won. Though I lost, I felt an overwhelming sense of happiness, relief, and pride that I was able to push through one of the most mentally and physically challenging days of my career. One of the benefits of being the athlete that is often overlooked is that it forces you to work harder, to keep your head down, and grind through whatever task lies ahead.

I ended the day's competition on the podium, thankful and with the bronze medal. I was absolutely ecstatic. Just that morning I had doubted I'd be able to even make it through one bout without collapsing, much less believed that I'd be going home with a medal, but I was proof that miracles do happen and that God answers prayers. I'd prayed for protection and strength and had been given more than I had even asked for. To this day, I say my performance in Greece had to be a gift from Allah.

———————

After the medal ceremony, I went and found my mother and Faizah in the stands. They were sitting near the American fencers. Mariel and her mother, Cathy, were seated nearby.

"I'm so proud of you, Ibtihaj," my mother said as I sat down next to her. She hugged me tight, kissing my cheeks. I could tell she had been crying, not because she was sad, but because she was as exalted as I was. She cried because she knew how sick I'd been the night before. My mom saw the roller coaster of emotions fencing put me through, and from the very beginning, I could count on her support to help me through even my darkest hour. She had always reminded me, who was going to believe in me if I didn't first believe in myself. It was a blessing to share this moment with both my mom and Faizah.

My mom then turned to Mariel and Cathy and said, "Congratulations to you, Mariel. Great fencing."

Mariel didn't respond, only half turning to barely smile in our direction. Her mother stayed silent, too. I was used to this cold treatment, but I couldn't believe that they would treat my mom, the most kind-hearted person I knew, this way, too. It was an awkward moment, and I was filled with anger, but chose to keep silent.

Back in our hotel room I exploded. "Why do you continue to congratulate them when they can't even respect you enough to say thank you?" I demanded, mad at Mariel and Cathy, not at my mom.

"It's not about them, Ibtihaj," Mom answered. "At the end of the day, I have to answer to Allah. That's it."

"But they're so mean! Even to you," I said, still fuming.

"Well, you have to show them that you're better than them. You have to always be kinder than them, and that's the way you hold up a mirror to their own dark reflections."

I shrugged my shoulders as a sign that I'd reached my limit in the conversation. I found their immature behavior exhausting. But my mom is a good-natured and religious person, and that's always been the way she has lived her life. She always tried to be a source of loving energy. It was a lesson I knew I needed to absorb more fully, because I wanted to be known as a good person, not just a good athlete.

––––––––

Back home in Maplewood, I dove back in to my regularly scheduled program. I didn't dwell too much on my bronze medal result in Athens because there were still a few qualifiers left and I had to get to work if I wanted to be prepared. On Monday morning, I sat down to plan my week, scheduling massage appointments, booking sessions with my trainer, arranging lesson times with my coach. Afterward I was getting ready for the gym when I started getting text messages from friends and family congratulating me on qualifying for the Olympic team. That struck me as odd, but I didn't pay the messages very much attention. I figured if I had really made the Olympic team, I would be the first to know.

As I brushed my hair into a tight ponytail and arranged my hijab, my phone beeped again, alerting me to another text message. I was so used to ignoring my phone, though, it was easy to block out the noise.

I went to the bathroom to brush my teeth, and when I came back to my room, my phone was beeping nonstop.

"Geez," I said aloud, grabbing my phone and scrolling through the email messages to see if there was anything of importance coming through.

And there it was. A Google alert flagging my name in an article posted on the United States Olympic Committee website, titled "Fencer Ibtihaj Muhammad Qualifies for Olympics, Will Become First Athlete to Compete in a Hijab." I had officially qualified for the 2016 Olympic team! I screamed, "YES!" Then I tore out of my bedroom, dashed down two flights of steps, and found both of my parents on the couch in the living room.

"I qualified for the Olympic team!" I screeched, my phone still in my hand. I pulled the article onto the screen so they could read the news themselves. While they read, I did my own version of the happy dance. I bounced around the room in excitement. I jumped up in the air once and then again, repeatedly screamed, "Oh, my God!"

Mommy and Abu joined in my wild celebration. They both hugged me and screamed with me. It felt surreal. I didn't realize that by winning the bronze in Athens, I had put myself so far ahead of my teammates that I qualified for the games before anyone else. But now it was official. At that point, no matter what happened in the last two months of the qualifying season, I was going to finish as either the number one or number two ranked saber fencer in the United States. No one could take that away from me. I was going to the Olympic Games to represent my country!

CHAPTER 16

The triumph can't be had without the struggle.

—WILMA RUDOLPH

2 sprained ankles

1 torn wrist ligament

3 pulled hamstrings

6 pulled groin muscles

Tendinosis of right elbow

Right shoulder impingement

Dehydration

I thought about the physical toll actually getting to the Olympics had taken on my body and then considered the emotional toll as well. Now that I had achieved the goal I had set for myself, it made me wonder if all the pain and suffering, of both my body and mind, had been worth it. Was I crazy for knowingly putting myself through the most strenuous journey of my life? Maybe from the outside looking in it would seem crazy, but for me, it made total sense.

For the first few days after I learned I had qualified for the Olympics—along with Mariel, Dagmara, and alternate Monica Aksamit—I felt like I could finally exhale, like I'd been holding my breath in anticipation for four years straight. There was this huge sense of relief lifted from my shoulders, and I felt an enormous sense of pride for accomplishing something most people could only dream of. But that sense of relief was shortlived as I quickly realized there was more hard work yet to come. In preparation for the world's most important sporting event, I would have to train even harder. The ante had been upped, and I had to be ready.

Once you qualify for the Olympic team, staying healthy up until to the day you compete at the games is critical, so optimum nutrition and adequate rest is just as important as what happens in the gym. Training becomes even more intense, and you have to take extra care to nurse every ailment. Additionally, the United States Anti-Doping Association (USADA) held random mandatory drug tests for the top athletes in each sport. Athletes could be tested both in and out of competition. Every quarter, we would have to submit our schedules for the next three months for possible drug testing. USADA doping control officers could show up at practice or home at any time to collect a urine sample. If you missed the test, failed the test, weren't where you said you would be on your schedule, or failed to submit your whereabouts for the quarter, that would count as a failed test. Three fails, and you'd be out. No Olympics.

Added to this pressure cooker of Olympic preparation came the media. For most athletes who make an Olympic team, there is going to be some media attention. Considering how many media outlets are dedicated to sports, not to mention society's all-consuming interest in the Olympic Games in particular, it's inevitable that a newspaper, magazine, TV show, or website is going to want to do a story or profile on an Olympic athlete. Whether it's the athlete's hometown paper or a *Sports Illustrated* special on first-time Olympians, it was understood that as athletes en route to Rio, we needed to be media ready. USA Fencing had a woman in charge of public relations who often helped schedule interviews. Because I had been flagged by USA Fencing in the past for posts on my social feeds that they may have deemed "too political," she always paid special attention to my interviews, perhaps afraid I would say something too radical or religious, but of course I never did. That was the thing about being the minority athlete, I had to be exemplary on the field to even be remotely acknowledged and conduct myself in a far more exemplary manner off the field to be acceptable. I didn't want to use my newfound platform as an Olympian to talk about my religious beliefs, but that didn't stop the flurry of attention I received because of my hijab. As soon as Team USA put out a press release announcing me as the first United States athlete in hijab to qualify for the Olympic Games, the phone didn't stop ringing. I thought the media requests prior to making the Olympic team were numerous, but this was a whole new level of attention.

I appreciated the media interest in my story, because our nation desperately needed to see that Muslims were just as American as anyone else. We could be athletes. We could be female athletes. We could be African Americans. We lived in suburbia, went to work every day, and cared for our families. Just. Like. Everyone else. I wanted the country—the world—to see that normalcy in me and in everyone I represented. This seemed logical enough, and yet there was never a more crucial moment for something or someone to change the narrative for Muslims in America. It was in that moment, in early 2016, during the run-up to the November presidential elections, that Muslim Americans came under vicious attack from then presidential nominee Donald Trump, who in turn normalized bigotry and emboldened an entire subset of Americans to act on their hate. There were numerous cases of hate crimes against the American Muslim community, particularly Muslim women who wear the hijab. But really no one was spared from the groundswell of hate. Physical and verbal attacks hit the immigrant and LGBTQ communities hard as well.

In late 2015 Trump had publicly called for a ban on all Muslims entering the country, and by the late spring of 2016 he was suggesting the United States ban all immigrants from Muslim majority countries. He'd even suggested creating a Muslim registry, which would force all Muslims to register with the government and carry special IDs. With a presidential candidate inciting fear and encouraging hate against Muslims, the floodgates had opened for a likeminded neo-fascist American populace to openly discriminate. Overnight we'd gone from our first African-American president to a presidential nominee who was openly endorsed by the Ku Klux Klan and the leader of the American Nazi Party.

I had a decision to make. As a United States Olympian, would I stand on the front lines and publicly challenge our so-called leaders who had normalized hate?

I thought about one of my personal heroes, Muhammad Ali, and his circuitous path to being an agent of change. Growing up, I knew Ali was a heavyweight champion and one of the greatest of all time in the world of boxing. And as I got older, I came to know Ali as more than just an athlete. His fame was also due to his activism against the Vietnam War, his efforts to fight racism with his words, and his devotion to humanitarian causes around the world. In fact, his public conversion to Islam in 1964 and his refusal to fight in the war thrust Ali into the spotlight for his beliefs as a Muslim, not his boxing. Ali never caved to the pressure to reject Islam or to fight in Vietnam, even with the threat of jail time and a suspended boxing license. Muhammad Ali is undeniably the most famous and influential American Muslim of all time. And it was Ali's legacy that inspired me to stand up to those who try to divide us along the lines of religion. He showed me what it means to have courage backed by religious conviction. Muhammad Ali put the question of whether one can be a Muslim and an American to rest. His reach extended far past the sporting world, and like many others before me, I was encouraged to stand my ground and share my truth because of his example.

So, as hate crimes against Muslims were increasing by double-digit numbers and Donald Trump's divisive campaign continued with no signs of slowing down, I made a commitment to myself to seize every opportunity to unify and lead in an effort to challenge Trump's hateful, anti-Muslim rhetoric.

What was encouraging to me was that the more virulent the anti-Muslim sentiment seemed to get in right-wing quarters, the more media outlets, brands, and companies wanted to talk to me, work with me, and/or hear my perspective on current events. I was often asked if I thought my outspokenness on social issues would affect my prospects to partner with big-brand companies. To my surprise, during a time when anti-Muslim sentiment was at its peak, a lot of companies sought to help elevate the conversation on the importance of diversity and inclusion by endorsing athletes who differed in thought, culture, and/or lifestyle. I partnered with a range of companies from Visa, to Nike, to United Airlines. Here I was an outspoken Muslim athlete, representing a relatively obscure sport, and these major companies were coming to me. I was also fortunate enough to find a management team whose interests were aligned with my own in using my platform to fight for justice and end bigotry. The firm was a powerful partner for me that helped me develop my platform as an athlete activist. Over the course of history, sport has played a dynamic role in shaping cultural discourse. While fencing was still my priority, using my opportunity as an Olympian to unify and to lead was the greatest call-to-action of my life. Meanwhile, the biggest competitive moment of my life was only months away.

My management team helped manage my schedule, so I could fulfill media requests between training. Most media outlets, like the *New York Times*, *ESPN*, *ABC Nightly News*, and *USA Today*, to name a few, would send over production teams to interview me at the Westbrook Foundation in New York. But some media requests required me to travel to them instead.

One day I got an email from a talent manager at *The Ellen De-Generes Show*. The email said they'd read about me in the press, loved my story, and wanted to pitch me for the show. I nearly dropped my phone in excitement as I read through the message. They said they would need to schedule time for a video call with one of their producers as soon as possible. A few days later, I Skyped with a producer named Kara, who went on about how she followed my career and wanted to know more about my life and story. She ended the conversation by telling me I had landed the gig, and she hoped her children would get the chance to meet me one day because she found my story so inspirational. I had to remember to act calm and not jump out of my seat in excitement. Instead, I tried to sound cool and professional, like I got a call from Ellen's people every day, and let Kara know that it would be my honor to be on the show.

After I hung up the phone, I smiled and took a moment to reflect. Here was this very successful white Los Angeles television producer telling me that she wanted her own children to meet me because she thought it was amazing how I had defied so many of society's expectations for myself as a woman, as an African American, and as a Muslim. Kara wasn't Muslim or a woman of color, yet she still felt an appreciation for my personal experiences, though our lives were seemingly worlds apart. It was a powerful realization about the importance of our individual lives, the impact we have on each other, and the diversity of the human family.

Being on *The Ellen DeGeneres Show* was beyond a fun publicity opportunity. Ellen had the most popular television show in the country and a massive global audience. She epitomized the attitude

I wanted to emulate, to be true to yourself, even when the costs are high, while simultaneously uniting people through love and laughter. That's what her show is all about. While a daytime television show may not be groundbreaking, I think Ellen is helping to make the world a little bit more tolerant and accepting in her own way. It was my hope that my appearance, as a Black Muslim woman in the sport of fencing who was on her way to the Olympics, would help alleviate anti-Muslim sentiment in mainstream America. I imagined that seeing a Muslim American in hijab who wasn't on screen to talk politics or terrorism but rather something positive and awe inspiring like my Olympic journey had to have a positive effect.

Once I was on my flight to Los Angeles to tape *The Ellen DeGeneres Show*, though, I forgot about my noble cause and started to feel more nervous excitement about meeting Ellen. For the segment, I would be interviewed by Ellen and then do a fencing demonstration with one of her producers. When I walked on stage and sat opposite Ellen in her comfy chairs, all of my media training went out the window. I forgot what I had planned to say, but Ellen was so funny and easy to talk to that our conversation seemed to end before we could really get started. It was a great experience I'll never forget.

I never thought so many amazing opportunities would be placed in my path after qualifying for the Olympics. It was amazing on top of amazing. I appeared on *The Late Show with Stephen Colbert* and even challenged him to a fencing match. At Team USA's "100 Days Out" celebration held in New York City, I had the opportunity to teach First Lady Michelle Obama how to fence and even got to meet with President Barack Obama a few times during his presidency. In April, I was named one of *Time* magazine's 100 most influential people in the world. I also had features in women's publications like *Glamour*, *Refinery29*, and *Allure*, where I was able to talk about my own self-confidence and beauty ideals. I was thrilled to be part of these distinctly women-focused conversations and bring my perspective as both an athlete and a woman of color, because historically society's standards of beauty did not include people who looked like me. It was empowering to help dismantle the definitions of beauty that too often erased women of color and almost never included hijabi women.

In many ways, I felt vindicated for all of the naysayers in my life, who had made me feel that, because of my race or my religion, I would never find success. It turned out the opposite was true. Despite society's misconceptions about my abilities as an African-American Muslim woman who wears hijab, I defied the odds. My success wasn't only measured by wins on the fencing strip, but also by the number of people I was able to touch and inspire by sharing my story of triumph.

Although it was tempting to get caught up in all of the media attention, I knew what was really important.

I was still fencing and taking lessons six days a week at the Westbrook Foundation; still cross-training at the gym with Jake, who ramped up the intensity of our sessions in anticipation of the games; still getting up in the early hours for morning runs; and still studying the videos of the women I would likely compete against in Rio. And on top of this hectic schedule, I was still competing for seeding at the games.

The insanity of my life had become nonstop. But in order to be truly prepared for the Olympics, there is a level of crazy required. You have to want to be successful more than you want to breathe. At least that's how I felt. In the final weeks leading up to the games, there were moments when the thought of my competitors training would wake me from my sleep and have me lacing up my running shoes for a sunrise run. I used every spare moment to train or recover from training. Sometimes, I would feel so panicked just watching television that I would throw myself on the floor of my bedroom for a core workout, pushing myself until my muscles cramped in pain.

Some days I would come to practice, and the exhaustion would just be dripping from my pores. A foil coach at the club, Buckie, saw me on one of these days and pulled me aside. His face was a mask of concern.

"You should go home," he said. "You look exhausted."

I tried to make a joke of it. "Do I look that bad?" I said with an attempt at a smile.

Buckie nodded. "You look like you need to rest," he said firmly. "Go home."

"But I have to practice," I said, panic making my voice rise.

Buckie shook his head. "Ibti, I've seen this a hundred times— training to the point of exhaustion day after day. You have to listen to your body. Rest and recovery are just as important as training itself. Think about how long you've been fencing. One day of rest isn't going to undo anything. In fact, your body will thank you for it later."

I could feel a knot in my throat. I didn't want Buckie to think I was weak. He was giving me permission to rest because I wouldn't allow myself, no, couldn't allow myself, to take a break. I started to say something more, to plead my case further, but he turned to start his lesson. The conversation was over, and I had my orders.

That day I went home and took a nap. When I woke up, I took a slow walk around Maplewood and then I helped my mother make dinner. Usually, whenever I missed practice or a session at the gym, I felt guilty. But Buckie had been right. After one simple day of rest, I felt so much better when I showed up at the foundation the next day. Clearly allocating a specific day for rest during the week wasn't such a bad idea.

Eventually, I learned to incorporate recovery methods into my routine that would help reduce fatigue and bouts of exhaustion. I became very aware of my body and how I was feeling. If I strained a muscle during practice, for example, or felt fatigued after a long trip competing overseas, I would not hesitate to take time off to give my body and mind a rest. I also started using acupuncture to treat old injuries and weekly massages and ice baths to help prevent new ones. I was doing everything I could to compete at the Olympics as healthy as possible.

Every night when I went to bed, my body and mind were both completely depleted from the day's relentless activities. It was the hardest season of my life, but I didn't regret a single moment of it. I knew it would be over far too soon, so I embraced the pain. I embraced the sacrifices. I embraced the opportunities and reminded myself along the way that every part of the journey was part of the dream.

CHAPTER 17

The bottom line is, if you stay home, your message stays home with you. If you stand for justice and equality, you have an obligation to find the biggest possible megaphone to let your feelings be known.

—JOHN CARLOS

Polluted air, bacteria-infested water, and the Zika virus. That's what we were told awaited us in Rio de Janeiro, Brazil, as we prepared for the 2016 Olympic Games. It was my first Olympics, so there was no way I was letting anything stand between me and traveling to Brazil to represent Team USA. I was far too focused and excited to be competing in my first games to let anything ruin a once in a lifetime experience.

Still, the horrifying stories about mothers trying to console their babies born with microcephaly and other tragic birth defects were heartbreaking. The images definitely made a lot of people reconsider their commitment to traveling to Brazil, and for my family, the high cost of attending the games was also a big factor. My parents never wavered on their promise to come to Brazil, but they knew it would be a financial hardship for the rest of my siblings. So my dad, with his entrepreneurial spirit, planned a fund-raising dinner at a local hotel, inviting some well-known speakers from the community as entertainment. I also participated by giving a speech. It was a brilliant idea, because it allowed me to connect with and thank many of the people who had supported me for years. The dinner was a great success, and coupled with another online fund-raiser that was created, eight members of my family—my parents, Asiya, Faizah and her husband, Qareeb and his wife and son—traveled to Brazil to cheer me on in my quest for Olympic glory.

Instead of booking a set of hotel rooms in Rio that were charging premium rates, my parents rented two apartments within walking distance of Olympic Park, located in the Barra da Tijuca area of Rio de Janeiro. Many Rio residents left the city during the games and rented out their homes for more reasonable rates than the hotels charged. For my family, this not only meant they would have convenient lodging, but they would also have access to a kitchen and laundry machines. They were all happy with their accommodations and were able to do a lot of sightseeing around Rio in between Olympic events. What they didn't get to do, however, was see much of me.

For starters, like most of the athletes competing at the games, I stayed in the Olympic Village. Going into the Olympics, I didn't know what to expect for accommodations, based on the alarmist media reports about Brazil's lack of preparedness, but our home away from home for the next two weeks put the media reports to shame. The Olympic Village was actually made up of more than thirty white high-rise apartment buildings meant to house the 18,000 Olympic athletes coming to the city. The buildings were constructed specifically for the games, with modern conveniences and accessible facilities for the Paralympic athletes who would be competing as well. I heard some of the apartments weren't completely finished, but my accommodations were perfectly comfortable. It was a relief to have a peaceful place to rest at the end of the day.

AUGUST 1–5

Every minute of my time during the Olympics was scheduled, from the moment I woke up in the morning until the blissful moment when I could lay my weary head down to rest at night. Both Ed and Akhi expected me—and my teammates, of course—to train every day. The games didn't officially start until August 5 following the opening ceremonies, but we arrived on August 1 to acclimate to our new home for the next few weeks and to everything in Rio that awaited us. I was enchanted by the city, the warm tropical air, the diverse faces of the locals, the bright pastel colors covering many of the buildings, the swaying palm trees that flanked the streets. Thanks to the miles of sandy beaches, Rio felt like a grand tropical island instead of a major city in South America's largest country. But as an athlete there was very little time to explore this enchanting, bustling metropolis before competition started.

In addition to training sessions twice a day, we had to sit for media interviews from the gaggle of media outlets—both national and international—camped out in Rio. Our first interview as a team was on the *Today* show the day after we arrived. We were one of the first team interviews on the *Today* show's beach set on the picturesque Copacabana Beach. That appearance felt like our official welcome to the games. And from there the interviews kept rolling. And as the United States' first athlete to compete at the games in hijab, I received a lot of additional media requests for interviews by myself.

Back home in the United States, Republican presidential candidate Donald Trump continued his campaign, all the while pushing his anti-Muslim agenda. He was so determined to cast a negative light on Muslims all over the world, not even a fallen American war hero—Humayun Khan—was spared in Trump's Twitter tirades. As the most recognizable Muslim American at the Olympic Games, my opinion on the current presidential campaign was in high demand. It was a lot of pressure to be at the center of so much attention, especially when the stakes were so high for Muslims in the United States. I didn't want to say the wrong thing or inflame already high tensions, but I felt a responsibility to use my platform to combat the negative ideas about Muslims that Trump kept feeding to the American people.

Sometimes the responsibility felt overwhelming, but I couldn't stop using my voice to fight bigotry. Though I embraced my simultaneous roles as athlete and activist, there were times at the games when I craved time outside of the spotlight. On nights when I would meet my family for dinner in Copacabana, I didn't wear US Olympic apparel and prayed no one would notice me. I couldn't believe my life had come to hiding from the media and trying to avoid yet another microphone thrust in my face. It wasn't always a pleasant part of my Olympic experience, but it was one I felt a duty to embrace. To not speak up and defend who I was as a Muslim American and what I stood for was not an option. Still, it was surreal. But I wasn't complaining. I knew I wasn't the only athlete who wanted to avoid the press. I'm sure people like Michael Phelps and Simone Biles, athletes whose stories had dominated headlines far before the games even started, were in heavy demand in Rio as well. So, if this was part of the price to pay to participate in the greatest sporting event in the world, I was happy to pay my dues. And really, the rewards compared to the cost were undeniable. It seemed like every day, despite the grueling schedule and media interviews, another gift was bestowed upon me.

August fifth was the day of the opening ceremonies. I finished a close second to Michael Phelps in the vote to determine who would carry the US flag at the opening ceremony. The flag-bearer was determined by a vote by my US teammates across all sports, and I was honored to even be in the running with world-famous athletes like Carmelo Anthony, Serena Williams, and Allyson Felix. I applauded Team USA in that moment, because their decision to vote for a Muslim American woman in hijab was a powerful rebuke to Trump's rhetoric. It was our collective act of resistance. It warmed my heart to be on that list because Team USA easily could have played it safe from the beginning and decided that a Muslim woman in hijab wasn't an ideal choice to carry the country's flag. In that moment, my teammates reassured me that they welcomed the diversity of our team and wanted to show the world what the United States truly stood for: inclusion and diversity.

The support didn't stop with the vote. As we marched into Rio's Maracanã Stadium that evening, I ended up walking in the front line only a few feet away from Michael Phelps and the American flag. Dressed in my white pants, navy blue blazer, and white hijab, waving to the cheering crowds, knowing that more than three billion people were watching all over the world, I truly felt all parts of my identity were being applauded. The indescribable sense of pride I felt in that moment was enough for a lifetime.

AUGUST 8

My first day of competing was the individual competition on Monday, August 8. Unlike our World Cup format, the individual event at the Olympics was held on one day. There were only thirty-two fencers competing in women's saber, using a direct elimination tableau, so there was no first day of pool rounds. Years of preparation and anticipation would come down to one day for individual events. The warm-up hall was adjacent to the main competition hall. It was small and cramped, with the thirty-two competitors, their coaches, officials, medical staff, and volunteers crowding the space. It was hard to find adequate space to run and stretch and even harder to find a quiet corner for my breathing and mantra ritual. Before my first bout, I stepped outside the venue for a brief moment alone. As I stood under the warm Brazilian sun, I reminded myself to fence from a place of happiness and gratitude. Competing at the Olympic Games was a gift beyond my wildest dreams, and no matter what happened I was proud of myself for making it this far. I came into the games ranked eighth in the world, and no matter what everyone else expected of me, I wanted to win. I always wanted to win and here on the world stage, I wanted to taste Olympic glory more than I ever had in my life.

My first match was against a Ukrainian named Olena Kravatska. We had fenced many times before, both in individual and in team matches, at World Cups and at World Championships. Any of the women from the Ukrainian team would have been a tough draw, and Olena was no exception. She was about six feet tall and a strong, relentless attacker. I'd already consulted my notes to see what information I had compiled about Olena over the years from previous bouts. What I discovered was that she used a lot of feints and depended on speed in her attacks, so I knew I would have to be patient and trust my technique and instinct in order to win. I wanted to fence my bout and execute my plans precisely. Before I stepped on the strip, I recited a quick prayer and reminded myself to fight to the end.

Olena was a strong opponent, but I managed to stay in the lead of our bout for the first few points. By the halfway point, she'd surged ahead to lead by two, 9–7. I was so nervous that I wasn't fencing my game. I was falling short in my attacks and getting hit in preparation of my attack. She was fast, and I needed to slow her down. One of Olena's strengths is her tenacity and unwillingness to give up. I would score and take the lead, and then she would follow up aggressively winning a point. Back and forth we went, exchanging the lead. Her primal screams, which sounded like an angry mountain lion, would ring throughout the stadium and then be answered by my own screams of triumph. We were deadlocked 13–13. I only needed a few more points to be declared a winner and move on. One of my fencing strengths has always been my sense of timing and my ability to use the distance and false actions to trick my opponent. My mind blanked in nervousness. When the referee said, "fence," Olena flew from the start, launching a long attack. I made two advances to close the distance, and matched each of Olena's advances with a retreat. I kept my blade out in front of me and could sense that Olena was holding back a bit. I unexpectedly shifted my weight to my front foot, while ducking, and hit Olena on her right arm. Oleana couldn't block my blade, and she slipped and fell to the ground without getting her light on. The point was mine! I now led 14–13. I only needed one more point. A win was so close, but there was no time to think. I was back at the starting line, saber raised. The sounds of the cheering crowds, the sweat rolling down my back and pooling in my armpits, the smell of my own breath filling my nostrils behind my mask were all inconsequential. I shut everything down except the instinct to score. I waited for the signal to begin. Olena came at me and just as before, I used the same action to score, ducking to avoid her blade, leaving Olena unable to get her light on. I did it! I couldn't contain my joy. My arms raised in triumph, I did a quick lap around the strip. I pulled my mask off and screamed in absolute joy and relief. The only sound louder than my screams at that moment were my brother Qareeb's shouts from the stands. He was so excited for me that he had everyone in the stands cheering, "USA! USA!" I turned around and saw my whole family on their feet fist-pumping, hugging each other, and shouting my name. I ran over to them and just let their happiness wash over me. I could not believe I was now going to the table of sixteen.

I ran down the steps near the edge of the strip and I stood on the bottom rail of the barricade reaching into the stands for my family's hands. Everyone was smiling ear to ear, with my mom crying tears of happiness and my nephew trying to squeeze his narrow limbs through the bars to reach me.

"Ibtihaj, you can do this," Faizah said, practically screaming down to me, projecting her voice so her words would reach me over all of the stadium noise. "You can really do this!"

I squeezed her hand and tried to convey in that moment how much I loved her and appreciated her. I knew that if weren't for Faizah working with me, supporting me, and keeping me sane in the midst of all the craziness, I wouldn't be in Rio. This win was just as much Faizah's as it was mine. I felt so emotional at that moment, I could feel myself start to cry. I owed everything to my family and their undying support for me. My parents had worked so hard to support my fencing career since I was twelve years old, and my siblings never complained about all of the time, resources, and attention my fencing had required of the family. With each of them in my corner, I actually felt like anything was possible, even bringing home a medal from the Olympic Games.

"Are you ready for your next bout?" Qareeb asked me. "I want to see you tear the next girl apart just like you did this one. You were amazing out there."

Before I could respond to my brother, we were interrupted by a volunteer who insisted I had to leave the fencing floor. As I walked back to the warm-up hall, there was a throng of reporters who were clamoring to get a comment from me following my first win. I think I counted ten microphones. I knew this wouldn't be a one-minute exchange, as every reporter would want a quote for their outlet. One minute would turn into thirty or forty-five minutes, and I just didn't have the time. At the Olympics, there wasn't a lot of time between bouts, and I needed every single minute to prepare for my next match. I gave my parents a quick wave and then turned to the pack of reporters and said, "Sorry, I have to go prepare for my next match." And then I ran off to strategize.

For my next match, I was fencing a woman from France named Cécilia Berder. The last few times Cécilia and I had fenced, I had won, but she was very good. She was the best saber fencer in France at the time and ranked ninth in the world, right behind me. She was a real fighter, but on paper I was better. I didn't go out on the strip overconfident, because I knew Cécilia would be a tough opponent and I had just proved in my last bout that the underdog can win. Akhi reminded me to fence smart and stay strong. I promised him I would, and I stepped out on the strip, game face on, ready for battle. I tried to calm my mind and shut out the sounds of the cheering fans. Right before the bout started I recited a quick prayer. I remembered the look of pride and hope on Faizah's face, and her words ran through my mind. "You can really do this, Ibtihaj." Yes, I could.

––––––––––

"USA! USA!" The fans were cheering, but I had to tune out all of the background noise and focus on my opponent. I came out on fire and jumped to a 6–2 lead. I could taste victory, but Cécilia rallied hard. She scored a few points, then we were tied, and then we traded turns taking the lead. But I was having trouble focusing. I got distracted by the noise of the crowd as I felt their desire for me to win.

The next point would be mine. When I heard the signal to fence, I exploded out of the box and landed a point on Cécilia right away. She barely had time to parry I came at her so fast. The match stopped, but the referee didn't call a point for me. I knew I had landed that touch, and I asked the ref to look at the touch again on his screen, but he still refused to give me the point. I couldn't believe it. I threw my mask to the ground in anger. "What?!" I cried. I knew it was bad form to argue with the ref's call, but I also knew I had scored that point. Instead of agreeing with me, the ref gave me a yellow card, warning me for false-starting. I was so mad, but I had to try to get myself back under control, to refocus and get back into the match. I put my mask back on and tried to use my anger to push harder. Celia and I traded points back and forth, but I couldn't seem to get my groove back. When the score was 12–14 in Celia's favor, I knew I didn't have any room for error. I was ready, by whatever means necessary, but after I fell short in my attack, Cécilia took over the attack, patiently staging her moment as she moved down the strip. We neared the end of my side of the strip. My foot slipped, and I ended in an awkward split with one foot out of bounds, losing the point. Celia won the match, 15–12.

It was over. I lost. My individual competition was finished.

I could feel the tears begin to well while I was still on the floor. I was absolutely devastated. I was mad at myself. I felt like I had let everyone down. I kept thinking I shouldn't have lost. How did I lose? I felt an overwhelming sense of shame as I peeled myself off the ground, shook hands with Cécilia, and walked off the strip. It seemed like only moments ago I was savoring the idea of a possible Olympic medal, and now my eyes were filled with the tears of failure. I dodged the reporters shouting questions and found a place with Faizah to lick my wounds. I needed to process my loss before I could answer any questions. I sobbed for more than thirty minutes. No matter how much you tell yourself you're just happy to make the team, losing is incredibly painful. Especially losing to someone you know you're capable of beating. I kept replaying each point in my mind and thinking what actions I could have done differently that might have changed the outcome of the match. I could barely look Faizah in the eye; I felt I had let her down more than anyone. I wanted to win so badly for her, for my parents, and for all of the people who had been following my fencing career and found hope in my success. Just thinking about all of the people who were cheering for me and praying for a win made me cry even harder. I felt this was their loss now, too, and I hadn't been able to spare them that.

———————

Thankfully, my family members joined us and came to offer words of encouragement and support. "You did a great job." "You never gave up." "We're proud of you." My mom reminded me that just competing in the Olympics was a win for me and for all of the people who looked up to me. I was an example for them—they could compete on the international stage, too. And even though I hadn't finished as well as I had hoped, I was one of the best female saber fencers in the world, and I should be proud of that. (For the record, I ended up finishing in twelfth place.)

Abu was the last person to speak. "Ibtihaj, it's okay. You win some. You lose some," he said, wiping my tears. "You gave it everything you had today. I'm so proud of you."

"But I lost my second match," I whispered.

"Ibtihaj, I've never seen anyone work as a hard as you do, especially out there today. In my eyes, you won that gold medal today."

"Thanks, Abu," I said, warming at my father's words. I knew my father wasn't the type to just say things to make me feel better. He was being sincere, and it meant everything to me.

Abu continued. "This has been the experience of a lifetime getting to see you compete in the Olympics. I couldn't be prouder, and you should be proud of yourself."

I took all of my family's words to heart, as I tried to cast out any negative voices still lingering in my brain. All told, it took me about an hour to compose myself. I knew the press was waiting for a statement from me, and I didn't want to come out tearstained and sniffling. I tried to get in touch with my rational self. I knew that while I could have done better, I had absolutely done my best. I searched inside my soul and knew I had no regrets. Losing on the world stage stings, but I knew in time the pain would fade and I was going to be okay. My family had reminded me that my attendance at the games went beyond winning or losing, and I would do well to remember that.

When I went out to meet the press, I tried to present a picture of resolve and acceptance. I knew what I needed to say because it was what I had been saying since I'd been given this unique platform. As I stood in front of the sea of cameras and microphones, I heard the same question repeated.

"How do you feel about losing to Cécilia Berder?"

I pulled in a deep breath and responded. "Cécilia is a great competitor and she bested me today. Win or lose, competing here today was bigger than any of my own personal ambitions."

The next question came as soon as I finished my last words.

"How do you feel as a Muslim woman competing in these Olympics, considering what's going on in your country?"

This was a critical moment for me. I knew how I responded to this question would get a ton of coverage. My answer was succinct. "I think that anyone who has paid attention to the news would know the importance of having a Muslim woman on Team USA, at this moment of time," I said. "In light of all the political fuss that's going on, I think my presence on the team challenges those misconceptions that people have about who a Muslim woman is and can be."

As I knew they would, the questions continued for close to an hour. I tried my best to represent my country and my family with honor and dignity.

As it turned out, no one from the United States women's saber team did well in the individual competition. Dagmara lost her first match, and Mariel lost in the second round just as I had. So the three of us were motivated to reclaim our glory during the team competition five days later. As a team, we were underdogs. Though we had medaled in the World Championships for the last five years, taking home the gold in 2014, we hadn't been able to secure even one medal at any of the World Cups this season. As a team, we'd been riddled with injuries and struggled to find our rhythm. We weren't going in overconfident. Personally, I wanted to win more than I had ever wanted anything before. The sting from my loss to Cécilia had transformed into a burning desire for revenge. To prove to myself—more than anything—that I could do better.

AUGUST 13

August thirteenth finally arrived after four days of grueling practices with Ed. Now that I knew exactly what to expect at an Olympic competition, I felt more confident than I had before my individual matches. Also, it was easier knowing that I had my team to support me on the strip. Mentally, knowing I didn't want to let down my teammates and that no matter what happened they'd have my back eased my stress level. There's something about team competition that brings out one's competitive spirit—especially when you are fighting for your country. It was a relief knowing that everyone could put their personal feelings that had defined our squad for the last several years aside for this one day. We'd done it successfully in the past at big events, and I just prayed we could do it again at the Olympics.

In the team competition, all three members of our team would fence against the three members of the opposing team. The first bout is to five points, the next bout to ten points, and so on. The first team to reach forty-five total points wins. Mariel, Dagmara, and I would be on the strip, with Monica waiting in the wings should we need a sub.

Our first match was against Poland. Not a bad draw for our first match, but I knew Poland would fight to the very end. We almost let an eleven-point lead slide through our fingers, but in a valiant last-minute effort, Mariel pulled us back for the win. In the semi-final round, we faced the formidable Russian team. I knew they would be our toughest opponents of the day, not only because they were strong opponents but because the referees seemed to love them. We hung in there most of the match, but had acquired a large deficit going into the seventh bout. I was up against Ekaterina Dyachenko, and I was on fire. I outscored her by a score of 13–4, giving us a narrow one-point lead. The score was 35–34 with Team USA ahead. But unfortunately, we couldn't hold on to the lead, with Dagmara failing to score any points in the eighth match, leaving the margin too large for Mariel to even the score and pull ahead. The Russians beat us.

We'd been in this position many times. Four times, to be exact. At World Championships, losing in the semifinals to either Ukraine or Russia, left to fence off for bronze. We walked into the call room, to have our equipment checked prior to the start of the bronze medal match. I could tell something was off about the Italian team. They looked defeated. It was clear that both of our teams had lost in the semifinals and now would fence off for bronze, but they looked as if they struggled to move past their loss. One of the things about losing in the semifinals was that you had to be ready to fence off for bronze. There was no time to sulk and ponder your previous loss. It was a position our team was far too familiar with, so we were ready. Dagmara nudged my leg, motioning me to look at the Italian team. She saw the same thing I did, a defeated Italian team we had to take advantage of.

Dagmara was the first one on the strip and Mariel, Monica, and I stood on the sidelines and cheered her on. The match started out well. Dagmara looked strong and decisive. She ended up winning that first bout 5–2. From then on, we took turns defending and maintaining our lead. After my second match, Mariel was up next. As I left the strip, prepared to give the ritual high-fives to rest of the team, I noticed Dagmara was hysterically crying. She and her personal coach, Yury Gelman, were having some sort of animated discussion, and she seemed really upset. As she walked away from her coach, I asked her what was wrong; all she could do was shake her head. I was really confused. We were winning. Why was she so upset, and would she be able to shake off whatever was bothering her so we could focus on the task at hand?

Just then, Ed walked over to me and said, "Good job. Monica will sub in for you."

I was shocked. I didn't need a sub.

Every team has a reserve fencer who normally was there to be substituted into a match in case of injury of one of the main three fencers or for strategic reasons. So why I was being taken out of the match? I was fencing well, and we had the lead. That's when the lightbulb hit. Now I understood Dagmara's uncontrollable tears. She was seething at the injustice of the act and maybe she was a little bit jealous, as she had been in the same position as Monica back at the 2008 Olympics in Beijing. Dagmara had qualified to be the team alternate in 2008, which meant she was ranked number four in the country, but she was never subbed in during any of the matches in the team event and didn't compete in any individual events. That meant Dagmara left those games with no Olympic merit to her name. In order to be named an Olympian you had to compete, and she never got that chance.

Monica was now going to get the chance Dagmara never had, and apparently that was a bitter pill for Dagmara to swallow, particularly because Monica hadn't impressed any of us with her work ethic or skills. But we all watched as her personal coach, Yury, insisted she be given a chance to fence, in this our final match. And despite the fact that I had been on fire on the strip, I was the one pulled. It was a bitter pill for me to swallow, too. But I accepted our coach's decision and focused on the win for our team.

When it was Monica's turn to fence against Rosella Gregorio from Italy, it was a nail biter. We needed Monica to hold on to the lead, but we knew it would be hard for her against Gregorio, who was a strong contender. Luckily for us, we had a sizable lead and she was able to win her match.

When Mariel scored the final winning touch, securing our forty-fifth point, we knew we'd done it. The three of us ran onto the raised strip and wrapped Mariel in grateful hugs. So much emotion was released. The final score was 45–30. I was so happy. We had triumphed as a team. Everyone had done what they had to do, and we had prevailed. I have never felt so proud. There on the strip, we hugged and high-fived and basked in our glory. For a moment I forgot about everything except the win. Every single sacrifice felt worth it in that beautiful moment. Every injury, every tear, every missed birthday, wedding—it all washed away as we stood there and reveled in the sound of the crowds cheering us on. I knew my family was among the roaring fans, and I hoped they could tell I was smiling at them, sending them my thanks for lifting me up.

Later that day during the medal ceremony, every single one of those feelings of gratitude and awe was magnified. I was so proud to stand under the stars and stripes in that arena. And even though I'd watched countless Olympic Games on television and sometimes even teared up during a particularly emotional medal ceremony, there was nothing that could have prepared me for the feelings that engulfed me when they announced the United States as the bronze medalists, first in Portuguese and then in English. At the sound of our country's name, my teammates and I clasped hands and held them high in triumph as we stepped up onto the podium together. Then one by one our names were announced and our medals were carefully placed over our heads. I felt a burst of pure unadulterated joy, pride, and awe. As an athlete, I had the ultimate prize hanging around my neck, an Olympic medal. Despite the obstacles and unbelievable odds, I had accomplished what I set out to do with my saber, and it was the sweetest feeling of satisfaction I'd ever had.

After the Olympic Games, I was physically and mentally exhausted. The day after I got home from Rio, I literally dropped my bags in my room and my sisters, my niece, and I got in my car, and we drove south to spend the week with my parents at the beach in Ocean City, Maryland. While everyone spent the day frolicking in the sand and water, I stayed in the hotel room so I could soak in the silence. As much as I love my family and was grateful to spend time with them, I needed the time alone. Thankfully, my family understood. They encouraged me to take as much time as I needed to relax and decompress after a crazy Olympic experience. So I did. For almost an entire week I lay in bed, getting some much-needed rest, occasionally joining my family for dinner or a walk on the beach. I tried not to think about fencing, training, or what came next. I let my mind wander and rest.

Of course, my self-imposed vacation from life couldn't last forever. I had previously booked speaking engagements and appearances. Not to mention my other responsibilities, like Louella. Our online store was growing rapidly, and my sisters needed me to be more than the face of the company.

Barely two weeks had passed post-Olympics, and I was with

my family in Chicago at the largest Islamic conference in North America helping to staff our Louella booths. Even though the Olympics had been the pinnacle of my athletic career, it had only created a jumping-off point for the rest of my life. But before I could take a moment to figure out my next steps, I had to deal with a more pressing issue.

Someone wanted me dead!

The email had come through USA Fencing. Some disgruntled American—a retired veteran—referred to me as "a thing that had to be destroyed." In a vile email, he'd threatened to kill me and my family, and threatened USA Fencing for having me on the team. It was the scariest thing I'd ever read. I'd never considered myself ignorant to the hate that existed in the world—my father had spoken to us several times about the dangers we'd face for being Black and Muslim in America. So, I knew there were people like that in the world, vicious in their hatred and willing to act on their desires to rid our country of anyone who didn't fit into their neo-fascist ideals. But this brought the threat too close to home. I was terrified, not just for me, but for my family as well. What was I to do in situations like this? Luckily, USA Fencing officials and my management team took the matter seriously right away and took it to the highest levels of law enforcement.

Because the man had made actual death threats against me and my family—threats that fell under the rubric of hate crimes— the FBI was quickly contacted. Investigators were dispatched to the man's home in Virginia, and it was eventually determined that he didn't pose a "real threat." He supposedly was just "blowing off some steam online." While I was grateful that the authorities had taken such quick and decisive action, this death threat only confirmed what I had feared all along—that with the rise of my visibility would come a rise in bigots who would make every effort to make my life and my family's life a living hell. My social media pages were already full of unsavory comments from people who had a problem with everything about me from my hijab to my taste in movies. Up until this point I had been able to brush off the online negativity as mere Internet nonsense, but this latest threat made it all too real.

I had to ask myself again: was it all worth it? As the nation became more racially and politically polarized, did I really want to take a stand at the risk of my own safety? One day I'd feel brave and resolute to keep speaking up even in the face of danger, but the next day I'd wonder how I would ever be able to go out into the world as a symbol of courage when I actually felt fear.

Both my mom and dad were extremely shaken by the death threat, even though it had amounted to nothing in the end. As a retired police officer, my dad wasn't convinced that the threat was truly over, though, and he blamed himself for not being able to protect me.

"You see, Ibtihaj," Abu said, "this is why sometimes it's just good practice to say nothing and let your actions speak for you. You've been a positive symbol for so many people, but maybe it's time for you to pull back from all the speeches and the media interviews. That just gives these guys more to use against you."

I didn't know what to say. My father was right—my increased visibility brought new opportunities, both good and bad. But if I went silent, I'd be letting the crazies win.

"But this isn't a game, Ibtihaj," he said. "This is your life we're talking about here. There are people out here with a racist axe to grind. People who don't want to see people like us getting ahead. That's always been the case."

I sighed. There was a lot of truth in what my dad was saying. And he was my father. His first concern—as it had always been—was his family's safety. "But, Abu, I've been given this opportunity. If I don't speak up, who will?"

"I don't know, Ibtihaj," Abu admitted. "But I can't let anything happen to you."

My dad would never have asked me to quit speaking out, but he also wanted to make sure I took the right precautions. For one, he wanted me to always travel with some kind of security team.

"You want me to walk around with bodyguards, Abu?" I said, laughing, as I imagined myself flanked by six burly men in dark suits and sunglasses at my next speaking event.

Abu wasn't laughing. "Yes, I do. And I know people who can provide the services."

My dad was serious, which made me immediately sober up. My father was career law enforcement, and if he thought I needed a security team, I really had a lot of thinking to do.

My head swam with the possibilities and the choices I needed to make.

On September 10, 2016, the city of Maplewood celebrated Ibtihaj Muhammad Day with a day's worth of activities and a parade. The event had been planned since before the Olympics, and bringing home a bronze medal only made the event organizers even more excited to celebrate my achievements. I was flattered by the idea, but the recent events with the FBI and my father's warnings had me a little skittish about the idea of walking through Maplewood with crowds of people around me. Even though it was Maplewood, I was still concerned about my safety. My parents were, too, and they demanded the city offer protection. Admittedly I was glad they did. The city police were terrific and made me feel as safe as possible. And the whole day turned out to be the most affirming experience—it cemented my purpose in the world.

Arranged by the mayor of Maplewood, the parade and subsequent activities far surpassed anything I had imagined. I was expecting a little walk down Main Street, but instead there was a motorcade of ten cars that traveled from the New Jersey Fencing Alliance all the way to the town library. My dad and I were seated together in a convertible in the front of the parade and my mom and sisters were in a car right behind us. I was so pleased to have my whole family involved because I wanted everyone to know that Ibtihaj Muhammad Day was their day, too. I'm sure most parade watchers didn't notice, but I was also surrounded by undercover police officers for the whole day. They were discreet, and even I didn't notice them after a short while on the parade route. I was far too engrossed by the outpouring of love I was receiving from my hometown. I was getting choked up just seeing it all.

I couldn't believe the number of people who came out to celebrate this day with me. The streets were packed with pedestrians holding signs and banners that said things like "Go Ibtihaj Muhammad!" and "Hometown Hero!" People were yelling and cheering for me as my car passed by.

"We love you, Ibtihaj," I heard more times than I could keep count.

When we got to steps of the library, the official program began, and I received a handful of official awards and proclamations from various city officials as well as artwork and letters from local artists. It was so humbling to have the city of Maplewood honor me that way. It still always shocked me when it wasn't just Muslim people or Black people who were moved by my story and who felt love for me despite both our different and shared experiences. Here I had the diverse citizens of an entire city singing my praises, congratulating me on my achievements, and that made me really think about the power of my story. I had the opportunity to touch people's lives and to make a difference in the world. I wasn't going to let the hateful rhetoric of a bigoted few define my life or change the trajectory of my journey. I wasn't going to live in fear. I refused to silence my voice when I knew I had the potential to change the world. I promised myself I would be more vigilant in taking measures to ensure my safety. Indeed, Allah had a plan for me, and I was going to keep riding this ride to see how far it could take me.

EPILOGUE

I decided to keep fencing. I had accomplished my goal to make an Olympic team, but I couldn't come up with a good enough reason to retire from the sport. I was still ranked number two in the country and number twelve in the world after the Olympics. And despite the fact that Louella was experiencing consistent growth and I was being asked to speak on panels and at conferences the world over, on topics that ranged from religion to body positivity in sports, at my core I still felt like a fencer.

But now my professional network and my opportunity to be a real agent for change had truly blossomed. Alongside four other well-known athletes, Michael Bennett from the Seattle Seahawks, WNBA stars Maya Moore and Breanna Stewart, and track and field legend John Carlos, I helped create a nonprofit organization called Athletes for Impact whose mission is to "connect athletes with communities to positively transform America." The organization addresses issues ranging from climate change to mass incarceration. With prominent sports figures—think Colin Kaepernick, LeBron James, and Aly Raisman—dominating news headlines for using their voices to speak on matters they believed in, we realized that if unified and organized, athletes could have an even greater impact on the world, and not just on the playing field.

It took me a moment to settle into my new role. I'm not sure what I would even put on a traditional business card: Olympic Fencer? Activist? Entrepreneur? All of the above? But I eventually came to understand that it's about embracing the flexibility and possibility of the unknown. I could define my own identity and I didn't need to explain myself to others or have them define me.

———

One of the most exciting things that happened to me post–Rio Games was that the Mattel toy company decided to make an Ibtihaj Muhammad Barbie doll. The best part, the doll would come dressed in a fencing uniform with a hijab. Like me, she would be a first, the first Barbie in a hijab. When the company showed me the prototype, I cried. Considering how much I had loved my Barbies as a child, the thought of little girls, both Muslim and non-Muslim, playing with a Barbie who chooses to wear hijab made me so happy. As I sat there in the conference room at Mattel, my mascara running from my tears, I tried to explain why this doll was going to be so important to so many little girls. "Not only does it give millions of little girls a doll that looks like them, it means you see us and that we matter," I said, trying to regain my composure. The Mattel executives may not have understood just how significant this was to me, but that didn't matter. Soon enough, the world would have its first Muslim Barbie.

The Ibtihaj Muhammad Barbie made her official debut at *Glamour* magazine's Women of the Year Summit and awards show in New York on November 13, 2017. Mattel came through by outfitting my custom Barbie in a Louella original. The immediate response to Barbie at the *Glamour* WOTY Awards was positive and the support and love for the first Barbie in hijab was overwhelming. I walked away from the event that night even more inspired to do more, more committed to standing up, and more determined to raise my voice.

If I've learned anything from this amazing journey I've been on, it's that the work never stops. The work ethic I developed as an Olympic athlete is the same one I'm calling on now as a change agent in a world that still hasn't figured out how to make room for everyone, regardless of their race, religion, or gender. Just as I defied the odds to make it to the Olympics in a sport that didn't have a place for me, I will continue to fight—to use all of my resources—for equality, justice, and peace. And I know this path I've chosen isn't going to be easy—the odds are against an African-American, Muslim woman being embraced as a spokesperson for building a better America—but easy has never been the way I roll. I've had to fight for every win, every place at the table, every ounce of respect on my path to world-class athlete. And I will continue to fight because the prize this time is an America that truly respects all of its citizens. And that is worth more than any medal.

Inshallah: so may it be.

ACKNOWLEDGMENTS

All praises to the Most High, the Most Beneficent, the Most Merciful. I thank Allah for giving me this beautiful life, the experiences of joy, of sadness, and everything in between. *Alhumdulillah.*

To my mother and father, I thank you for seeing potential in me even when I had a hard time seeing it in myself. My parents' efforts to instill values like hard work and dedication have shaped me into who I am today. They have taught me the importance of sacrifice, preparation, and responsibility. It is through them that I have learned to have an unwavering love for Allah, His plan, and my faith. It is my hope that I will continue to make them proud and that their love and guidance help me in every step along my journey.

To my sister Faizah, thank you for being the calm in every storm and the wind beneath my wings. Though we are six years apart, I like to think of us as twins, coupled on this adventure into the world of elite fencing. We trained together every day, helped each other through the moments that mattered most, and never stopped rooting for the other's personal success. This Olympic medal is as much Faizah's as it is my own. Here's to always being best friends.

To my brother Qareeb, sisters Brandilyn and Asiya, and Auntie, I am forever grateful for the endless support and love. To my niece Maliha and nephew Zayd, because of them I strive to leave the world a better place.

ACKNOWLEDGMENTS

To my personal coaches, Akhi, Frank, Alex, trainer Osei, and other coaches that helped me along the way, Achiko and Zoran, thank you for preparing me physically, tactically, and mentally to become the best version of myself.

To Peter Westbrook, thank you for paving the way for black and brown kids everywhere and for making this dream a possibility for me. To my Foundation teammates and mentors, friends Isis and Paola, thank you for your unconditional love and support. What a blessing it is to have family by your side during your wins. What an even greater blessing it is to have family by your side during your falls.

To Joel Hirschhorn and Andrea Buccino, thank you for putting the pieces back together again.

To Lindsay and Mary, I will be forever grateful for your guidance and friendship, and for encouraging me to awaken my inner activist.

I want to thank Greg for showing me the importance of deadlines and guiding me through the book-writing process. A big thank you to Krishan and the team at Hachette. Writing this book was as intense as it was gratifying, and I am indebted to Lori Tharps for her patience and brilliance in helping me tell my story.